Willamette Interlude

Willamette

INTERLUDE

By SISTER MARY DOMINICA, S.N.D. de N.

PACIFIC BOOKS, *Publishers*

Palo Alto, California

To the
Pioneer Sisters of Notre Dame de Namur
on the Pacific Coast

Author's Note

Historical research affords satisfactions other than sojourns which our confreres set down, with a degree of truth, as vacations. One of its pleasant by-products is the element of surprise, the sudden discovery that sets calculations along new lines or furnishes the lacking step in a teasing problem. Best of all is the generous sharing by others in the researcher's undertaking. Since I have experienced this pleasure many times in writing *Willamette Interlude*, I am happy now to acknowledge my indebtedness.

I am sincerely grateful to Mr. Thomas Vaughan, director of Oregon Historical Society and editor of *Oregon Historical Quarterly*, for making available to me the Society's archives, collections, and extensive files in Portland; to Priscilla Knuth, OHS research associate, for the benefit of her experience and ability, both in Portland and in subsequent correspondence. For archival material I am greatly indebted to Reverend John R. Laidlaw of Portland; to Sister Margaret Jean, head of the Department of History, Marylhurst College; to Mr. David C. Duniway, Oregon State archivist; to Mrs. Hazel E. Mills, reference assistant, Oregon State Library; to Mr. Guy H. Pace, County Clerk, Clackamas County, Oregon; to Miss Vara Caufield, curator of McLoughlin House, Oregon City, and descendant of one of Oregon's pioneer families; to Mr. W. Van Cauwenberg, Consul General of Belgium in San Francisco; to Mr. Jan-Albert Goris, Belgium Government Information Center, New York; to Reverend Sister Maura, S.N.D. de N., Sisters of Notre Dame de Namur in Rome. For other valuable information I am very grateful to Most Reverend Francis P. Leipzig, D.D., Bishop of Baker City; to Reverend Martin Thielen, Ph.D., S.T.L., Diocesan Superintendent of Schools, Portland;

to Very Reverend Theodore J. Bernards of Oregon City; to
Reverend James L. Maxwell of St. Paul, Oregon; to Mr.
Carl Landerholm, secretary of Fort Vancouver Historical
Society; to Dr. Burt Brown Barker, vice-president emeritus
of the University of Oregon; to Sister Agnes, S.H., Provi-
dence Hospital, Seattle; and to Sister Mary Ida, Mt. Angel
Women's College, Mt. Angel, Oregon.

Vignette drawings are by Sister Marie of St. Joseph,
S.N.D. de N.

SISTER MARY DOMINICA, S.N.D. de N.

College of Notre Dame
Belmont, California
April 10, 1959

Foreword

It is said that for the unknown there is no desire. *Willa-mette Interlude* might be considered a refutation of this apt philosophical axiom. Certainly, not one of the six Sisters of Notre Dame de Namur who volunteered for the Oregon mission had ever seen an Indian.

Despite this, the six were but a few of the Community who would have willingly embarked on the gallant ship *l'Infatigable* and braved the perilous waters of the stormy Atlantic and treacherous Pacific.

On these pages of high adventure on sea and on land, the phantom spirits of pioneers are once again clothed with flesh and blood. Each one of the Sisters enjoys a distinct personality. We come to know the strength and the weakness of each character that plays a part in the coming of the Sisters of Notre Dame de Namur to our own West Coast.

If we think that travel by sea is an adventure of our day, this odyssey causes us to revise our notion of the meaning of adventure. The almost seven months' trip from Antwerp to the Willamette Valley in Oregon has its present day parallel only in ventures like that of Kon-Tiki or the Lehi.

In an age when the church is in dire need of more Sisters, this true story of courage and dedication should win more vocations than formal treatments of the beauty of the religious life. In the reader's mind, the conviction must grow that if the six who braved so much for God and the "noble savage" in 1844 were heroines, their kind of courage was not interred with them. It is still to be found in our convents of Sisters throughout the world.

In the writing of the *Interlude,* Sister Mary Dominica was not thinking of a possible Hollywood production. Nonetheless, this account of a journey and a mission has everything that fiction might suggest with the plus factor that it did happen.

Most Reverend HUGH A. DONOHOE, V.G.
Bishop of San Francisco

Preface

The story of *Willamette Interlude* has four claims to distinction. First of all, its theme is magnificent. In the second place it is concerned with beginnings, and to true lovers of history nothing is more absorbing than origins. There is, moreover, a wealth of four-dimensional character portrayal and vivid incident that only devoted scholarship and rich primary sources can provide. The narrative, finally, is a masterpiece of lucid and fluent English.

So far as theme is concerned it is difficult to imagine anything more dramatic than this epic of valiant Belgian women, the Sisters of Notre Dame de Namur, at grips with the raw Oregon wilderness of the early 1840s. Here is a confrontation of Christian zeal with pagan inertia, of civilized refinement with the incredible squalor and misery of frontier construction. What writer could ask for a subject more exciting and significant? There are no false notes struck in this account, for this is not fiction but history. We are presented with no easy conquests, no comfortably satisfying resolutions to fictitious problems. Here is struggle, marked at times by heart-rending setbacks, by human misjudgments and miscalculations, by failures as well as triumphs. But their failures were chiefly in the material sphere. In the realm of spirit the triumphs are real.

The series of events traced in this volume will have an absorbing interest for all persons who value frontier history, and particularly for those who seek to penetrate beneath the surface and study the molding forces which were at work. This is an important contribution to the mosaic of local monographs which will eventually fill in and round out the the larger picture of the American Frontier. Its principal setting is the old fort of the Hudson's Bay Company at Vancouver on the Columbia River, the settlement at St. Paul, and early Oregon City. There are also tantalizing glimpses of San Francisco and San Jose, California in the 1850s, the area to which the Sisters transferred their labors after leaving Oregon. Major attention is given, however, to the earlier northern efforts. A good deal of illumination is shed upon the crises and conflicts which were to determine the development of Oregon. The observant eyes of the missionary Sisters provide fresh and revealing insights into the personalities of the chief actors and into the drives and purposes which moved them. These are the more valuable since the sharpest focus is upon religious issues and personalities which, though important, have been generally less well known and understood.

In addition to the documents preserved in episcopal archives and in those of her own Order, the author has been able to utilize a wealth of material in the form of records, reports, and letters exchanged between the Oregon Sisters and their Superiors in Belgium, as well as a number of diaries kept by the Sisters and by pioneer priests. The detail these provide is so vivid and colorful as to give one at times the impression of reading a work of fiction rather than history. No one will complain of this, except, perhaps, those misguided persons who have been conditioned to believe that sound history must be dull. Actually, of course, the past was not dull but exciting. An historical narrative which fails to convey this excitement to the reader is, to that extent at least, a falsification. This charge cannot be leveled against the account given in *Willamette Interlude*. In these pages the past is vividly recreated, its experiences relived. The reader will know intimately what it was like to sail in a cramped, rat-infested ship from the north of Europe around the Horn to the Pacific coast of North America. He will see the virgin wilderness and its people, Indian and white. He will have an exact knowledge of the primitive accommodations, the privations and hardships that early Oregon offered. He will feel too, if vicariously, the determination, courage, and rugged faith with which these obstacles were met. In the end he will have deepened his awareness at once of the tragic as well as the heroic dimensions of life.

A word remains to be said about the narrative skill with which these elements are blended together. The writing is quite obviously a work of love, done with great care, with understanding, and with sound craftsmanship. It will be unnecessary to tell the reader that the author is no novice at this art. The text itself will tell this quite clearly.

EDWIN ALANSON BEILHARZ

University of Santa Clara
March 1, 1959

Contents

Illustrations

PART I

CHRISTMAS ON
THE SCHELDE

CHAPTER 1

Deck Promenade

For nearly two weeks fog had brooded over the Schelde, heavy winter fog with no breeze to disturb it. In Rammchen Roads above Flushing, Holland, some twenty or thirty ships rode at anchor, ghosts of ships in the half-light of that Christmas Eve, 1843.[1] On their decks, officers and sailors shouted pleasantries or curses from ship to ship as their moods prompted them, frustration weighting the general temper as the morning wore on. There was little of the spirit of Christmas in their observations.

One of these ships was the sturdy little two-masted brig, *l'Infatigable,* built in Antwerp in 1840 and boasting 242 tons. Thus far she had fulfilled the promise inscribed in the books

1

for her by the examining experts, who had assured her owners
that she was fully seaworthy and appropriate for long voyages
"on both sides of Cape Horn and of Cape of Good Hope."
Though her earlier triumphs are not on record, she had
already won the title of *Passepartout* from her somewhat
silent and dour captain, S. J. Moller, whose recurring moods
of pessimism were the result of illness which he refused to
recognize as he planned *l'Infatigable*'s course around the
Horn, up the Pacific Coast to the Columbia, and thence to
Manila.[2] Captain Moller knew that to avoid running into
the heaviest weather in the southern seas, early winter departure was best. Now the protracted gloom and failure of
wind made him withdrawn and grim, as it made other seamen
in the Schelde loud and profane. Captain Moller was a gentleman. That was Father Pierre DeSmet's reason for seeking
passage on *l'Infatigable* for his missionary group.[3]

Six Belgian Sisters of the Congregation of Notre Dame
de Namur walked slowly to and fro on the ship's deck that
Christmas Eve morning, for taking air was an item of their
daily routine. Two were praying, their black rosaries slipping
between their fingers. The other four clutched French-
English exercise books, puzzling over impossibilities of
Anglo-Saxon speech and rendering phrases triumphantly to
one another in patterns unrecognizable by Briton or American. At least, they assured one another, they were making
headway in this difficult and unlovely language. Perhaps the
delay in departure was a blessing in disguise. It was giving
them a running start with their lessons before rough seas
made study impossible. They might be speaking English
with a degree of ease at the end of their voyage. Even now
Father DeSmet was pleased with their progress, though he
made no comment about their success with Chinook. Well,
perhaps a bit later. But the fog was lifting a little over the
desolate stretches of Walcheren, and the six gazed with relief
at a vista of inviting green fields lying between stretches of
silver. In those few moments of light it was pleasant to see
the roof tops and church towers of Flushing, and here and
there little knots of farm buildings sheltered by clusters of
dark trees, and the silvery sail of a canal boat that seemed

to be making its way right through a meadow. Again fog wrapped them around. In the grayness they stood chatting gratefully about the brief interval that had made them forget the monotonous motion of the ship and the unending lapping of water around the hull, motion and sound mocking their longed-for conquest of distance.

Unlike the rough seamen, whose language they regretted, these six Sisters knew how to accept delay even in the attainment of their high adventure. They were bound for the ends of the earth, for faraway Oregon, where they hoped to share the joys of their Faith with savages and to rekindle them in the hearts of white settlers. But God's work, their Superior, Sister Loyola, reminded them, is done in God's time. She made the remark as timely though she was one of the less patient of the group, a person of quick initiative and ready adaptability. Because of these qualities, Mère Constantine had selected her to lead the others, not however without strong advice about patience and deliberation. As much as the delay irked Sister Loyola, she would not allow the others to surmise her annoyance. Besides, she had a still more serious problem than delay. Below, in the smaller of their two cabins, Sister Reine, the seventh member of the band, sat huddled in a depression that grew darker each day. None of their attempts to cheer her, not even Father DeSmet's gentle counseling, had thus far availed. If the sun would only come back again and stay, they might coax her up on deck, Sister Loyola thought, and, as if reading her mind, the others began to talk anxiously about their poor Sister's trouble. Nothing at all to worry over, Sister Loyola assured them. She had consulted Father DeSmet again, and he felt as she did; it was all a temptation of the devil to prevent Sister Reine's becoming a wonderful missionary. She would surely recover her good spirits on Christmas morning; if not, they would send word to Mère Constantine and have her returned to Namur. Father DeSmet said a mission was certainly not the place for a person with persistent moods, so they must unite in prayer for Sister Reine. The Sisters promised, but they prayed without the sure hope they felt as they prayed for a strong east wind.

Better to send the poor thing home, ran the undertone
to Sister Marie Catherine's petition. Even if she came out
of this depression, she would be bound to have recurrences.
Forthright as she was, Sister Marie Catherine dared not offer
this opinion for her new Superior's consideration. She would
have offered it with no hesitation to the Mother General herself, but Sister Loyola was different. Her suave speech was
tipped with finality. For the present, at least, Sister Marie
Catherine would set her ideas aside unless they were requested. Only the Good God knew how hard that would be.
Well, hadn't she been looking for some special self-denial to
make her a little more worthy of her grand mission?

While the Sisters stood talking together, Father DeSmet
came up on deck with Father Nobili. They greeted the
Sisters and went directly to a small table in a sheltered corner.
Seating themselves, they unfolded a large sheet of paper.
Father Nobili followed eagerly as Father DeSmet pointed
and explained. That, Sister Mary Aloysia whispered, must
be Father DeSmet's sketch of the Oregon country; he would
show it to the Sisters when he had finished it. Presently genial
Father Accolti appeared with Brother Francis Huysbrecht.
Father Accolti sat down to join in the map lesson, but as usual
Brother Francis stood at the rail to watch the occasional port
steamers and tugboats winding their way cautiously but im-
portantly, their movement accenting the helplessness of the
ships. Now the Sisters went below to leave the deck to the
Fathers. It was their hour to care for the "chapel," the ship's
social room, which Captain Moller allowed his passengers
to use for this purpose. That morning, under Sister Mary
Aloysia's artistic guidance, they would decorate it for Christmas.

As they swept and dusted the room, Sister Loyola opened
a large box on the bed beside which Sister Reine sat with
hands folded listlessly. Carefully she took out shining silver
candlesticks and silken, red flowers, and spread them in tempting array. These, she said cheerfully, were the very flowers
Sister Reine and Sister Mary Aloysia had made for their
first Christmas in Oregon. Wouldn't she come now and help
to decorate? They all knew how artistic she was. It was

useless. When the Sisters came to gather up the Christmas splendor, Sister Loyola shook her head in disappointment. The Sisters went back to their work all a bit depressed until Sister Mary Aloysia observed that they had special need of keeping up their spirits just because of their Sister's mood. Sister Reine's nature was especially fine, she told them, and such souls often had a greater capacity for suffering. It was too bad. She had been so zealous and insistent in offering herself for the mission. Sister Marie Catherine looked dubious; she was beginning to think of Sister Reine's initial fervor as a bit of romance. It seemed quite simple; God was not calling Sister Reine to Oregon and He was withholding the wind until she should leave the ship. Sister Reine had fancied herself heroic, but now twelve days on the waiting ship had quite sapped her strength.

Sister Marie Catherine again repressed her desire to speak her mind on this matter. She talked to God about it instead, adding a prayer that she herself would have grace to accept the dominant note she detected in Sister Loyola. That was going to be her own particular difficulty. There would be hardships, of course, but she had no fear of physical trials. Thus far, her Superiors had understood her, had enjoyed her exuberance, her quick way of plunging into the hardest of situations, her shrewd evaluations, and even the somewhat emotional extremes of her piety. For she was a combination of visionary and resourceful business woman, the product of a unique childhood, the memory of which warmed her heart through the dark days on the Schelde and through even darker days to come. Daughter of middle-class parents, Pierre Cabareaux and Marie Dignole, Marie Thérèse was born in 1813, in the little town of Couvin in the province of Namur, only a few miles from the French border. She was a rollicking youngster, a little too noisy for her day, but faith-centered from the start. Faith was the one tremendous interest that opened up to her greater and greater vistas of wonder. Religion was not just a list of do's and don't's, though her sensitive child conscience bothered her when her impulses led her into courses that her more code-minded little contemporaries would have avoided. But these worries never lasted

long since she possessed a wonderful friend who always viewed
her motives kindly and discouraged fretting in any case. This
was Brother George. To the end of her days she loved to
recall him bent over his books and paintings in her father's
study where his "library" was piled high on tables, chairs,
and window sills. Her father never objected; he had himself
invited this Brother Minim, an exile from France, into his
home.[4] An old saint, he called him.

Partly in gratitude, and partly because he realized her
worth, Brother George undertook the education of little
Marie Thérèse. That was the least he might do, he insisted,
to repay her parents for a comfortable room and three good
meals a day. When lessons began, Brother George found his
pupil somewhat spoiled as the result of a long illness. But
presently Madame Cabareaux noticed that the child's
tantrums subsided at a word from Brother George. Even
the sight of him sitting alone in his room, his eyes closed in
prayer, was enough to calm her. As a reward for a good
lesson, he would let her sit at his table and watch him make
rosaries or paint or, best of all, print motto cards with wooden
type from his type box. In fine weather, he would set out
with tools and brushes to repair a neglected shrine or calvary
on the roadways. If the distance permitted, he would take
his little pupil along and let her sit on the grass while he
worked. The work finished, he would sit beside her to rest
a while and tell her a story. The best story teller in all the
world was this old Brother George. Then they would
both discuss his repair work with extreme satisfaction and
pray a little before the shrine in its renewed beauty. Those
were happy days until, to her bewildered sorrow, they came
to an abrupt end in her ninth year.

One night Madame Cabareaux awakened her little
daughter and told her that her eighty-eight-year-old friend
was very ill and wanted to see her. At his bedside, the child
was struck with fear; he seemed not to know her, not even
to hear her mother's words. But when Madame Cabareaux
took her hand and placed it in his, he opened his eyes and
smiled at her. A few minutes later, Monsieur Cabareaux
entered the room and his wife whispered to him that Brother

George had just gone to God. One is not surprised that after
his death Marie Thérèse suffered an "illness," probably an
emotional upset, for though her attachment to old Brother
George had in no way interfered with her normal child life
of home and play, still it had opened channels in her ample
spirit before reason and experience could control the cur-
rents.

When the child recovered, her parents wisely sent her to
the village school where she made a normal adjustment in
the face of double difficulty. On the one hand, she read like
an adult and possessed a general knowledge far beyond her
age level; on the other, according to her account, she had
still to learn to write. This may mean that she had not
learned to execute the copybook models on which her companions had spent three or four years of daily practice. Whatever she means, penmanship was the cross of her schooldays.
She never mastered it. All through her life, she wrote a large,
bold, angular hand, most unlike the delicate tracing of her
contemporaries. Imitation was not for her. She liked her
teachers and companions; she needed them as people. But
she found the stilted classes a bit boring and so didn't mind
being stricken down by one or other childhood illness. It
was quite nice to sit up in bed with books from Brother
George's library strewn over the coverlet. Making her own
choices, she dipped into the abounding affective piety of the
time. It went to her head, firing her active imagination and
paving the way for a somewhat troubled adolescence. But as
a nervous, introspective eleven-year-old, Marie Thérèse was
not neurotic, not even badly adjusted; she was too friendly
and generous for that. But she loved to pray. She read and
reread her favorite visionaries and worried over her inability
to keep pace with them. Finally, she had what she believed
to be a vision of her own in the parish church one Sunday,
a vision that involved her future life as a religious. Without
a doubt of its reality, she told her mother, who seems to
have guided her wisely and patiently through this troubled
period, requiring her assistance in her never ending rounds
of charity in the village as a means of distraction. Though
Marie Thérèse emerged from her nervous worries quickly

enough, she clung to the reality of her childhood vision. When in her old age she was told to write her story just as she recalled it, she set it down as her best remembered event; it was part of her tremendous faith.

From childhood she found prayer easy. When Father Michael Accolti acted as spiritual director to the Sisters of Notre Dame in Oregon, he considered Sister Marie Catherine something of a mystic. Her adult life was not marked by visions; still she never wavered in acceptance of her one taste of ecstasy, perhaps because that era was credulous of visions while it frowned on and feared mystic states of prayer. Of this she was always certain, that the influence of Brother George was the great blessing of her childhood; the suggestion that her early years had been abnormal would have annoyed her. Actually the brief crisis left her healthy and fun-loving, so much of an outdoor tomboy that her mother feared she would never measure up to accepted standards of manners.

Families that could afford it were sending their daughters to boarding school for a year or two. That was just the thing for Marie Thérèse, Madame Cabareaux decided, and she hurried her daughter off to the nearest convent boarding school, requesting the gentle Daughters of Mary to correct her "numerous defects if possible." Apparently Marie Thérèse co-operated wholeheartedly with their efforts. She became politely subdued, at least by comparison with her former self, and if she could not completely control her enthusiasms, she channeled them into the directions of piety fostered by convent life. In a short time, she was the center of a somewhat overpious group. Under her directions, they formed a "community," and even elected a superior, though she fails to say whom. They made daily meditations and were in general quite pleased with themselves. But they were not prigs; they got on with the unorganized and with their teachers.

Less enthusiastic about the conventional program of studies, Marie Thérèse still managed to deserve reports that pleased her parents. But her classes must have offered her some challenge or she would have mentioned the fact; unfulfilling experiences would have aroused resentment in her.

She accepted the manner of her education as she knew of no other, but one cannot help thinking how she would have expanded under the Socratic approach. As it was, she returned home at about fifteen, astounding the neighbors with her sedate manners and filling her mother with pride.

Her family raised, charitable Madame Cabareaux was now devoting most of her time to the poor and sick. To her delight, her daughter wanted to accompany her on every errand of mercy. Together they bathed and medicated the neglected ones, often spending entire nights at their bedsides, their goodness leading darkened spirits again toward light. Between these acts of charity, Marie Thérèse often delved again into her old friend's book collection. Looking for a favorite volume one day, she came upon some old numbers of *Annals of the Propagation of the Faith* and opened one idly. Presently an article on foreign missions held her spellbound. Her hard-won sedate manner abandoned her. She was a missionary, teaching mobs of savages. As the scene grew real, she mounted a chair, the better to reach them all with her message. The exalted moment past, she got down and sat on the chair in dejection. After all she was a girl; men always had much better opportunities. Still, at school she had heard about religious women going to foreign lands. She opened the *Annals* again. There it was: Sisters were wanted in mission lands, real missions, not cities and towns in settled countries. And allowing for the decade since the printing of the article, perhaps numbers of Sisters had answered the call. Of course she would have to join an order. Marie Thérèse began to consider her fitness, or lack of it, for religious life and decided to wait until her seventeenth birthday. She might make a better impression then.

The former teacher on whom she counted for encouragement proved disappointing. Marie Thérèse was too young to know her mind, she said. She should just go on living as a fervent young Christian and wait for light on the subject. Much as she detested waiting for anything, Marie Thérèse seems not to have questioned the advice. She settled down to work and pray at home. With an ear to the ground for chance news about foreign missions, she lived on happily enough for another two years. Then an unforeseen circumstance brought her one day to Namur and the Mother House of the Sisters of Notre Dame. Here she met Mère St. Joseph, the co-foundress and second Mother General of this young institute. Since the day that two daughters of a neighboring family had entered Notre Dame, Marie Thérèse had been wondering whether this new venture in religious life had perhaps something special to offer her. What she had heard of it sounded vigorous and to her liking. Encouraged by Mère St. Joseph's gentle smile, she told her of her aspirations. And as the chilly reception of her ardent offer two years before had given her a humble self-estimate, it seemed only honest to acquaint this kind superior with the facts. She was not at all gifted, she said; in fact, she was an ignoramus, but she was willing to try anything. Her frankness won Mère St. Joseph and the other Sisters who met her that day. She was accepted, perhaps not quite as a "gift from heaven," as was her contemporary, Caroline Neujean, the tried and true product of a Notre Dame school, but certainly with a kindly welcome.

Excitedly announcing the news at home, Marie Thérèse suddenly realized her family's deep attachment to her and hers to her family. The younger members failed to understand her decision and declared they would prevent it if possible. But her parents and at least one sister took her part, and when she left for Namur, these three accompanied her. Parting with them there was much harder than she had anticipated. As she recalled that day, she knew some tremendous grace had steadied her resolution when for the first time she saw tears in her father's eyes.

Fortunately for her, the novelty of the postulate swept her along. This was the life! For the time she forgot about foreign missions. She was just going to be the best possible sort of Sister and leave the rest to God. She entered into every duty assigned her with such gusto as somewhat to disturb novitiate serenity. And she was happy, the happiest postulant the Sisters could remember, if perhaps the most emotional; her joy overflowed in tears as well as in laughter. In an amused sort of way, the Mistress of Postulants was satisfied with Marie Thérèse. One had to explain religious decorum to her, partly in the interests of furniture and dishes, and allow her time to fit herself more closely into the scheme of things. To be sure, Marie Thérèse was different; for one thing she was quite bewildered by the meditation book used faithfully by old and young in that day as a *sine qua non* of progress in prayer. She could not understand these deliberate steps, or planning of any kind, in one's approach to God. But she passed so successfully the acid tests of charity and humility that the Mistress and the Mother General both closed their eyes to her heretical attitude toward points and preludes. Besides, what could one do in the face of such general approval? Everyone liked Marie Thérèse.

What her Superiors did astounds the twentieth century novice. They clothed Marie Thérèse in the holy habit at the end of six weeks. Those were uncanonical days in which fitness of the subject and need of workers combined to shorten training periods. Lengthy reports of Sister Formation Committees were unheard of. The index was good will, which, if it stood up well under the stress and strain of six weeks in the postulate, was considered abiding and dependable. So with the name Sister Marie Catherine ringing strangely in her ears, the new novice splashed tears of joy on the starched white cape as Mère St. Joseph placed it over her shoulders. One hopes the wilted linen was replaced before she was presented in the novitiate, for there among the Sisters preparing for their vows was her future Superior, Sister Loyola. Practical and efficient even as a novice, Sister Loyola would have disapproved of both tears and disorder.

In those days, a novice was thrown at once into a whirl of preparation for teaching. If possible, her work was planned along lines in which she had shown promise in school. Experienced teachers instructed her in both academic subjects and methods. So Sister Marie Catherine soon found herself rushing from class to class, enjoying it all, especially science. She was even tried at the piano, which exercise, while it proved an excellent means of using up her energy, had to be discontinued in her case. When the musicians in the house heard her practice, she records, they excused her from further pursuit of musical studies. In general, she says, she needed a great deal of help, which everyone, especially the other novices, seemed most willing to give. As she had never quite lost all her boyish manners, the older novices took turns at making her more dignified. The brightest hour of her day was her evening charge as assistant to the infirmarian. Her mother's training and her love for the sick made her invaluable as a nurse's aide.

The unbroken flow of happy days began to puzzle Sister Marie Catherine. A dedicated life, she thought, should have a cross now and then. Crosses were signs that one was growing up spiritually. Perhaps she should assure God that she would not object to a few difficulties. Then as she was praying over this problem one day, the growing-up process suddenly began. Word came that her father had met with a fatal accident. There was no question then of even a novice going to visit a sick or dying parent, but her sympathetic mistress talked kindly to her and sent her to the chapel to pray. Within a few days, a letter from her mother told her of her father's death and of his last message to her. His greatest happiness, he had said, was her dedication of her life to God. For Sister Marie Catherine the event was a fulfillment. Growing up, she found, was not a realization of one's strength under trial; it was the discovery of Divine love and grace waiting quietly for one in the straitening hour. When the next blow came, she met it calmly.

A few months before the summer retreat at which Sister Marie Catherine expected to pronounce her first vows, Mère St. Joseph sent her to replace the sick mistress of resident pupils, ninety-two in number, at the house in Gembloux. The novice rose to the challenge in completely adult fashion. She had the qualities that spelled success in a Belgian boarding school, order and control. Unfortunately everyone praised her, so that the experience was stamped in her mind as a pattern for dealing with girls; a pattern that later proved unacceptable in America. But for the time success was hers, and that it failed to turn her head speaks volumes for her maturity.

At the close of classes, Sister Marie Catherine returned to the novitiate and plunged into preparation for her vows, as humble and earnest as ever. Presently Father Louis Vercruysse, himself to be one of the band on *l'Infatigable,* came to conduct the summer retreat. A stickler for method like the earlier Jesuit author of the same name, Father Vercruysse clung tenaciously to Ignatian points and preludes and expected his retreatants to do likewise. Mystic prayer, he thought, had led many astray; it flattered self-love and pride, it caused deception, it just didn't belong to the active life. So Sister Marie Catherine was again faced with the problem which her novice mistress had decided to ignore in her case. Not that either novice or mistress knew much about genuine mysticism, or its dangerous counterfeit, quietism. But Father Vercruysse, who knew the distinction, seems to have held prayer of quiet and affective prayer both dangerous for religious souls. He presented each meditation in deliberate steps, a rigid outline of progress. Her soul thus cribbed and cabined, Sister Marie Catherine decided the thing must be done. To hold out would be disobedience and pride. Book in hand she struggled morning after morning to contain her soul in method, until long afterwards in Oregon Father Michael Accolti set her at peace forever in this matter.

Sister Marie Catherine considered the years between her profession and departure for Oregon excellent preparation for hard mission life. At Namur, she assisted crippled old Sister Madeleine, a brilliant instructor in her day, who still clung to a little teaching though unable to move about without help. Leaning heavily on Sister Marie Catherine's arm, she moved at a snail's pace about the house; it seemed to require hours to get her started, or again to get her settled, but her glad way of sharing her life's experience was always compensation. Still, this curb on youthful speed was nothing compared with the difficulties at the house in Liége to which Sister Marie Catherine was sent as head mistress. Here the elderly Superior was fast losing her sight, and as a result there were problems of disorder in the classes. Everyone looked to the new first teacher to bring order out of the chaos. The speed with which she did so attracted the attention of the zealous and energetic Sister Victoire, who seems to have been occupied at the time almost entirely with parish projects. Before long Sister Victoire swept the new first teacher into the orbit of her apostolate, utilizing her energy and profiting by the renewed spirit of order and work among the pupils. It happened that about this time aid for foreign missions began to take priority among Sister Victoire's varied interests, and with this kindling Sister Marie Catherine's dormant hope burst again into flame. Then presently excited whispers fluttered along the interconvent grapevine of the little Notre Dame world, outrunning announcement from authoritative sources: Sisters of Notre Dame were wanted in America! Cincinnati! Where on earth was it, and how was it spelled?

Soon Reverend Mother Marie Thérèse announced Bishop Purcell's request for missionaries and asked for volunteers.[5] He wanted teachers for a school in Cincinnati, and though that was not quite what Sister Marie Catherine had in mind, still it was missionary work such as any Belgian would consider venturesome. She submitted her name as convincingly as possible and, while waiting for a reply, talked so eagerly about the project that everyone took her acceptance for granted; her local Superior even began to prepare things for her long journey. Poor Sister Marie Catherine was disappointed but not discouraged when her name failed to appear on the list. She knew that once the movement had begun, there would be a series of calls to the new world. She must just keep her missionary desires before the Mother General's eyes.

The second call was well worth waiting for. Oregon! Distance alone placed this venture on an epic scale and made it worthy of a St. Francis Xavier. As Sister Marie Catherine read her letter of acceptance, throngs of natives once more advanced toward her, this time in a broad, green valley in the far Northwest. Now she must hasten to learn English and Chinook; both would be needed in her valley. But alas, both were learned only with great difficulty unless one came by language easily, which she did not. On the deck that Christmas Eve, she recalled her first amazement at the sight of the words in the little Chinook handbook that Father

DeSmet had sent each volunteer. And here she was, months later, still trying to master those dreadful words. How slowly everything was moving! After all the hurried preparations in the Liége convent, here she was waiting, waiting. But it was comforting now to think about all the admiring wonder of the Sisters at having an apostle in their midst, about Sister Victoire's encouragement, about that last visit with her young nephew who came to say goodbye and could talk of nothing but ships and America. And her class! In the end she had slipped out and left her successor to explain matters. She loved them all so much, her pupils, her religious Sisters, her family. Like Homer's heroes, she didn't consider it cowardly to shed a few big tears at the thought of it all, though it might be more seemly to be cast in Sister Loyola's harder mold. There at that very moment that unemotional Sister stood eyeing her, catching her in a bit of sentimental indulgence, and a honed edge of scorn was sheathed in her look.

About this fascinating head of the group too little is known before the Oregon story begins. Sister Loyola was Rosalie Duquenne, another middle-class daughter, born in Louvain, May 10, 1810, and thus two years older than Sister Marie Catherine. That her ability was recognized early is clear from the fact she held two successive superiorships at Brussels before her appointment to lead the missionary band. In fact, she planned and supervised the building of the second foundation at Brussels while governing the first. When she opened this second house, a boarding school in l'Arbre Bénit, in the suburb of Ixelles, she was only thirty-two but an already experienced and successful Superior, so highly admired in Brussels as to cause general regret by volunteering for the Oregon mission. The beautiful gold monstrance given her as a parting gift by the pupils of the two Brussels schools and their parents indicated their esteem.[6]

In naming Sister Loyola head of the mission group, Mère Constantine was counting on her unusual initiative and ability to get things done quickly and well. A certain elasticity in her character would enable her to meet situations that failed to fit into traditional grooves, while at the same time her loyalty would maintain the spirit of the congregation. It was true that thus far all her opportunities for inventiveness had occurred within easy reach of consultation with the heads of the institute at Namur. One could not foretell how things would turn out on the far Pacific Coast, but thus far there had been no indiscretions in Sister Loyola's management. She met difficulties with optimism and ingenuity, always found a way out. Success attended her plans with promptitude; people liked to help her. She seemed altogether the perfect choice for the great venture. Mère Constantine regretted giving her up, but she knew of no other so apparently fitted to head the project. And as her assistant, the retiring and somewhat conservative Sister Mary Cornelia would act as a check should initiative run to impulsiveness.[7]

Twenty-eight-year-old Sister Mary Cornelia, self-effacing and generally loved, had been appointed Superior of the convent in Fleurus just a year before the sailing of *l'Infatigable*. Though she was destined to make the most significant contribution to the enterprise, she lacked the inventiveness of either Sister Loyola or Sister Marie Catherine. All her life she tended to lean rather heavily on someone more forceful than herself. By nature and because of her extreme cultivation of humility, she found it easy to submit. Under Sister Loyola's increasingly dominant leadership, she fitted gracefully into obscure positions during the first decade of her life in America. But Sister Mary Cornelia's lack of initiative was compensated for by unusual gifts of judgment. When she emerged as leader of the group in California, her decisions, always a little timid and always based on consultation, were close to center and unregrettable. Her own interior life she led with watchful fortitude, and thus occupied, her critical eye looked gently on others. She admired ability in her religious Sisters. She found it easy to regard as masterful in others what she would have considered aggressive in herself.

On that Christman Eve, Sister Mary Cornelia's thoughts could dwell on a very placid childhood in a well-ordered, upper middle-class home in Liége. At a chance meeting with Mère Julie Billiart, her pious as well as successful father, the cloth-merchant Neujean, was so impressed with the holiness of the foundress that he insisted on bringing her home to meet his wife. Everyone knew the story of how Madame Neujean, quite as deeply impressed, placed baby Caroline in the holy woman's arms to be kissed and blessed. And Mère Julie knew from that moment, said all the early Sisters, that little Caroline would grow up to be one of her daughters. Certainly the child began very early to speak about being a Sister, perhaps not too surprising a thing in that pious family. At the advice of her uncle, the formidable but revered Dean Neujean of St. Nicolas, her parents enrolled her at the age of four in the school of the Sisters of Notre Dame in his parish. Six long hours a day with no afternoon nap! The poor baby struggled bravely through that first year, but the next year was better for then her idolized little sister, Jeanette, was enrolled with her for the same Spartan treatment. Duly chaperoned they set out each morning to no attractive kindergarten; these tots sat on hard benches from which they could not reach the floor even with their toes; they did "sums" and copied words and sentences laboriously on noisy, creaking slates. For Caroline compensation came at recess and noon-hour, when dainty little Jeanette became the cynosure of the playground.

When Caroline was a seasoned schoolgirl of eight, Dean Neujean presented a second suggestion to her parents. She should be sent to boarding school in preparation for her First Communion. There was no argument. The Dean was always right. Caroline was sent straightway to the Notre Dame Boarding school in Liége. It was well that she liked it, for there, perhaps also at the Dean's advice, she remained for eight long years. Looking back on those years, she could recall only two unpleasant memories. One was that her stern uncle postponed her First Communion for a year because he found her "rather playful and inclined to fun." The other was her frequent "bad marks" for tardiness to class. She straggled in last so often that the Sisters dubbed her "Little Sylvester," recalling the saint of the last day of the year. But her teachers overlooked her inexactness in view of the

combination of humility and fine mind that gave her at
fifteen "a ripeness of culture far beyond her years" and a
balanced and genuine piety.

In her early teens, Caroline fell under the spell of masterful Sister Victoire, with a schoolgirl's complete dedication.
From the day that Sister Victoire lined Caroline up among
her selected young leaders, she was a changed girl. Soon the
malcontents in the boarding school found her a power to
consider. Reporting was apparently now laid upon her as a
duty, but one she disliked so thoroughly that she tried to
render it unnecessary by a personal warning to each offender.
If the erring one mended her ways, Caroline let the matter drop. In case of relapse, however, she "aided Sister
Victoire." In that day, of course, the meddling attitude
ranked as related to loyalty and respect, but it seems a block
that fitted badly into Caroline's design. Even so, in this as
well as in other lines of action, Caroline became so helpful
that Sister Victoire recommended her as head of a pious confraternity in the St. Nicolas parish, an organization which
Dean Neujean had established at the behest of Mère Julie
herself when her Sisters began their work there. So when thus
recommended, the naturally timid Mademoiselle Neujean
returned home with all the schooling usually possessed by
the "finished" girl of her day, she threw all her energy into
confraternity work under Sister Victoire's direction. From
the start, the members accepted her leadership despite her
youth, partly perhaps because they were for the most part
workers in her father's extensive cloth mills. But they seem
to have liked her on her own account, too. Regularly she
read to worker groups, explaining the more difficult passages,
imitating Sister Victoire's assurance as she spoke. At the day's
end, she prayed with this or that group of workers. She
exhorted them all to attend Sister Victoire's large sodality
meeting after Mass on Sunday, and was on hand after that
meeting to dispense books from the parish library. It was
a dangerous game. In her tremendous admiration for the
attractive Sister Victoire, Caroline was running the risk of
outdoing her zeal. She felt responsible for her father's
workers; she watched over them, warned them, even had

their sodality membership suspended when they disregarded her warnings, all of which is most unlike her later diffidence in assuming authority over others. It was, of course, her abiding and generous love for all, that prevented her becoming a zealot and arousing resentment in the workers.

When Dean Neujean died, Caroline came under the direction of a certain Father Groetuclas, a less exacting and gentler counselor. On his advice she left off regulating the lives of the mill hands and asked for admission at the novitiate of the Sisters of Notre Dame in Namur. Even though her relatives might reasonably have expected this announcement, it came as a blow to all of them, especially since her brother had shortly before entered the seminary. But their spirit of faith soon brought them around to Caroline's point of view, all, that is, except Jeanette, whose hysteria indicated her difficulty in seeing any point of view other than her own.

With her storied aura of Mère Julie's predilection, the general esteem in which her family was held, and the glowing epithets of Sister Victoire, Caroline ran the risk of becoming a spoiled postulant. But her Superiors saw this danger and so spared her none of the rigors of novitiate training, which included the calculated humiliation then considered necessary. They were perhaps not entirely surprised to discover that in Caroline's case the planned attack on pride was less necessary than usual. This very prayerful nineteen-year-old was reaching for humility as a plant for the sun. She was the least of all; it was as though she had never known Sister Victoire's urgent prodding toward leadership. In a very short time everyone recognized that absolute selflessness that marked her life as it did that of her priest-brother, who died heroically among the cholera-infected coolies of Serain. It was no wonder that in a matter of weeks Caroline was clothed with the habit and white veil of a novice and given her reverend uncle's name lest that sternly good man should be forgotten.

Before she was quite used to novitiate life, Sister Mary Cornelia's Superiors entrusted her with the copying of papers important to the institute, not at all the sort of task usually assigned to novices. Far from being impressed by such self-

satisfying incidents, the new novice plunged eagerly into
the most menial tasks. Now the once tardy pupil was first at
the dishes, first to don wooden shoes in the laundry. But
as admiration for her grew, her humility kept well in advance
of it. When she pronounced her first vows in 1836, she was
steeped in nothingness. In her occasional interviews with
the now ailing co-foundress, Mère St. Joseph, she drank in
deep draughts of the institute's primitive spirit; her one aim
was to resemble as closely as possible the humble woman
who had smiled upon her babyhood. This, she believed, was
what God desired of her. To attain it, she began a life of very
intense prayer. It was this tremendous beginning that carried
Sister Mary Cornelia safely through a peril cleverly disguised
with enticement.

As Mère St. Joseph's health grew frailer, she entrusted
the government of the Namur house to her Assistant, Sister
Marie Thérèse, reserving for herself the supervision of the
secondary houses. Sister Marie Thérèse, herself something of
an invalid at the time, began to delegate her authority to
the persuasive and dominant young Sister Borgia, whose
craving for power was in turn being fanned into flame by a
self-deluded visionary, who had abandoned community life
on the score of ill health. With pious talk and subtle flattery,
Sister Borgia exploited the visionary, leading even the best-
intentioned to her for spiritual guidance. The visionary's
advice always included the highest praise of Sister Borgia, who
now began to make high-handed and ill-advised changes in
both school and convent. Presently the "saint" revealed to her
clientele that Mère St. Joseph was too old to govern; that
they must break off and make a new start under the leadership
of Sister Borgia. All this had been revealed to her in ecstasy,
she claimed. Seemingly poor Sister Marie Thérèse in her sick
room was completely deceived by the plotters. Certainly
some of the more stalwart members of the community were
taken in. And deeming it an advantage to have the much
admired novice in their number, the leading instigators approached Sister Mary Cornelia. She really must come to the
visionary's room, they told her, and hear from her lips the
will of Heaven.

Tactfully and without the least self-righteous note, the

novice refused to see the visionary, nor would she join with the conspiracy in any way. She refused, on the other hand, to judge or condemn them. She did not think it her duty to report the affair. It was not her place to interfere. God would take the matter into His own hands. Perhaps her attitude had something to do with opening eyes to the truth. At any rate, all those involved finally professed loyalty to Mère St. Joseph and the primitive spirit, and the deserted leaders left the house.[8]

Two effects of the rebellion were the general strengthening of the institute and the stature gained by Sister Mary Cornelia, especially in the eyes of two future Mothers General, Mère Ignace and Mère Constantine. Both were stationed at the house in Jumet when she was assigned there after profession, the former as Superior. Knowing the stand she had taken, these two watched her carefully and were not surprised at the prudence and judgment that went hand in hand with her humble self-estimate. When Mère Ignace assumed the generalate, one of her first acts was to place Sister Mary Cornelia in full charge of the school at Jemmapes, in which serious discipline problems resulting from destitute homes were resisting all efforts at solution.

The new first teacher's achievement of order and good will were due to her training under Sister Victoire, said onlookers. Undoubtedly that preparation helped in her plans for alleviating the wretchedness of her pupils' homes, but now her work was marked by profound charity and sympathy rather than by high-powered organization. At any rate, the change in the school was unbelievable. Then before complacency had time to tempt Sister Mary Cornelia, she received her third assignment. At twenty-five she was appointed Superior of the house in Fleurus. Completely stunned, she could not appeal to Mère Marie Ignace, whose fatal illness was swiftly ending her short generalate. She decided to lay the matter before Sister Constantine, who was then the local Superior at the Mother House and who had been delegated to install her at Fleurus. With her fine judgment she would surely see the need of changing this decision made by a dying Superior.

When Sister Constantine arrived at Jemmapes, Sister Mary

Cornelia presented a convincing argument. It might be true, she argued, that she had succeeded with mill hands and bad-mannered children, but direction of a community of Sisters was quite another matter. Besides, she was too young and inexperienced, even if she had native ability for such a task, which she had not. She lacked all the necessary qualifications. As she began to enumerate these, Sister Constantine cut her short with a blunt and all-embracing agreement that bordered on sarcasm. Of course, she lacked ability. So had the Apostles. It was God's way to use weak things in his work. And now, as time was pressing, they must set out at once for Fleurus.

As they trudged along on foot, Sister Constantine broke the monotony with crisp bits of advice of such an unflattering nature that it was a relief when a messenger in a carriage over-took them with a letter for her. She must return to Namur at once as the Mother General had taken a turn for the worse. For a moment, Sister Mary Cornelia glimpsed an escape, but only for a moment, for Sister Constantine bade her go on to Fleurus alone and introduce herself to the Sisters there; in fact, introduction was scarcely necessary since they would have had official notification of her appointment by this time. And Sister Constantine, all kindness and encouragement now, bade the new Superior a loving goodbye and climbed into the carriage.

Right up to the door of her new home, Sister Mary Cornelia prayed for confidence but failed to feel it; even as she knocked she wanted to run. Light-hearted and gentle Sister Bernardine admitted her, cut short her stumbling declarations of incapacity, and hurried her into the presence of the pleased community where her diffidence disappeared in the general buoyancy of spirit.

Sister Mary Cornelia's stay at Fleurus was a happy recollection as she waited in the Schelde, a calm and gentle preparation before her call to Oregon, during which she learned how to head a community. Still, her entire life was to be marked by diffidence. Not the diffidence of pride that fears failure. It sprang rather from the genuine humility that she had cultivated in girlhood and that led her to accept easily the more masterful leadership of a Sister Victoire or a Sister Loyola.

As soon as Sister Mary Cornelia had volunteered for the Oregon mission, she was wrapped in doubts about her fitness for it and immediately sent a follow-up letter about her worries to Mère Constantine. She might, in fact, be rather a hindrance to the project. Should she withdraw? Reading the letter, Mère Constantine decided that the writer needed a still deeper plunge into selflessness. She answered briefly. She had no doubt, she said, that God had inspired Sister Mary Cornelia to offer herself for the mission precisely because she lacked all merit. It was a work that called for complete trust, and the more totally unworthy the subject, the more complete her trust could be. The volunteer folded the letter gratefully, wound up her affairs, and packed her things, including eight pairs of winter shoes and another eight pairs for summer, as each of the seven missionaries had been directed to do. Then she went to Namur and entered with enthusiasm into the preparations going forward there for the journey and mission. She herself supervised the packing of thirty large boxes, following closely the precise suggestions sent by Sister Louise from Cincinnati. In all this she passed Mère Constantine's acid test; her reaction to severity was humble and enthusiastic obedience. She could be counted on as a cornerstone for Notre Dame's venture in the West.

The finest spun and gentlest of the group was Sister Mary Aloysia. Artistic and poetic, she was also their nearest approach to the intellectual. In her case, the memoir writer is not satisfied with the cliché "rare talents"; Sister Mary Aloysia was an entire "university faculty" in herself, a walking dictionary, even from childhood. She was, of course, just another product of the finishing school of her day, but a highly polished product. In the boarding school in Jumet, the Sisters had singled out this motherless child, a real little wonder, who walked up for first prizes on "Exhibition" days then and all through her school years. Frail Jeanette Chevry was by far the most docile and sweet-tempered child in every one of her classes, one to be counted on to say and do the correct thing in any situation, a cause of frustration to all competitors. Each summer she returned, laden with honors to her wealthy, upper middle-class home, to be petted and admired by her father and relatives. She enjoyed it all without being in the least spoiled by it and at each summer's end returned without murmur to the restrictions of boarding school.

When the school in Jumet had bestowed its last and highest honor on Jeanette, her father sent her, on her teachers' advice, to Notre Dame's boarding school in Namur. Here she continued her unbroken line of victories while her relatives awaited her entrance into brilliant society. Yet they were not entirely surprised, when after her last prize-laden return home, this lovely bud announced that she meant to return presently to the novitiate at Namur. She carried out her wish in the summer of 1837 despite their attempts to dissuade her, especially on the score of her frail health. At the novitiate, that obstacle to admittance was overlooked in her case in consideration of her other qualities. Jeanette was received as another "gift from heaven," it would seem. It was not until the twentieth century that the athletic maiden, in whose high-school picture gleam laughing eyes and two rows of strong, white teeth, became the promising novitiate prospect. In Jeanette's day smooth manners and external piety weighed heavily in the aspirant's favor. Both could, of course, be entirely external, but they often represented, as in Jeanette's case, genuine charity and a deep spirit of prayer.

A certain quiet but firm resolve marked Sister Mary Aloysia's novitiate days and her subsequent three years of successful teaching in the boarding school at Namur. When Mère Constantine accepted her offer to go to Oregon, some wondered how she could deprive her most important school of so promising a teacher, and how she could send one so delicate on such an arduous mission. But no one really doubted Sister Mary Aloysia's will to see it through. Those who worked with her knew her way of confronting difficulties with vigor, as in the case of Nanny, the little goat on *l'Infatigable.* As all the missionaries found the ship's black coffee unpalatable, Father DeSmet made use of the long delay before sailing to search for a goat among the nearby Walcheren farms; a little milk, he said, would make the coffee less bitter. When he returned to the ship with his purchase, the somewhat recalcitrant Nanny, it was delicate

Sister Mary Aloysia who grasped her horns and held her while Sister Marie Catherine milked her. Sister Mary Aloysia's secret weapons were, of course, the tact and good will that accompanied her vigor, as Nanny recognized. The goat's response was good behavior during the long journey, and her reward for it all was the wondering gaze of many an astonished young native in Oregon.

But it is easier to picture Sister Mary Aloysia writing pious poems and doing oils of mountain scenes for convent parlors and corridors. None of her verse has survived her, but it must have been, like her prose, filled with proper clichés and quite uncreative. Some of her time-blackened paintings still exist, at best skillfully made copies. She played the piano well and sang sweetly. She was not in the least original, nor was she expected to be; there were no creative classes in the girls' school of her day. In the new world, her chief asset was to be her way of meeting persons as individuals. Sister Marie Catherine envisioned swarms of natives coming to be saved; Sister Mary Aloysia met them singly at the door of her heart. To some extent, certainly in dealing with Sisters, Sister Mary Cornelia shared this attitude, but it was not the common attitude of teachers in those days; the important thing was to stamp the ideal pattern on all. In later days in California, daughters of Spanish dons and newly rich miners, alike spoiled and pampered, found it hard to conform to the Belgian standard of girlhood upheld in the first decades of Notre Dame's boarding school in San José. But one and all, they blessed the name of Sister Mary Aloysia. One of these, a schoolgirl in the seventies, who found that even Sister Mary Cornelia stressed the pattern too heavily, said fondly at the age of ninety-four, "But Sister Mary Aloysia was a princess." [9]

Because Sister Mary Aloysia died before historic interest began to center around this pioneer group, we lack incident and detail in her case. She was not a leader. She seems to have had little to do with building or finances. Even as first teacher she never spoke of herself as head of the school. She was a cheerful, self-effacing sister, always on hand to help with tactful word and willing hand.

The expedition to Oregon was fortunate in having these four Sisters, whose contributions were complementary to a degree that proves Mère Constantine to have been a gifted director of personnel. And the two less known pioneers were equally well chosen. The community in Ghent parted reluctantly with forty-four-year-old Sister Norbertine, Séraphine Verreux, whose physique was tremendous even for a Belgian woman, and who was blessed with a green thumb that had turned the convent garden into a park. Of peasant origin, she seemed to hold the key to the world of plants. She had a way with workmen, too; a gardener would have to be an unredeemable idler not to be spurred into action by her interest in plant and tree. And idlers didn't stay long; she had as little use for them as for a neglected landscape. Mère Constantine knew the acres attached to the mission house on the Willamette would offer Sister Norbertine sufficient scope. And last there was short, robust Sister Mary Albine, Joséphine Gobert from Thuin, whose smile reminded the older Sisters of Mère Julie herself. An expert infirmarian, she would fill an important mission need. Besides, as there was no more perfect maker of church vestments in all Belgium, the poor missionary priests in Oregon would be grateful for her presence there. She knew, of course, that her elaborate creations in gold embroidery would not be in demand. The Jesuits on *l'Infatigable* knew they would have to celebrate Mass in dingy hovels; they would be grateful for fresh altar linen and the plainest of vestments.

Only two of these Jesuits were to be closely associated with the work of the Sisters of Notre Dame in the West. One was Father John Nobili, who worked heroically among the natives of British Columbia (formerly New Caledonia), and preceded the Sisters to California, where he founded Santa Clara College.[10] During the short period of his rectorship there he guided the beginnings of Notre Dame in nearby San José. Father Michael Accolti, jovial and enterprising, was assigned as spiritual director of the Sisters during the voyage, an office which he resumed at times in Oregon. Fathers Anthony Ravalli and Louis Vercruysse were to be associated with the distant Rocky Mountain mission, an arrangement that must have pleased Sister Marie Catherine in the case of the latter; she could never forget his insistence on formal method in prayer. Fortunately for the Sisters, Brother Francis Huysbrecht, the one lay brother in the group, was to be near them at Willamette during their building days. Little is known of him except that he possessed a happy combination of rugged strength and willingness to help.

Forty-three-year-old Father Peter DeSmet was already a seasoned missionary when he led this little band to Oregon. In a way, he was conditioned to missionary life from boyhood by a sort of discontented restlessness.[11] Far-off hills were always green. Even in the matter of schools, he always had to try the as yet untried; he was in and out of a remarkable number of boys' schools before his seminary days. To his father's disappointment, Peter's instability failed to disappear with adulthood. With the priesthood in mind, he made two futile starts before he finally enrolled in the Junior Seminary of Mechlin, where he fell under the spell of the famous missionary, Father Charles Nerinckx, who was on a recruiting tour for the American missions. This at last was what Peter wanted. With six others he signed up to accompany Father Nerinckx to America. But there was the matter of his father's assent. Almost certain of not obtaining it, he borrowed passage money and sailed without even seeing his father; thus he created an estrangement that he always regretted. His five companions, too, it seems, met with or had reason to expect parental opposition; each had to pawn his personal possessions to raise funds for the journey.

A fairly smooth forty-day voyage brought the six to Philadelphia, a thriving city, to their surprise, and not a village in the wilderness. Soon they entered the Jesuit novitiate at Whitemarsh to begin their long preparation for the priesthood. Less than two years later they were transferred to the new novitiate at Florissant near St. Louis. It was so new, in fact, that they helped erect the buildings, which meant much hewing and fitting of timber, work that afforded an outlet for young DeSmet's extraordinary strength and nervous energy.[12] He was a good student, too, so satisfactory that he was chosen to teach in the new college at St. Louis before his ordination

in 1827. All went well, it seems, up to the time of his first
trip to Europe in 1833. Then with impaired health and a
sense of frustration, he left the Jesuits for a time, being
released from his vows early in 1835.[13] But loyal to both order
and missions, he continued his very successful begging tour
for the work of his recent associates.

Soon young DeSmet found again that change had not
altered his state. He grew really unhappy. But this time instead of trying something new, he returned to the Jesuits
and to Florissant. From then on his life was one long and
tremendous dedication to the Indian missions. And certainly
missionary life such as his was the one for which he was best
fitted. His long and arduous journeys, taking him frequently
into unknown territory, were interspersed by voyages to
Europe for recruits. He lived dangerously, never long off the
path of adventure, never losing the single sight of his
glorious purpose. For the hankering after change that had
worried his family in his boyhood was no mere wanderlust;
it was the early sign of epic impulse, which in his case was
blessedly allied with consecration. A true hero, he knew
the interest value of his Odyssey and to the end he told his
story with compelling zest. As a small boy, the grandfather
of a present-day Jesuit was completely captivated when the
famous missionary visited his father's house in 1865.[14] The
boy's wonder was not entirely due to the Indian bow and
arrows that Father DeSmet thoughtfully presented to him,
nor to his animated narrative; it was the priest's tremendous
love for the Indians that made a life-long impression on the
lad. He could never forget the commanding but gentle
presence, the face "full of intelligence, and to me, beautiful to
look upon."

Father DeSmet was a poet, too. He loved nature, especially
in its gorgeous and dramatic scenes. Change, contrast, movement delighted him. He must have been the most sorely tried
of all by the dull days of waiting for wind. But because he
loved grandeur of soul still more, and recognized it in his
volunteers, a great happiness overcame his impatience. He
taught and entertained them, he planned their future with
them, but most of all he prayed with them. Their initiative

delighted him on their first day aboard *l'Infatigable* when he saw Sister Mary Aloysia and Sister Mary Albine convert their square piano into an altar while Sister Loyola and Sister Marie Catherine transformed the ship's social room into a convent chapel. And now they borrowed splendor from their mission boxes to make their chapel lovely for this gray Christmas on the Schelde. At the sight of it all, Father DeSmet whispered to Brother Francis, who went directly to unpack a lifelike wax Bambino, the gift of the Jesuits in Rome. When he returned with it, Father DeSmet laid it reverently on the altar and knelt before it to pray. Presently all his little flock except one knelt praying with him, praying for a peaceful Christmas, for good will in the hearts of men, for a strong wind to fill their sails, but most of all for the one who would not join them. For Sister Reine sat listless and sad in her cabin, caring not at all for their Christmas preparations. Now she was beginning to mutter that she could not go on. The mission was not for her, Father DeSmet decided. He would go ashore after Mass on Christmas morning to consult the Jesuit Rector at Flushing about having Sister Reine returned to Namur. For some reason, Sister Loyola waited a few days before sending a message to Mère Constantine. Perhaps she still hoped that the dark mood would pass before sailing. Sister Marie Catherine thought otherwise. God was withholding the wind, she felt sure, because of this one troubled, dissonant note in the harmony of high adventure.

CHAPTER 2

Eyes to the West

Sister Louis de Gonzague shares credit with Father DeSmet for setting Notre Dame's Oregon Odyssey in motion. Herself a recent arrival on the American scene, she wrote a series of most compelling letters to the Mother House on behalf of far-western missions. These letters puzzle the reader at first, for Sister Louis de Gonzague wrote them as the head of the first American foundation of Notre Dame, in the development of which she might have been expected to find sufficient interest and excitement. In 1840 she and her Sisters had arrived from Namur at the invitation of Bishop Purcell. They opened their first school in Cincinnati in January, 1841. From the start, the Bishop was pleased with their work and the people showed their appreciation by friendly helpfulness.

Yet the situation was not what these missionary Sisters had expected. The zeal that had given them the heart to leave their homeland had been fostered by articles in *Annals of the Propagation of the Faith.* They had pictured prairies and thundering buffalo herds, and themselves teaching "savages" on the fringes of wilderness. They knew there were centers of population in America but they had not expected them to be so advanced, so separated from the life of the Indian. For Sister Louis de Gonzague and for most of her community, the discovery was disappointing, especially when they began to hear of missionary ventures being made by the Religious of the Sacred Heart. There was Mother Duchesne, for instance, well past seventy, heading for the West.

Sister Louis de Gonzague's disappointment was increased by her difficulty in learning English.[1] Her efforts to master it yielded such discouraging and sometimes hilarious results that before long she slipped into the habit of leaving business contacts and affairs of school to Sister Louise, who had studied English while waiting her father's consent to enter the novitiate in Namur. Yet Sister Louise, too, cherished a longing to work among the Indians until Mère Constantine bade her set aside the notion once and for all. Thus with the majority of the new community in Cincinnati sighing for real missionary labors, Father DeSmet found an assured hearing when he first visited their convent in February, 1841, after his first journey to the tribes of the Northwest. That journey was only a taste, he said. There were two Canadian priests in western Oregon, and he had written to one of them, Vicar-General Blanchet, promising to return with reinforcements. In fact, one purpose of the publicity-begging tour which brought him to Cincinnati was to obtain Sisters for this far-flung Quebec mission. To his surprise, perhaps, Father DeSmet found a strong ally in Sister Louis de Gonzague. Without her pleading, which amounted almost to the impact of modern advertising, Father DeSmet would hardly have secured Sisters for so distant and untried a mission from cautious Mère Constantine. Sister Louis de Gonzague certainly possessed the art of stirring enthusiasm in others. For she wrote with a dash and an absence of the usual nineteenth-century cliché that too often prevented conviction. Now at the word of Father DeSmet she begins to point to the West as the most attractive field for missionary endeavor, her strongest argument being her own intense desire to set out as soon as possible.[2] How she would like to share in the unbelievable good that Father DeSmet is accomplishing in the Rocky Mountains! In a short time, she says, he has baptized six hundred Indians.

Geographically, Sister Louis de Gonzague is a little uncertain, yet when the name Oregon emerges as her western attraction, her faith in it as a promised land is quite as unqualified as though its boundaries lay mapped before her. Father DeSmet hopes soon to visit western Oregon, she announces, there to plan a golden future with the Canadian priest who is about to build a school on a wooded river bank.

Later she writes with urgency that the Ladies of the Sacred
Heart are preparing to set out for "an Indian country."
Clearly, Sister Louis de Gonzague would prefer not being
second in the glorious adventure. Next she relates the visit
of another Jesuit missionary, Father Gleizal, who reports
that "where Father DeSmet is now" would be "a good place."
With a chuckle of relief, she adds that this location (Oregon)
is "even farther away than where the Religious of the Sacred
Heart have gone." She has high hope now that the school
on the river "will be ours." In December, 1842, she announces to Mère Constantine that Father DeSmet will soon
be in Cincinnati again. He is on one of his far-flung tours
collecting funds and securing workers. He will certainly
visit her convent, and this time she will ask him "whether he
does not wish us for his savages." She is preparing her
Superior for a direct request for far-west missionaries, taking
it for granted that these will include herself and some of her
Sisters. And to point out the vastness of western possibilities,
she states that to date the Fathers have converted nineteen
thousand natives in missions beyond the Mississippi.

After Father DeSmet's second visit, Sister Louis de
Gonzague wrote a high-pressure letter to Namur. Despite his
heavy schedule in Cincinnati, she says, she managed to
persuade this wonderful Jesuit to talk to her community.
Either she or one of her Sisters took notes of that talk, and a
very long talk it must have been, judging by the lengthy
quotations, interspersed with her own humorous comment
that she included for the delight of some community hour at
the Mother House. But these astounding stories of Father
DeSmet's life among his Coeur d'Alênes were merely for
the Sisters' entertainment, she explains. Ma Mère is not to
conclude that he is proposing that sort of life for her Sisters;
"il y a de trop mauvais sauvages." No, but he has gone to
Oregon at last and there has visited with Father Blanchet,
the Vicar-General of the Quebec Mission in the Northwest.
And it is true; this good Canadian priest is building a house,
seventy-five feet long to be exact, for a community of Sisters.
How wonderful that would be for Sisters of Notre Dame!
With Father Blanchet is another zealous Canadian priest
named Demers, and with these two Father DeSmet has drawn

the blueprint for a golden age. Oregon! Valley of the Willamette! Future center of the Faith in the western world!

And surely Mère Constantine will be happy to know that, realizing the particular fitness of Sisters of Notre Dame for the situation, Father DeSmet has had the forethought to tell Father Blanchet all about the community in Cincinnati and their excellent work there. What is more, Father DeSmet intends to include Europe in his current begging tour. Of course, he will visit the Mother House and ask in person for volunteers for the mission on the Willamette. When he arrives, her letter will be there ahead of him, with volunteer offers from her community, herself among them. She adds that Father DeSmet has wisely cautioned against withdrawing too many from the house in Cincinnati. Bishop Purcell would certainly object to that, and justly. Still, Father DeSmet thinks the house can spare a few, not more than four; of course, if they all insist on volunteering, they may draw straws. The full number, seven or more, can be made up from Belgium, he suggests. It was all wonderful, but certainly not the least of Northwest attractions to Sister Louis de Gonzague was the house, seventy-five feet long, though its location was as unfixed in her mind as that of Calypso's island.

By way of contrast to her pictured house on the Willamette, Sister Louis de Gonzague packs her letter with gruesome details called from Father DeSmet's own western experiences. With humorous gusto she relates his life with his savages, worst of all his sharing of their diet. Often, she says, they live on insects. When the hunt fails them, they know where to find ants bigger than flies and grasshoppers "as large as your thumb." Father DeSmet says one doesn't like this diet at first, but that when one is hungry anything tastes good. And even when the hunt is rewarded, the feast that follows the kill is disgusting in point both of etiquette and satiety. Sitting around the fire, the ravenous savages devour unbelievable quantities of roasted buffalo, fearing, as they well may, that they will not taste it for many days again. But again, these are pictures of life in the wild. The Sisters' life will, of course, be hard, but it is quite unlikely they will ever have to eat grasshoppers. Father DeSmet will see to that.

"Where our house is," Sister Louis de Gonzague writes

with assurance, "there are twenty Catholic families, some speaking French, a sort of patois . . . not very difficult." A little English, such as some of her Sisters have mastered, will be a great help, too. And certain that this last argument will incline the Mother General to select missionaries from her community, she adds her hope that soon "the gate to the savages will be open to us." Speaking for herself, she reminds her Superior of her "iron constitution," since the mission calls for "robust health." And now the final argument. Sister Louis de Gonzague has taken a poll of her community and discovered that every single Sister would be ready in an instant to dedicate her life to work among the savages!

Though this readiness was temporary in the case of two or three, still Father DeSmet certainly convinced them all for the moment. For one thing, he had dwelt eloquently on the natural goodness of the Indian and his readiness for instruction. And to Belgian women struggling with the difficulties of the English language and the independence of the American character, the "noble savage" idea might understandably appear attractive.

Before Sister Louis de Gonzague ended her long letter, another Jesuit missionary, Father de Theux, called at her convent. She added excited paragraphs about that visit. This once delicate missionary, she announces, is now the picture of good health, a fine example of what life in the wild West does for the weak and frail. She has asked him about the place on the Willamette, and he has confirmed Father DeSmet's words exactly; this mission would be entirely suitable for Notre Dame Sisters. A house, the beginnings of a white settlement, and yet proximity to the dear savages. And she has just heard, perhaps from Father de Theux, that some European Sisters have left for Madras, "and we, Sisters of Notre Dame, shall we remain so at ease?" She even furnishes the formula of permission; all that is needed now is, "Yes, you may go." And, of course, a few Sisters from Belgium will be needed to fill the number. Father DeSmet will be on his way to Europe presently. All Mère Constantine has to do is to entrust a few missionary Sisters to him, and the grand Notre Dame project in Oregon will get off to an early start. And "It's Yes, Ma Mère, isn't it?" she ends irresistibly, and folds and seals her ardent plea. It will be all to the good to have Father DeSmet deliver it in person. Cautious Mère Constantine will be taken by storm. Sisters of Notre Dame will be first in the very farthest West and Sister Louis de Gonzague will be one of them.

In Europe, Father DeSmet found himself something of a celebrity. Everyone seemed to have at least a reading acquaintance with him.[3] Noble, merchant, and worker received him cordially. For the most part, he had himself to thank for this happy fact, as on his earlier visit to the continent he had laid the foundations of publicity for Jesuit missions in the West. Since that time, his letters and published travel accounts had reared a spectacular superstructure. He was his own most successful press agent. But he was both too humble and too purposeful to suffer ill effects from all the heady adulation. He liked it simply because it meant aid for his beloved missions. He certainly neither saw nor sought personal aggrandizement in all his flattering receptions. In fact, when he became aware that Pope Gregory XVI thought of appointing him bishop in the Northwest, he secured the help of his Father General to dissuade His Holiness.

The pontiff received the two together. Rising, he clasped the missionary in his arms, and then perhaps to his astonishment, listened to their arguments against the appointment.[4] Father DeSmet suggested Vicar-General Blanchet as his senior, and as the one to whom praise for work in the Northwest was really due. Nevertheless, Father DeSmet was human enough to rejoice that his name had been considered for episcopal dignity. He was still happier to know of Pope Gregory's intense interest in American missions, but his greatest satisfaction was the promise of his Father General to send five more Jesuits back with him, and the decision of Mère Constantine to call for seven Sister volunteers.

Yet Mère Constantine made that decision hesitantly. She listened with deep respect and interest to all Father DeSmet had to say. She followed his accounts of progress, his records

of conversions, with ejaculations of controlled enthusiasm.
Then she asked four days to consider the matter of Sister
missionaries, four days to pray and think, and to ponder over
the long letter from Cincinnati. It was difficult to know just
what to conclude from that letter. Mère Constantine
wondered whether she had ever really known Sister Louis
de Gonzague. Wanting to leave her quite successful establishment. To go "farther off." The Rocky Mountains! Even
farther! Was this what America was doing to sensible Sister
Louis de Gonzague? Rereading that letter, Mère Constantine permitted herself some little of the mirth it provoked.
But no, she must not allow herself to be swept along by such
persuasive eagerness. While the proposed mission in Oregon
seemed to offer her Sisters security enough even by her conservative standard, there were terrifying hazards on the sea-
voyage. Still, other orders of religious women were planning
long voyages to distant missions. Mère Constantine had
known that even before Sister Louis de Gonzague, and
despite all her caution she was quite as unwilling to be found
lagging behind in the new movement. She believed, though,
as did her assistants, too, that the personnel for this venture
should be drawn entirely from the Belgian Province. Since
everything needed in the new mission would have to be transported there with the missionaries, it would be more practical
to make a single voyage; sending supplies from two points
might result in lack of necessities at the journey's end.

Besides, the house in Cincinnati was doing well despite
difficulties. The Sisters worked in harmony under the direction of Sister Louis de Gonzague. It seemed unwise to remove
any of the group, much less the Superior. And Mère
Constantine could scarcely have failed to detect a note of
adventure, a hint of desire on the part of the writer to plan
her own future. To a Belgian Superior of that day, these
seemed dangerous American trends. Adventure might accompany a mission, but it was not to be sought. A missionary
Sister should advise her home Superior of needs and possibilities, but should not insist too much on action, or on being
herself chosen as agent. And work in the mission must be
guided along European lines. The pattern of mission schools

as well as that of mission convents was in the homeland. This
insistence on as perfect an identity as possible is clear in Mère
Constantine's letters to her Sisters in the West. It is equally
clear in their letters to her that she had instructed them
thoroughly in the matter before their departure. Again and
again they assure her that the likeness is all she could desire.

This fear of American freedom, this wish to conform
American youth, white or native, to the old-world model,
was not due to narrow prejudice on the part of Mère Constantine; in the end she displays more adaptability than do
some of her missionary daughters. It was the result rather of
the still-fresh memory of revolutionary excesses. It was also
due to the fear that age-old experience and culture, as well
as faith and piety, might easily suffer in a thoughtless, young
country. So in accepting the Oregon mission Mère Constantine decided to select and train an all-Belgian group to staff
it. In the light of Sister Louis de Gonzague's eloquent plea,
this seems a thousand pities. It must have seemed so to
Father DeSmet, who knew so well what an advantage even a
year or so of American experience would give those about to
open a new mission.

Still, Father DeSmet left the Mother House rejoicing that
Mère Constantine had accepted the project and was so
evidently determined to do everything possible for its success.
She would send a circular letter at once to the secondary
houses, she promised. She had asked his advice about qualifications and preparation of the Sisters chosen, and about the
material needs of the foundation as well. In all it was quite
clear that since she had decided in favor of the project, she
would see it through to the best of her ability. Now the
next thing was to let Vicar-General Blanchet know about his
good fortune. It might be possible to send him a message
by some ship sailing for New York or Boston, hoping it would
reach him overland, perhaps with the next Hudson's Bay
brigade. In fact, with good luck, the message might reach
the Willamette even before the departure of the mission
band. If they sailed around the Horn, they would hardly
leave before December; captains chose this month so as to
avoid weather in the southern latitudes. And that would

allow Father DeSmet time enough to complete his begging tour and secure suitable passage for his charges.

Mère Constantine's energetic approach to the Oregon mission lighted a spark of fervor greater than she had anticipated. Letters from volunteers came in with every post. Unfortunately, none of these applications are extant, but the memoirs indicate that while they contained the usual platitudes expressing complete unworthiness, they also presented certain special claims to fitness. One of these claims indicates by its frequency that Mère Constantine had called for versitility as a qualification. Each aspirant seems to have considered herself a "bouche-trou," a sort of Jack-of-all-trades, a humble phrase which today might be dignified by the term initiative. But all told, the applications added up to the presence of tremendous zeal and willingness to endure hardship. For this reason the choice was difficult; still, with the exception of Sister Mary Aloysia, who being present at Namur could plead her cause the more urgently, Mère Constantine wrote out her list without much hesitation. Writing to Sister Louis de Gonzague, the Mother General expressed grave doubts about Sister Mary Aloysia's health, which had always seemed delicate. Finally, however, she yielded, though this also meant the sacrifice of the most promising young teacher in the Namur boarding school.

At once Mère Constantine notified her choices and called them, except Sister Loyola, to Namur for intensive preparation. Because of her incomplete building project at Ixelles, Sister Loyola's presence was necessary there, it seems, right up to the time of sailing. Besides, she had to instruct her first teacher, Sister Mary Xavier, who was to replace her as Superior. It seems to have required a good deal of special training to enable this Sister to follow in such successful footsteps. Certainly this exemption from the preparation afforded to the other six seems unfortunate in the case of the leader of the band. Following the courses with her future community, she would have enhanced the importance of the training and gained more of their affection. But in those days the very fact of office, implying at it usually does some special fitness, was thought to supply in some way for special training. And the term "grace of the charge" carried more practical implications than it does today.

Preparation began with a special retreat for the missionaries. Then a course of lectures was given, perhaps by a priest with missionary experience. But whoever gave the course, it did not prepare the Sisters as their successors are prepared today, to approach the mentality of Indian, French-Indian, or American. They were not at all prepared for the sulking relapses that scowled at them through the first cracks in the veneer of novelty. Without an English-speaking instructor, their study of that language was unsatisfactory. Their texts were patterned after Latin grammars, and in their conversation exercises they perpetuated their uncorrected first errors. Their geography course was more helpful. Inexact though it was, it enabled them to trace their journey on globe and map, it gave them notions of distance and relative location, it made them conjure up pictures of strange flora and fauna, of great, rushing rivers and mountains that shoulder the sky. Materially, their preparation was generous and well adapted. All those months they sewed interminably and packed boxes and hampers as the Mother General and the secondary Superiors filled up the long list of possible necessities. Mère Constantine even insisted that Sister Mary Aloysia take with her the square piano which her family had given her in her girlhood. No wonder Father DeSmet beamed with pleasure on his occasional calls at the Mother House.

Early in December, Father DeSmet came with the great announcement. In a few days they would sail from Antwerp in the brig *l'Infatigable*. At once all the baggage was on its way, and Mère Constantine and the six Sisters set out for Brussels, to the fine new (though still unfinished) boarding school on rue l'Arbre Bénit in lovely Ixelles, where Sister Loyola would join them. Ixelles was the beauty spot of Brussels, a restricted area of fine homes and extensive gardens. How heroic Sister Loyola must be to leave it and her new school! But of course, she would do wonders in Oregon. Such was the general comment.

At Ixelles the party found Sister Mary Xavier, with all her

preparation for superiorship, suddenly on the verge of a breakdown. Mère Constantine was so distressed that all the Sisters expected her to withdraw one of the missionaries; they knew well that in sending seven to Oregon, she was leaving the province shorthanded. That was not the way to treat the Good God, Mère Constantine said; since He wished the seven Sisters in the mission, He would easily make up for the incapacity of one at home. But knowing, nevertheless, that the Good God expected some little effort on her part, the Mother General began to cast about in her mind for a substitute for Sister Mary Xavier. She was struggling with the problem when Sister Loyola announced an important visitor. The Apostolic Nuncio had called to convey the blessing of his Holiness, Pope Gregory XVI, to each of the missionary Sisters. With pride the Mother General presented her seven to Monsignor Joachim Pecci, the future Pope Leo XIII. Touched with their enthusiasm and courage, the prelate spoke such words of encouragement that the Sisters could quote them years later as they displayed the treasured little memento picture that he presented to each that day.

Leaving the Ixelles problem unsolved for the time, Mère Constantine hurried the missionaries through farewells. They must allow time for a stop at Mechlin, she told them, to call on the very mission-minded Cardinal Sterckx. To be complimented and blessed by two prelates in one day, in addition to receiving the papal benediction! It was all quite elating. The seven left the Mechlin audience in such high spirits that, as they resumed their journey (in a private carriage, it seems), Mère Constantine thought she might leave them to their own resources and indulge in a few minutes of worry about Sister Mary Xavier and Ixelles. But they began to notice the little frown that always accompanied her concentration, and one by one they grew pensive. At this turn, their Superior began to relate such "amusing and edifying ancedotes," relates Sister Marie Catherine, that they were soon in good spirits again.

When they reached the convent in Antwerp, the Sisters there were adding last minute touches to a grand farewell celebration and submerging their awe of heroism in waves of gaiety.

All that was very well for a day, Mère Constantine knew, a wholesome experience before the great separation, but as there would be a delay of at least three days before embarking, she announced a spiritual triduum for the missionaries. In view of all their recent spiritual preparation, the seven wondered a little at this, but of course, on second thought they saw her purpose. Being genuinely spiritual themselves, they realized that strength of soul slips away in the tension that arises from excitement, and that souls rise stronger out of periods of silence. So they began the retreat with zeal, and seeing them thus wrapped in recollection, Mère Constantine went back alone to Ixelles to care for Sister Mary Xavier. But she had scarcely arrived at the house on rue l'Arbre Bénit when a messenger rode up to the door with an excited message from Sister Loyola. Mère Constantine could barely believe what she read. Sister Mary Cornelia had succumbed to a bad case of nerves; she was weeping in a manner unheard of in her case and was quite unable to attend the triduum. She wanted to see Mère Constantine. But on second thought, the Mother General was not too troubled at the news. She knew this little break was a passing disorder, the combined result of a heavy cold and the severe ordeal of parting with her family a few days before in Namur. Years later, Sister Marie Catherine described that parting. On that day, she said, Sister Mary Cornelia and her aging father exercised great restraint so as to offset Jeanette's completely hysterical behavior and insistence that her older sister must give up her plan to leave Belgium. Sister Mary Cornelia's sudden loss of grip was reaction to that scene, and with it returned her worries about her fitness for the mission, about everything in fact.

Mère Constantine decided not to return to Antwerp before sailing day; that would magnify the gravity of the case. Sister Mary Cornelia must not be treated like a weakling, and Mère Constantine was the last one in the world to contribute to the making of such. Instead, she sat down and wrote little responses to the last farewell notes the others had sent along with Sister Loyola's letter in case they should sail on short notice and so not see her again. That done, she wrote

a long letter to Sister Mary Cornelia, not a stern letter as
was her wont with this promising daughter.[5] She knew this
was the moment for affection, but this letter reveals more
than great affection for Sister Mary Cornelia; it indicates the
great detachment that she herself is making in parting with
her. She is the poor mother who needs comforting, "who
makes so great a sacrifice in separating herself" from her
daughter. Reading this admission, Sister Mary Cornelia recovered calm and courage. Even Mère Constantine shared
her weakness; from that common footing, she found it possible to face her fear and reduce it to rational proportions.
From then to the end of the long voyage, Sister Mary
Cornelia was, in her quiet way, a dependable source of
strength which her Sisters never forgot.

When Father DeSmet sent word to Mère Constantine
that Captain Moller intended to sail Tuesday, December
twelfth, she hurried to Antwerp the evening before departure for a last surprise visit. In the morning, she and two
of the Antwerp Sisters were on board with the missionaries
to help them store away boxes, trunks, and other luggage
that had been preceding them to the ship during the last few
days. What a tremendous pile, the result of additions from all
the Belgian houses to their original plan! But first Mère
Constantine wanted to see the Sisters' cabins. She was amazed
at what she found. Contrary to promises that their comfort
would be cared for, only two small cabins were assigned to
them, the larger with scarcely space for three. There was no
appeal. Nothing could be done about it. But the seven
laughed and joked about it, hurried their bedding into the
tiny, airless compartments, and demonstrated to Mère
Constantine their plan for taking turns sleeping on the floor.
They breathed sighs of relief when the last of their boxes
and trunks disappeared from the deck. If the cabins were
small, they said, at least the hold must be commodious to
contain all their belongings. It really seemed, Sister Marie
Catherine remarked, as though they were transferring a
good part of Europe to America.

Probably some of the Sisters went below to see how their
belongings were stored. If they did, they must have learned

about the rats. Rats darted into corners of that hold, rats nibbled their way into boxes of food supplies and into wooden pantries. The ship's cook didn't need to see them. Their presence assailed his nostrils when he opened cupboards in his kitchen. No modern inspector would have trusted that infested ship as far as Dover. Absence of alarm over this matter on the part of both ship's officers and passengers seems irrational now. But in any period the ordinary has a way of appearing rational. What if a few rats did scamper about? Rats belonged to ships. Of course, if they became too numerous and got underfoot, so to speak, the vessel could be fumigated in the next port. At any rate, if the Sisters did notice the rats, they said nothing about it to their Mother General. She might make a fuss and anyone could see that would be quite useless. With her cautious and logical mind, Mère Constantine certainly would have made a fuss; she would have seen the fatal possibility. But she was spared that worry. And nobody else really worried. To officers and crew, to the thirteen who made up the cabin-passenger list, *l'Infatigable* was their lovely ship, with her two little masts and her sails beginning to breathe and swell, a vessel as goodly as black-hulled ships drawn up on Trojan sands.

There were few cautious thoughts in the minds of those Sisters and even these few enjoyed short entertainment. They were more concerned with the coincidence that they were sailing on the Feast of Our Lady of Guadalupe, the one American feast they knew about. Since childhood they had heard the story of the Mexican Indian boy and the roses. The silver medal commemorating it had been worn by each Notre Dame Mother General in turn, an inheritance from Mère Julie. There it hung below the edge of Mère Constantine's white linen cape, the image of the Blessed Virgin as first limned upon the blanket of her simple Indian client in Mexico City. Standing around their spiritual mother, the Sisters chatted about this good omen for their sailing, about the humorous incidents of the morning, about light things that would keep both her and themselves from realizing that they would more than likely never again see either her or their native land.

As the Sisters were talking, a small boat came alongside bringing the Jesuit missionaries. Father DeSmet was in his most optimistic mood as he greeted Mère Constantine. They would be out of port and on the high sea with no delay, he assured her. And the voyage itself would be much less wearisome, he added, if there was no long wait in port. Then, in order to go ashore in the boat that had just brought the Fathers, Mère Contantine and the Antwerp Sisters bade hasty farewells. On deck the seven watched their dangerous descent down the rope ladder, and waved goodbyes as the boat crossed over to the wharf where a carriage was waiting for them. Apparently the driver was in a hurry, for the three climbed up at once and the carriage was presently out of sight. It was a heavy moment, but Sister Loyola dealt wisely with it as she led her Sisters quickly to their cabins. There they plotted and planned to secure the maximum of space, and laughed together at their clever maneuvering. Until sailing they must keep reality out of their minds.

By the time the carriage reached the convent in Antwerp, Mère Constantine was quite overcome by sadness. She should have stayed longer on the wharf, she thought, despite the driver's impatience. At the door she turned and called to him just as he was starting his horses. She must return to the wharf, she told him. Then she asked her astonished companions, to find the young and nimble Sister Gonzales to accompany her. On the way she explained her purpose to Sister Gonzales. If the ship had not weighed anchor, would Sister mind crossing over in one of the boats that were always standing by for such emergencies, to bear her last messages to the Sisters on board? Sister Gonzales thought it a grand idea. Unlike her Superior General, she considered the rope ladder a bit of fun; she wasn't the cautious type. On board she rounded up the surprised Sisters and pointed out Mère Constantine seated in the carriage on the wharf and waving to them. As they waved back, Sister Gonzales recited her Superior's messages with emphasis of her own, kissed them all goodbye, and scrambled down the rope ladder with a seaman's skill. From her seat in the boat, she signaled in both directions; to the Sisters on the deck more fond goodbyes, to Mère Constantine assurances that she had fulfilled her mission. Now surely, she thought, the Mother General must feel satisfied that her Sisters on *l'Infatigable* knew her care for them.

But while any possibility of communication remained, the urge to use it was too much for Mère Constantine. That afternoon at two she wrote the travelers a letter, addressing it to "The Sisters of Notre Dame on board *l'Infatigable*," and sent it by river steamer to Flushing where the ship would stop before leaving port.[6] With its flashes of humor, this is one of the best of her long series of letters to the Oregon Sisters. She will always keep up with their ship, she promises; in fact, with this letter, she is getting a sort of head start. And who can say, she asks, that she will never see them again? Quite possibly she may be a missionary to Oregon herself some day. A surprisingly adventuresome statement that, in view of her attitude toward rope ladders. But in that letter one sees Oregon becoming her cynosure. The fact that her Sisters are bound for that land makes her supremely happy. She is proud of them. She spurs them on though her heart aches through the lines. She names each and lingers over the names. She reminds Sister Norbertine to take special care of Sister Reine and Sister Mary Cornelia until they are entirely over their colds. Playfully she admonishes the latter, who was almost the least likely linguist in the group, "to say good little Indian words at recreation." She tells them all she must return to Brussels that very evening and hopes the next day to go on to Namur, "without ever being separated from the happy passengers of *l'Infatigable*." She is sure they will send her messages from Flushing and will count the hours until their notes are in her hands.

Her letter finished, she hurried off to catch the stage for Brussels. As she sat waiting for the coach to start, tired and heavy-hearted, two gentlemen entered. They were friends of Father DeSmet, they told her, and had come to Antwerp to see him off. They praised him highly and assured her emphatically that her Sisters could not be in better hands. Mère Constantine thanked God for this chance meeting. Though she had felt great confidence in Father DeSmet all along, this enthusiastic assurance of his friends was just what she needed at the end of that trying day.

Meantime Father DeSmet spent the afternoon hours telling his missionaries about Oregon, the good Vicar-General, and the plans they had made together. Father Blanchet and his co-worker, Father Demers, were heroic missionaries, he said, adding that he had great hopes that Father Blanchet would be the first bishop in the Northwest. He said nothing about his own close call to that honor. If he thought of it that afternoon, it was to rejoice at his escape, his freedom to work among his Indians. With this small band of dedicated workers under his care, he seemed to be rid of his old restlessness. Now he was an assuring and tranquilizing leader, disturbed at nothing, not even when the wind suddenly fell off and sails in the harbor sagged helplessly. In getting to Oregon, he said, as in all efforts, one must wait for God.

As they settled themselves to wait, a last visitor came aboard, a certain "good friend Marie," from Brussels, who had set out that morning with *bon voyage* messages for the Sisters from the convent in the rue de Kint. Chatting with her, the Sisters scribbled hasty thank-you notes, and each except busy Sister Loyola wrote last farewells to Mère Constantine. All was well, they told her, the wind was in the sails again, and they would soon be on their way. She must not worry about the cabins. They would really manage to be quite comfortable in them. In fact, at that moment Sister Loyola was working wonders toward that end. Hoping these indefinite statements would keep their Mother General's mind off the fact of their sleeping on the cabin floors, they consigned their notes to Marie and said what they thought would be their last goodbye. A few minutes later, the monotonous underfoot roll grew uneven. The ship shuddered, veered, and was soon moving in the strong river channel.

Presently the thirteen missionaries were summoned to supper at the Captain's table, which, as Sister Marie Catherine noted, was scarcely large enough for eight. Though the food was well prepared, the dour expression on Captain Moller's face and his refusal to join in conversation cast a gloom over the diners. In an attempt to dispel his mood, the Fathers supplied bits of humor, but it was as though he heard neither the witty remarks nor the laughter that followed. Evidently his passengers must not expect much mirth from him. It was not that he disliked them, nor that he objected to their merry conversation; in fact, they sensed his secret pleasure in their presence. So ignoring his gloom they set a convivial dining precedent for the voyage at that first supper. Later Father DeSmet led night prayers and announced that there would be five Masses each morning throughout the voyage when the sea was not too rough.

Sister Marie Catherine declared it required nothing short of heroism to maintain the conventual "great silence" as the Sisters tried to settle for the night in their cramped cabins. Wrapped in blankets, she and Sister Mary Aloysia laughed as their makeshift beds slipped about on the floor with the movement of the ship. They were grateful now for the very small space.

After the last Mass next morning, Father Accolti, the appointed spiritual director of the group, read the daily program for the voyage. As a health directive, it called for an early morning promenade on deck to offset the effect of airless cabins. But their first promenade proved depressing; sails were going limp, the ship was inching along in a lazy breeze that fell off at last and left them waiting for hours. By dint of occasional and undecided wind, they were carried next day into Rammchen Roads above Flushing, the little Dutch town at the mouth of the Schelde which appears as Vlissingen or Flissingue in the old accounts. Here *l'Infatigable* joined a number of ships that had been waiting for sailing. Presently the wind arose and decks were alive with hurrying officers and seamen. Pilot boats made their quick appearance like summoned servants. One of these came alongside the brig, its officer signaling to Captain Moller that *l'Infatigable* would require his assistance at the river mouth. But the captain was not in a mood to be told what he must do. He had made his own way through that passage many a time, he declared, without benefit of pilot, adding that he had no wish to waste his money. The officer shouted back that the danger was much greater than usual. It was. Starting off on his own, Captain Moller ran *l'Infatigable* on a sand bank with such straining of timber and rattling of tackle that Father DeSmet was certain she was wrecked.

One by one the other ships were piloted safely past Flushing and out to sea. The missionaries sadly watched them glide past, dipping and raising their flags to *l'Infatigable*. The rejected pilot master, in mockery it seemed, returned to rescue the stranded brig, with other nearby craft giving a hand. Hours of struggling and groaning, of shouting and swearing, and at last *l'Infatigable* was rescued from the sand. Too late. The wind fell off again, and this time Captain Moller had one long month to rue his independence. In his chagrin he shut himself in his cabin for the next three days, leaving his ship in complete charge of his first mate, a man of loud and obscene speech. And the otherwise decent crew joined in the vile language as a vent for their annoyance over the accident and delay. Actually all the chagrin and annoyance was a bit unreasonable; the ship had sustained no worse damage than a break in the deck railing, and it was easier to wait out a calm in port than at sea. The real annoyance was *l'Infatigable*'s ignominious loss in the race out of port.

Father DeSmet attributed Captain Moller's three-day seclusion to his illness as much as to his chagrin. But his poor health was not a matter for worry, he assured Sister Loyola; it would certainly improve after they were a few days at sea. The captain was competent and good, he went on, and if he seemed uncommunicative at times, they must all remember that he was not accustomed to a passenger list of missionaries. And Father DeSmet promised to stay near the captain as much as possible when he seemed to be in a dark mood. Above all, he would try to persuade him not to leave his authority so completely in the hands of his first officer again. For if Father DeSmet feared anything it was blasphemy, a vice to which the mate was very prone; he could not understand Captain Moller's allowing it on his ship.[7] And that language, Sister Loyola answered, might easily have caused Sister Reine's disturbance. Being Flemish, she understood the speech of officers and crew. Their obscenity, especially that of the mate, had shocked her from the start.

Lacking reports on weather and movements of ships, Mère Constantine thought *l'Infatigable* had sailed directly from Antwerp and wondered why the Sisters failed to send their promised message from Flushing. At last a letter arrived late Sunday afternoon, but as it made no mention of either the accident or the ship's location, she asked the messenger to wait while she wrote a hurried reply to be sent by packet to Dover, where Captain Moller intended to stop.[8] She had just had a visit with Bishop Dehesselle, she told them, and had presented him with the gift they had sent him from Antwerp. It had pleased him greatly, and they must know he was all enthusiasm over their mission. For her part, she was preserving their "pencil" notes that Marie had brought from the ship "as relics," and from this fact they must know how heroic their departure made them in her eyes. "In the eyes of all, and of course, in the eyes of God, too." She cannot help worrying about their cabins, she says. She can still see Sister Marie Catherine and Sister Mary Aloysia preparing their beds on the floor. They must go on being so gay and united, and Sister Loyola must never be too busy to write. They must all write, for already their messages have done her "so much good." Especially the note from Sister Mary Cornelia, "she knows why." But it was nearly a month before the Sisters received this little gem of half-humorous encouragement.

Communication being what it was, the wonder is that people managed as much correspondence as they did in those days. A letter entrusted to the pilot of a harbor boat, the captain of a passing vessel, or a fur-trading brigade, might or might not reach its destination. Forgetful messengers sometimes found letters years later in their pockets, but even with the best of care, a letter might be a year, or even two, on its way. To cut down time, as well as to practice grateful charity, Mère Constantine served tea and cookies to each courier. While he enjoyed it, she wrote an answer at her tremendous speed, and handed it to him with his fee when he arose refreshed. In such a deliberate person, this rapidity is surprising. When word reached her in Namur on December 22, that *l'Infatigable* was lying in Rammchen Roads, she managed one of her quick return letters, hiding her disappointment in playful teasing.[9] God was only making them "languish" for their "beautiful mission." First days are always hardest, and the little trial would soon be forgotten in Oregon. She even tucked in a note for Sister Mary Cornelia, just in case her morale still needed a little support.

On Christmas Eve, Mère Constantine wrote again as there seemed no prospect of wind.[10] A severe cold, "like yours, my dear Sister Mary Cornelia," prevents her going to see them as she had planned, but she is trusting Miss Marie with her Christmas greetings. Until they sail, they must write often. She watches for each arrival of the post to bring a letter; "several would be better." On this Christmas their "little parlor," and still more their narrow cabins, must be their stable of Bethlehem; their hard beds, the straw in the manger-bed of the Christ Child. This last she addresses to the meticulous Sister Mary Aloysia. She has asked the Sisters at Brussels to buy the church music that they wish and send it to them. And they must know that at Namur the Sisters are invoking all the saints for a good, strong wind.

CHAPTER 3

Wind After Yuletide

Christmas brought no wind, no sun to the Schelde. As if in despite of the season's joy, the scowling fog held cold and stubborn possession of wide harbor and flat countryside. But in the social room of *l'Infatigable,* glowing candles were symbols of conquering joy as the five Jesuits celebrated the Holy Masses of Christmas Night and Morning and Day, and the Sisters sang Noël canticles sweetly harmonized, with Sister Mary Aloysia's voice running through like a golden thread. Now and again, Sister Loyola cast a sidelong glance, hoping against hope to read in their one sad face some flicker of response to so much genuine peace. If this joy of Christmas would only prove the needed link with Sister Reine's childhood, with her happy days as a novice! If only Sister Loyola would not have to admit this defeat to Mère Constantine. She hated the thought of losing even one. She needed them all and it was too late to prepare a substitute. Besides, who could calculate the effect of one desertion on the others? On the other hand, Sister Reine's dejected presence accentuated the trials of weary waiting and might easily weaken the morale of the less patient Sisters, Sister Norbertine, for instance, good as gold but a bit crotchety. But Sister Loyola's distraction was cut short as Sister Mary Aloysia handed her an open hymnal. They were going to sing *Adeste Fideles* as an Offertory hymn. Turning to nod her thanks, Sister Loyola caught sight of the captain standing in the doorway, his usual dejection replaced by wonder.

All along Captain Moller had found his passengers an unaccountable group. They never complained, not even at the long failure of the wind. And they were radiantly happy at the thought of the hardships that awaited them. They prayed so much, too; he saw them morning and night kneeling there together absorbed in prayer, and through the day walking on the deck in silence with rosaries or books. And when they were not praying, they studied; in fact, they had turned his ship into a sort of combined church and school. Captain Moller knew almost nothing of his passengers' religion, but he was coming to feel that their presence would bring some sort of blessing on his ship. He was beginning to take a sort of proud interest in their studies, too. There was Father Vercruysse rounding up his French class on a corner of the deck the very day after Christmas. Those students were three Italian Fathers, who would need French in the Willamette Valley or anywhere in the Northwest, Father Vercruysse told the captain. There they would be working among French-Canadians and half-breeds. During the voyage they must learn enough to get on with both, for after their arrival they would have almost no time to study. And they would learn enough, their teacher added; they were still fairly young, and their studious habits were a great asset.

Even in the Chinook tongue, the widespread native jargon, Father Vercruysse said, there was an element of French, a growing element since young half-breeds tended to add French expressions to the Chinook of their mothers.[1] As he explained this to the captain, he showed him one of the little printed books that Father DeSmet had given to each of the missionaries. It was merely a list selected from the four hundred or more words that made up the ugly hodgepodge of Chinook, which was not rated as an Indian dialect at all. It was rather an assortment of Clatsop and Flathead words with a few mutilated French expressions thrown in, but it was important because it had become the intertribal and interracial speech medium of the fur-trading Northwest. At that moment Father DeSmet joined the two. He remarked that Chinook was the very poorest sort of speech medium, that it derived its name from the Chinook tribe, and that these Indians displayed their very low intelligence by adopting it. To please the captain, Father DeSmet uttered a few

Chinook words, accompanying them with exaggerated facial
contortions. He had heard these words often in Oregon, he
said, but still could not manage the entire list. For that
matter, he added, he had never succeeded in learning all of
any Indian dialect. He was a little too old, a little too impatient, but that didn't matter as he was always able to find
a satisfactory interpreter.[2] En route he would teach his
companions what he had picked up of the cacophonous
Chinook. Then Father Demers would give them a few brief
lessons in Oregon. Father Demers was an expert with Indian
dialects.[3] One after another, he mastered them with incredible speed.

But why, the captain wished to know, were they also
studying English if the whites in Oregon were French-
Canadians? Father DeSmet explained that the daily English
lessons the captain had heard him giving his companions were
in a way the most important of all. Even then, he said, there
were settlers from the States in Oregon, and before he left
for Europe he had heard that a great throng was gathering
to take the overland trail. Americans, he said, would ac-
complish whatever they set out to do. They were adventuresome and had a keen eye for opportunities; the fertile
Willamette Valley was certain to attract them. In fact, Father
DeSmet thought it quite conceivable that the Americans
should some day inherit the Northwest or some large part
of it. Captain Moller nodded. In that case, English would
be necessary, and being slightly acquainted with the language
himself, he would call it a hard necessity.

To make the long delay more bearable, Father DeSmet
punctuated his lessons with descriptions of Oregon that
bordered on the romantic. His savages, waiting to be edged
easily into abiding good life, are reflected in Sister Mary
Aloysia's voyage journal. But it was as well that the Sisters
saw their future charges in this idyllic light. The vision eased
tensions during the long waiting in the Schelde and drew
them like a beacon on their epic journey. Sometimes, too,
Father DeSmet spoke eloquently of the great Hudson's Bay
leader, John McLoughlin, and of the fur trade that he had
built up with honor and generosity as well as success. He

described the company's thriving farms, much to Sister Norbertine's delight. One of these at Nisqually, he said, was producing fifteen bushels of wheat to the acre, besides fine crops of oats, peas, and potatoes. But this farm's greatest development was its dairy; its seventy milk cows produced butter that brought a good price from the Russian traders. In fact, between traders and long-voyage vessels that entered the Columbia, there was always a market for produce in excess of the company's own needs. And then there was McLoughlin's plan to settle Indians in the company's employ on fifty-acre lots of their own, and thus to give them a taste for civilized life and productive work.[4] To Sister Loyola this was the best news of all. She was always impatient with the unimproved status quo. The child of the forest was very well in poetry; in real life he should have his feet set in progressive paths as soon as possible. She was a bit taken aback then when Father DeSmet said that the change from wild to civilized life would be necessarily slow, even in the case of those settled on the company's acres. Most of the Indians would be affected chiefly through contacts of their rising generation with the missionaries. And Father DeSmet kept the background for these contacts alluringly before his companions' eyes. They saw their "dear savages" under giant trees, in an always green valley, so fertile a valley that wild berries were large and luscious and wild grasses grew vigorous and tall. And the beauty of it all! On the Columbia, Father DeSmet had seen falls unbelievably high and fed by the eternal snows of mountain peaks in plain sight of the Sisters' new home.

As they listened to Father DeSmet's picturesque phrasing, Sister Mary Aloysia thought of her oils and brushes tucked away in one of their trunks, and Sister Norbertine smiled at her own happy inspiration to bring a good supply of choice garden seeds. But on the whole, the Sisters were fairly realistic in their expectations; they knew that when Father DeSmet indulged in poetic flights, the picture he presented needed toning down. They knew they would have to teach the child of the forest order and cleanliness. That was one reason for considering some kind of boarding school a necessity. They

would begin with abandoned waifs. Then they would persuade French-Canadian parents to entrust their daughters
to them. The child of inferior training, as well as the waif
of the wilderness, needed constant vigilance. Even those
blessed with better homes benefited by it. Thus the boarding school loomed high in Sister Loyola's plans, an institution
lowly in its beginnings, no doubt, but approaching the European standard. In a Belgian boarding school, parents waited
for their daughters in commodious and well-carpeted parlors.
Even in the wilderness, Sister Loyola would establish these
signs of civilization as soon as possible. Paying less attention
than the other Sisters to Father DeSmet's descriptions, real
or romantic, she kept her mind on the task before her, sharing the results of her concentration at times, usually as finished products, with astonished Sister Mary Cornelia.

Directly after Christmas Father DeSmet announced that
he was beginning a journal of the voyage, as was his custom
when traveling. Father Vercruysse would write one also, he
said, and it would be well if one of the Sisters would do the
same. The three writers might thus check their notes for
certitude, and all the travelers would have these journals for
reference when writing letters. Sister Loyola assigned Sister
Mary Aloysia to this duty, and as things turned out, she
became the most accurate and satisfying recorder of the
voyage. Father DeSmet's method, or lack of method, was
to let days and even weeks pass without entries and then
to catch up with events in a dateless total review, his long
descriptive paragraphs interspersed with literary quotations
and verse of his own making. At first, however, he wrote
faithfully and often, and the other two used his notebook
as their model. Father Vercruysse, in fact, seems to have
decided he could do no better than to make a fairly close
second copy of this notebook. Entries and letters were
written in the ship's social room or, in fine weather, on the
deck; there was neither room nor light for writing in the
tiny cabins. And as that small vessel tossed about in rough
seas, writing demanded greater patience; but from the start
the scribes were rewarded by the sight of their companions
reading their entries with interest.

They waited for sailing day to begin their journals. They wanted to forget the stagnant darkness of the Schelde, more intolerable, they were certain, than the roughest of seas. Yet they kept their joy of spirit through those days after Christmas as the recurring feasts of the octave shone like candles in their gloom. Finally, on New Year's Eve Father DeSmet decided that some form of diversion was necessary. He had gone ashore himself to visit the Father Rector of the Jesuits at Flushing, but Captain Moller had been nervous about his absence and had refused to allow his other passengers to leave the ship. If wind should rise suddenly, he would want to sail without delay, he said. But on New Year's morning he yielded. There was no sign of wind, and in the fitful moments of sunshine, they might enjoy exploring Walcheren Island. And he assigned sailors to row them to a long arm of low land extending into the Schelde on the north.

Laughing at the almost forgotten feel of land beneath their feet, the missionaries stumbled on the uneven, hand-laid flags of the road that led into Flushing and through the little town on into the countryside of this land of dykes. Father DeSmet led them first to the ruins of an old convent on the walls of which they saw marks of many an inundation. What a dismal land! Sister Marie Catherine couldn't understand how anyone could want to live in such a place. Nothing but floods, and broken dykes, and general gloom! She had scarcely spoken when the sun came out and turned the gray flats into green fields. The sight was breath-taking. Flowers everywhere and here and there a single-sailed canal boat that seemed to be riding through the meadows. It might have been a day in spring.

Finally they stopped at a Dutch farm where the "good lady" and her seven comely daughters received them with wondering politeness; they had never seen Sisters before. Somehow they managed a Flemish-Dutch conversation. No, the Sisters were not the Fathers' wives, Sister Loyola explained as she struggled to convey the idea of a religious congregation of nuns. Wonder turned to admiration when the family understood that the group was on its way to

Oregon, a very distant land, to teach savages, and that more than likely they would never return. But awe gave place to friendliness as Father DeSmet asked questions about farming in Walcheren and as Sister Norbertine expressed high approval of the good lady's barns and livestock and gardens. Time did not permit the visitors' acceptance of this kind Dutch woman's offer of refreshments; they had promised to dine early with Captain Moller. Disappointed that they could not taste her excellent beer and cakes, she hastily wrapped up one of her fine cheeses and handed it to Father DeSmet. If their ship didn't sail soon, she said, they must come again to her home. Her daughters echoed her invitation in chorus.

That evening Sister Marie Catherine noticed that Sister Reine's spirit had been only temporarily revived by the outing, that being away from the ship for a few hours had actually increased her loathing for it and her fear of the voyage and mission. Now her few upward glances were haunted. It was soon plain to all that she could not be saved for the enterprise; even Sister Loyola had to admit defeat. But that same evening, Sister Marie Catherine's sharp eyes also took note of a happier omen. When the missionaries gathered around the beautiful Bambino to pray and sing, as they did each evening of the Christmastide, Captain Moller entered and stood smiling and pleased till the hymn was finished. Then as they left the room, he came and studied the lovely face for a reverent moment.

Before New Year's Mère Constantine wrote another gay letter to encourage her Sisters on *l'Infatigable*.[5] At Namur, she told them, the Sisters were elated by the accounts they had written of their Christmas on the ship. In fact, some were quite jealous, she said. As for herself, if she did not feel certain they would be sailing at any minute, nothing would prevent her going to see them again. She had scarcely sent that letter on its way, together with a great pile of mail and packages that the Sisters of Brussels had left with her for Sister Loyola, when the regular post brought her first knowledge of Sister Reine's condition. Sister Loyola begged her to come or send for Sister Reine, but if they should have wind

before anyone could arrive, Father DeSmet would entrust
her to the Father Rector in Flushing, who would have her
returned safely to Namur. The Mother General left at once
for Antwerp with Sister Augustine, the Superior of the
Namur community. At Ghent another Superior, Sister Mary
Julia, joined them.

From there on to Antwerp, the two joined forces to
persuade Mère Constantine that her mission project would
still succeed. The long delay was a trial from the hand of
God, they said, quoting her own advice on other occasions;
and no great work for God had ever begun without some
such cross. They told her, too, that Sister Reine's failure
would only strengthen the others. She had but to recall
Sister Loyola's staunch way of facing difficulties, and Sister
Mary Cornelia's tremendous fidelity even as a novice. And
of course, everyone recognized Sister Marie Catherine's
sterling worth even if she was a bit emotional at times. Mère
Constantine had great need of these reassuring words. It was
hard to find herself mistaken in so important a choice as
this. She had felt extremely confident about Sister Reine,
always so intelligent and so balanced. It must be that God
did not will her going to Oregon. Perhaps the long delay
was His way of preventing it.

It was well into the afternoon when the three reached
Antwerp and secured places on a little harbor steamer bound
for Flushing, the master agreeing to take them directly to
l'Infatigable. Considering the fog, that seemed a feat that
called for an excellent pilot, but he spoke with assurance;
besides, one must trust the Good God. Meantime the missionaries assembled at three that afternoon to dine with
Captain Moller, or rather to dine in his sad presence. There
he sat, refusing all that was set before him, and apparently
taking no notice of Father Accolti's humor. Sister Marie
Catherine sensed a general flagging of spirits as the meal
progressed. She watched Sister Mary Albine's smile die after
each brave effort. Nobody else was even attempting to smile,
and there was a sort of panicky look in Sister Loyola's eyes.

Suddenly the cook's assistant spied the three Sisters boarding the ship. Excitedly he popped his head through the little

serving window and called, "Schwesters!" In a few minutes
the missionaries were all on deck greeting the visitors. And
gracious even in his moods, Captain Moller went up to pay
his respects, but finding the somewhat excited talking too
much for his nerves, he merely bowed and withdrew. Then
more out of habit than of hope, he glanced at the compass
indicator as he passed. Unbelievingly he looked again. It
was moving. Wind! He raised his head and saw the fog
lifting, breaking into irregular drifts edged with pale light.
The Fathers were standing at the rail, fascinated by this
beginning of movement, pointing out wraith groups of masts
and spars emerging into misty half-light and swaying gently
as the water roughened. But the Sisters were talking intently
with Mère Constantine, explaining to her that Sister Reine
was moping in a corner below, listless and mute. Captain
Moller approached the group, smiling and bowing to the
Mother General. They must all know, he said glancing
around at the Sisters, that their good Mother's coming had
brought a great blessing. Wind! Nothing else could account for his smile. With one accord, the Sisters turned to
the east. As the light breeze fluttered their veils, Mère
Constantine studied their faces and knew she had been right
about these six; after their four weeks' trial, their mission
still beckoned them. They were brave and strong, she told
herself, as Mère Julie herself would have them to be. Then
in her brief conversation with the captain, she discovered
that, silent and remote as he was, he had appraised them
correctly, too.

Lacking means of transportation back to Antwerp that
evening, Mère Constantine and her companions had to spend
the night aboard the ship. They must have a little rest before
their journey back to Namur, Sister Loyola insisted, and
thus the three visitors made firsthand acquaintance with the
hard beds in the larger cabin, while the other Sisters took
cat naps in turn in the smaller one. Nobody rested much as
the crew made noisy preparations through most of the night;
besides, by nightfall the Schelde had grown so rough as to
cause disturbing qualms.

Long before morning, wakeful Mère Constantine made

serious reflections about the ship and the voyage her daughters would make in it. Though she was not more fastidious than other Belgians of her day, she was shocked at the sanitation, the lack of air, and the whiffs of food spoiling even before the vessel put to sea. But her Sisters had chosen to go. It was God's will and He would care for them. And like a brave mother, she made light of the straitness of their apostolate.

Profiting by his earlier mistake, Captain Moller had bargained with the pilot of a harbor boat to take his ship safely to sea. When the wind arose, the pilot appeared and agreed to be ready at two in the morning. That hour was a bit early, but there were other ships waiting in Rammchen Roads, and Captain Moller wanted to be clear of them all and on his way to sea before they weighed anchor. This time *l'Infatigable* would lead the line! So at two o'clock Captain Moller began to pace the deck, growing more impatient each minute and quite unaware that the convivial pilot had fallen into a stupid slumber after an overmerry evening with his Flushing friends. When he did come aboard at sunrise, the Captain saw at a glance that he was quite unfit to guide *l'Infatigable* to sea. There was nothing to do but wait for the man to sober up, since every other harbor pilot was now engaged. But it was bitterness to Captain Moller to hear the glad shouting of sailors on nearby ships, and to see Father DeSmet trying to make light of it all. The poor man could not look at his passengers; he had failed them again. He kept out of sight as one by one the ships got under way and passed *l'Infatigable* in a morning-long procession, "a pleasant sight," recorded Father DeSmet ironically, for the Oregon missionaries, who had "the honor of receiving their salutes." Tiresomely *l'Infatigable*'s flag was hoisted and lowered again and again in a show of good will as the line passed, a second such procession in one sailing.

At noon Captain Moller secured the service of a pilot who had just returned from the river mouth, but now two vessels moved into positions that blocked *l'Infatigable*. The larger of these, bearing emigrants bound for Texas, weighed anchor first and seemed to be slipping easily into the channel when she swerved suddenly around and struck *l'Infatigable*. In horror, the missionaries saw the afterdeck rail broken to pieces, while the shock of the impact foreboded even more serious damage. The Sisters turned to Mère Constantine. Was it that after all the Good God was opposed to their mission? Amid the loud babel of the Swiss and German emigrants on the other deck, the Superior assured her daughters, for she saw Father DeSmet approach them smiling. Neither vessel was seriously injured, he told them. Besides her rail, the ship had lost a window shutter; that was the extent of her damage. The Texas-bound vessel had suffered a smashed-in plank and a broken anchor; she would have to wait for repairs. *L'Infatigable* could go right out to sea. Her railing had probably been weakened by its former accident, he said, but it could be repaired, perhaps in Valparaiso; meanwhile passengers had to be careful on deck, especially in high seas. With good wind in his sails, a sea captain could not be expected to delay for the repair of a railing. In fact, while the two irate crews were shouting their last imprecations at each other, "with the usual delicacy of sailors," as Father DeSmet noted, all three vessels got under way. And as they headed toward Flushing in that brisk wind, not even Captain Moller cared how many ships had sailed on ahead.

The stop at Flushing was very brief, as the master of a passing harbor boat caught Captain Moller's signal and came quickly alongside to take the four Sisters ashore. But those few moments were frightening as well as poignant. With the river so disturbed by the wind, descent into the boat was difficult and hazardous. Then, when the four were seated in the boat, the carelessness of one of the oarsmen caused it almost to crash against the side of the ship. Poor Mère Constantine! She had just managed her last descent from *l'Infatigable* with a certain degree of seamanly competence. Now her fear of water and boats gripped her as never before. On the deck, her Sisters breathed relief as the boat pulled out of danger, but in another moment they

were all thrown into a second state of dismay as the irate
master of the boat cursed the absentminded oarsman in
Flemish.

Silence fell on the missionaries as *l'Infatigable* got under
way again and the little boat made off toward the wharf,
bobbing in and out of sight among the river craft. At last
they saw the four Sisters standing on the wharf waving to
them, four indistinguishable forms that quickly merged and
dwindled from sight. Two of these, Sister Marie Catherine
reflected, were nervous; cautious Mère Constantine, who
measured difficulties but accepted them bravely, and poetic
Sister Reine, who could not live her dream Odyssey when
she felt its sternness. But her six Sisters had none but kind
thoughts of her as they lost her from sight. She was a noble
soul, they said, but somewhat too fine. As she left them,
"déjà assez sourde," listless and broken, their hearts ached for
her. She would be better soon, they said, in her accustomed
surroundings and occupation. She was. Fortunately she
was spared the long delays and ego-satisfaction of psychiatry.

Father DeSmet described the last farewells of the two
groups of Sisters as a touching sight.[6] He made the parting
easier for his six charges by a few minutes of cheerful encouragement. Then Sister Loyola led the way briskly to the
"chapel" to pray for a safe return of Mère Constantine and
her companions. And as they prayed and meditated, trying
not to notice the effects of the tossing waves, *l'Infatigable*
entered the sea. The pilot left her and she sailed gallantly
into the evening.

PART II

PASSEPARTOUT

CHAPTER 4

Stars and Storms

It would be a thousand pities to miss the gorgeous sunset, Father DeSmet told the Sisters. They followed him up on deck, even Sister Loyola and Sister Mary Cornelia, whose miserable reaction to sailing was now becoming acute. There they stood spellbound by the splendor of the west and the wealth it cast on the waves. As though lured by the flashing gold, their ship kept its course in that long, narrowing lane of light. The silence of the sea was touching their ship with its spell, silence broken only by the beating of halyards against the mast and the washing of waves around the hull. How this silence had transformed the cursing sailors! Now they worked purposefully, each serious with his responsibility, an obedient and intelligent crew.[1] A dignifying assurance marked their every movement; it was their skill that was keeping the full strength of that wind in bellying foresail and mainsail. Now they were part of their ship and subject like her to the spell of the sea.

But presently the rolling of the ship broke the spell for Sister Loyola. She had never felt so ill before. Was it that she must die at sea and never reach Oregon? She had heard of such things. And now her new house and unfinished chapel at Ixelles swam in wavelike fashion before her closed eyes. She tried to bring the picture into focus, first for distraction's sake and then with a terrible longing. Why had she ever volunteered? Why hadn't she stayed and finished her task? In something like despair she looked at Sister Mary Cornelia, but instead of a comforting response she read her own anguish in that usually serene countenance. The other Sisters, too, were beginning to look strained and sad, all except Sister Marie Catherine, who still gazed smilingly at the sunset. If only she wouldn't smile that way; it made her look quite sentimental. But there! Sister Mary Aloysia was humming in that sure, exactly-on-pitch way of hers, and Sister Loyola joined the others as they moved into a close, little group. *Ave! Ave! Maris stella* they sang, with no note in their harmony betraying their distress. At once the Fathers came and sang with them. And to this hymn that holds the loneliness of the sea in its cadences, they added the *Litany of Loretto*, and the two comprised their evening song for the long voyage. Father DeSmet loved this singing at sunset; afterward he wrote with pride that perhaps the Atlantic and Pacific never resounded with hymns sung so regularly and for such a long period.

Captain Moller paused near the singers that first evening to listen and smile his approval. At the end of the *Litany*, he returned to them again still smiling and pointed toward the west. There a ship was bowing in stately fashion, dark and graceful, with the sunset as backdrop. Then another. These, the captain told his passengers, were their neighbors in the Schelde and had weighed anchor hours before *l'Infatigable*. And for all their headstart, he added, she was gaining on them. For the first time, his listeners heard him chuckle. And why should she not gain? Spreading his hands expressively, he addressed the question to Father DeSmet but immediately supplied the inescapable answer himself, *"l'Infatigable! Elle est un passepartout!"*

As the sun dropped suddenly into darkness, the ship's course turned south toward Dover. Now she had to struggle at the same time with opposing wind and the turbulent waters of the strait. The passengers began to feel quite wretched. It was the courteous thing, of course, this first night at sea, to appear at the captain's table for supper. Sensing the distress masked by their forced smiles, Captain Moller gave them first-voyage advice. To overcome the inevitable *mal de mer,* he said, one must eat well, have a good glass of wine with meals, and take plenty of fresh air on deck. His listeners tried bravely enough to follow his advice, but most of them found quite repelling even the well-prepared fresh vegetables and meats brought aboard from Flushing that very morning. One by one they arose, bowed wretchedly at the captain, and departed. This was no ordinary indisposition; it was agony, aggravated that night by the sudden storm. Until late the following day, *l'Infatigable* was a floating hospital, its silence broken only by groans. Headed by Sister Marie Catherine, the less prostrate Sisters administered what restoratives they possessed with such kind insistence as to win high praise from Father DeSmet.

Through that dangerous night, Captain Moller was more than once at the point of making for an English port, though the stop at Dover scheduled for the December sailing had been canceled. There were moments when he feared that *l'Infatigable* would be driven on the coast of France, but he managed to trust Father DeSmet's advice that his crew could avoid accident and even make some headway. Father DeSmet had no desire to stop at any port before Valparaiso. He had been delayed long enough.

After they left the strait and the sea had abated somewhat, the anguish of the stricken passengers began to ease, too. On the second morning even the worst cases were able to mount on deck, enjoy the lively wind, and see that *l'Infatigable*

was still outstripping vessels that had started ahead of her.
That sight was enough to make the journalists turn to their
notebooks. Father DeSmet set the example. But he did not
begin with *l'Infatigable*'s victories. Instead, he entered with
facetious realism the plight of his fellow Jesuits in the grip
of seasickness. Peering over the writer's shoulder, Father
Vercruysse saw that he himself was the chief subject of
caricature; with every detail magnified, he was being pictured in ridiculous dejection. Pretending not to notice, he
waited until Father DeSmet had closed his notebook and
departed. Then he copied the account almost word for word
in his own diary, taking care, however, to insert Father
DeSmet's name wherever his own occurred. Having thus
secured sweet revenge in nicely turned paragraphs with very
little effort, he closed his notebook until Father DeSmet
should provide him with a second installment. Sister Mary
Aloysia started her record, too, with an eye on the model
journal, primly leaving, of course, certain details to the
reader. She left off writing when someone sighted an
"enormous fish," probably a seal, which "agreeably diverted"
everyone. That entertainment was followed by the discovery that the ship had lost her metal nameplate. At once
Captain Moller prepared a written message about the loss and
sent it by a passing vessel for publication in British newspapers. This, he said, was to prevent a report that *l'Infatigable* had been lost, in case the metal piece should be washed
up on the English coast.

They had their closest view of that coast toward evening
as they passed Point Lizard with its great light, a single one
in those days, telling of the rocky shoreline jutting southward. Soon they would pass Land's End and enter the
Atlantic. With the wind behind them, they were making
good time; Captain Moller was quite satisfied with his performance.

But the fourth day brought a return of sorrow to most of
the passengers, as *l'Infatigable* was tossed about in the rough
Atlantic. They could not write or study or go up on deck.
To move about at all was almost impossible; even the most
agile of them could not keep their footing. And the terrible

sickness was upon them again, more prostrating now than on the dreadful first night. When Sister Marie Catherine could manage it, she stumbled about, grasping at railings or other immovable objects, to bring help to the others. It was becoming evident that she was the best sailor in the crowd and that Father DeSmet was one of the worst.[2] All through the voyage he suffered more than the others because of the malady which really never left him. But when the sea smoothed out after three days of this rough sailing, they all recovered quickly enough. Father DeSmet was able to celebrate Mass and even to give a short lesson in English. Captain Moller noticed with relief that his passengers were taking the air on deck again. And on this first day of quiet sea Sister Marie Catherine found the secluded spot she had been seeking, "a spot very favorable to the disposition of my soul." It was the platform of the cannon, hidden in a recess on the deck, where she found she might "contemplate the ocean and its inhabitants" quite undisturbed. The ocean, she discovered, was a great vestibule to union with God. So all through the voyage, except when weather kept her below, she spent her free time in her little corner and all her companions respected her seclusion.

In this quiet period Sister Mary Aloysia began, perhaps at the advice of Father DeSmet, to polish up her diary notes for publication. In a way, this was unfortunate as her letters might have been a little more spontaneous and natural if she had written them only for the communities of Notre Dame in Belgium. Her idea of fine writing was the studied and stilted exercise that won first prize in girls' finishing schools on commencement days. And when the writer added the platitudes that most nuns of the time considered edifying, the total effect could be wearisome. Sister Mary Aloysia's word pictures of the sea are studies of a model just as her paintings were. When her entries are not copies of Father DeSmet's, they stand quite in contrast to them. Father DeSmet's nature descriptions, even the more verbose of them, hold the reader with their grandeur and feeling, as well as with their sense of reality. He writes swiftly with an eye on the total picture. Sister Mary Aloysia is more intent

on phrase-by-phrase correctness; as she searches for the fitting
term, feeling escapes her. She is prim and fastidious, omitting
in her narrative much of the sordid detail which Sister Marie
Catherine parades dramatically across her page.

When desire to live returned, the six Sisters began to
realize how impossible it was to improve conditions that
amounted to nightmare. To gain some little room in their
cabins, they tried putting the two or three chairs in the little
hallway at night. But there was no way of letting in a breath
of fresh air, and worse, especially for those who tried to sleep
on the floor, no relief from the rats. To avoid being bitten
they wrapped themselves well in their blankets, but as soon
as they dozed, they were awakened by rats making "processions" over them from head to foot. At last they devised the
plan of taking turns sitting up to frighten off the rodents
while the others slept. In the dark, the one on guard could
at best make uncertain passes at the intruders, which served
only to awaken the sleepers.

Before long, food also became an acute problem. Perishable foods spoiled rapidly because of the complete lack of
refrigeration. Captain Moller, who kept a close eye on the
supply, had to order a large consignment of corned beef
thrown overboard even before they left the Channel. Live
chickens brought on board just before the ship sailed died
within a few days. And the obnoxious rats found their way
into everything; even the ship biscuits, kept in zinc con-
tainers, came to the table nibbled. Little Nanny, with her
good supply of fodder, alone seemed dependable, and goat's
milk took on a hitherto unsuspected value.

But *l'Infatigable* was well-stocked with rice and other
grains, with smoked and dried meats, and with seasoning
which helped to offset the permeating offensiveness. With
ordinary good sailing there would be no need to ration
provisions, or water, or the excellent wine that Captain
Moller always carried. But from the first, the taint of that
rat-ridden brig offered challenge to the strongest stomach.
Poor Father DeSmet with his precarious digestion suffered
as much from that taint as from his tendency to *mal de mer*.
On the way down to the Horn, he was unable to teach for

days at a time, an unfortunate thing since his classes distracted his students' minds quite completely, a feat which Father Accolti's more humorous manner could not always achieve. So the deck and the wind became the most dependable sources of relief, and none made more constant use of these than Sister Marie Catherine. Except in rough weather, she could be found in her corner, her cloak wrapped about her, the wearisome English book forgotten, repeating Chinook phrases for the sake of her dear savages, or just lost in the sea's illimitable reaches into the Everlasting.

Off Madeira, on the eleventh day, a sudden drop of temperature to nineteen degrees Centigrade forced Sister Marie Catherine to leave her corner and pace the deck. A strange, cold stillness settled on the sea, which Sister Mary Aloysia described as "a lake of ice furrowed by a prodigious number of fishes," creatures which she found her knowledge of aquatic life too limited to name. Her equally ignorant and curious companions donned cloaks and shivered with her on the deck for the sake of a look at the "monsters." They knew salmon, and cod, and trout, "which are similar," Sister explained, "in grace and symmetry"; but these creatures, "with their tails where their heads should be," seemed to them the sport of Nature. Their school days had not been varied by trips to tropical aquaria. But as they grew accustomed to what at first seemed grotesque, they recognized new forms of beauty. Spellbound they watched the gorgeous colors flash in the water. How charming the dolphin! How fascinating the giant shark with "its two pilots," and the shoal of "little, old women" that made fishing easy for the crew and a good dinner possible for all by their suicidal eagerness!

Here, in their comments on the tropical seas, the two chief diarists of the voyage first appear in contrast. Of the shark and its pilots, Sister Mary Aloysia writes: "About noon a shark of uncommon size paid us a visit with its two pilots, which are superb fishes a foot and a half in length, traced with bands of shining white interspersed with others of bright blue."

In Father DeSmet's account the scene is real and dramatic. The shark was "accompanied by its pilots, (*centronati*

ductores), little fishes a foot or two in length, marked by
bands of dazzling white, crossed with others of brilliant blue.
They piloted the shark to a piece of bacon, attached as bait
to a hook of one-inch iron: the shark seized it, and feeling
himself caught, turned about with such violence that the
hook was straightened and pulled out of his mouth. Blood
appeared on the surface, but as for the shark, he returned to
the abyss."

Often enough Sister Mary Aloysia is attracted by Father
DeSmet's fine phrases, as when relating the catch of fish for
dinner, she describes the fishes as "rushing on the murderous
iron." But most of her borrowings merely add ornament
to her already decorated statement. After the same figure,
Father DeSmet achieves actuality which she does not: "We
stopped after we had taken twenty-seven, because we were
tired. . . ." [3]

This contrast runs through the diaries. Uninhibited and
nervous, Father DeSmet rushes his impressions into his notebook, heightening his convincing action pictures with generous splashes from his rich store. Sister Mary Aloysia fits
her impressions into the framework furnished her as a bright
and overdocile schoolgirl. Even when she writes with his
notes before her, she thus falls short of his lifelike touches.
But the difference is not surprising; she had learned her
clichés as she had her spelling. Her reading had been limited
to prudent selections. She had never known the liberty of
browsing through great books as Ruskin recommends for
the better education of girls.

As the second day of the calm brought nothing exciting
in the line of "monsters," the Fathers got out their glasses
and swept the sea in search of diversion. Soon one of them
spotted a small boat leaving a larger vessel and moving
languidly toward them on that glassy sea. Probably pirates,
one of the Fathers observed, and was immediately sorry
when he noticed the effect his words had on the Sisters.
But as the boat was manned by only five men, they decided
against the pirate theory. Captain Moller called down a
gracious invitation to the strangers to come aboard *l'Infatigable,* but they declined, explaining that their ship, the

Fourmi, was bound for Marseilles. In order to escape quarantine in that port, they must swear that they had not set foot on another ship en route. The pilot explained that he was captain of the French ship *Félicité*. She had been wrecked on the coast of Africa, he added sadly, and he and his crew had been taken aboard the *Fourmi*. They merely asked the longitude, for after their long and aimless voyage in the *Fourmi*, they wanted to know how near they were to France. The Fathers gave them what news they could of their native land and sadly watched them row away. Now in that disheartening calm *l'Infatigable* knew a doubled loneliness.

By way of distraction, the Sisters utilized the clear weather to wash their linens. Sea water! No boiler! Sister Mary Albine shook her head. The afternoon justified her forebodings. Amices, corporals, Sisters' capes, all hung dry on the line, far from the dazzling white she loved to see in convent laundry yards. Sister Loyola clucked her tongue at the grayness. There must be something one could do about it. But the appearance of Father DeSmet ended the fussing. Surely, he said, nobody would expect a white washing at sea. And what difference did it make? It was much more important to learn English, so they must resume classes at once. With his digestive well-being restored by the smooth sea, he was ready for a vigorous attack. Classes and singing practice from now on, he said. And that evening they sang Vespers on the deck, a devotion which became their fair-weather custom for the voyage. These activities were blessings during the calm; for moving thus from one duty to another created a feeling of progress that helped to offset the ship's immobility. Neither journal states how long that calm lasted, but they both report a moderate wind on Sunday, January twenty-eighth, and such a swell that it was impossible to celebrate Mass, though the weather was still clear, and calm enough for Vespers on deck.

February brought *l'Infatigable* in sight of the Cape Verde Islands. Brisk wind, clear skies, and the ship making fine headway. Then their first sight of flying fish, which Sister Mary Aloysia described in detail. And as the second of February was a feast of the Blessed Virgin, Sister Mary Aloysia

prepared a special concert for the evening. As she called the
pages, they sang litanies and hymns, everything they knew.
They were still singing at nine o'clock, Captain Moller and
his men thinking they had never heard anything more beautiful. Then they stood watching the stars, for the night was
very still and clear. The sea was becoming smooth again.
Too smooth. *L'Infatigable* was moving into another calm.
On the sixth, Sister Mary Aloysia wrote that the calm was
"still reigning," and Father DeSmet recorded 88 degrees
Fahrenheit, adding that subsequently it went no higher in
the tropics. Sister Mary Aloysia explains his relief; he feared
losing weight "under the ardent rays of the equatorial sun,"
a strange statement in view of the great missionary's tendency
to overweight.

Alternating periods of calm and light wind marked the
second week of February, yet there was no sense of dragging
time as all were well enough to follow the daily program.
To this they studiously adhered except when interrupted by
interesting incident, as when one evening hundreds of fish,
in full flight from two immense sharks, "assailed" the ship.
When darkness fell, the ocean was alight with flashing
streaks of phosphorescence, and the scene of cruel pursuit
changed to one of *Ancient Mariner* beauty under that starlit
tropical sky. Spellbound Sister Mary Aloysia wrote that the
tropical sea at night "has a charm that captivates the heart;
there is a sense of peace brooding over its vast basin."

But in a way the beauty emphasized the loneliness. If
only a ship would appear and lessen the feeling of distance
and isolation! So the twelfth was a red-letter day when word
passed quickly around that not one but several ships had been
sighted. They counted ten in all, counted and recounted
them, hoping that one at least was bound for Belgium. They
were disappointed; the long line passed too distant for
recognition. Then in the quick breeze that arose the following evening, a Dutch prison ship passed *l'Infatigable* as her
passengers were singing their evening litanies and hymns.
On the deck of the passing vessel, the Dutch soldiers were also
singing, their lusty "chansons militaires" in strange contrast to *l'Infatigable*'s peaceful strains. The two ships ex-

changed information about their home ports and destiny; then the rough soldier chorus faded into the night, but it was good to have had this brief encounter with humanity.

Distraction of another sort marked the next two days. On the fourteenth the captain remarked noncommittally that they were nearing the equator, whereupon he and Father DeSmet exchanged knowing glances. All the uninitiated wondered at this and at the unusual and somewhat furtive actions of the crew. Something was up. But apparently it was nothing to worry about, for suppressed laughter followed hushed bits of conversation and Father DeSmet looked wise when he heard it.

That evening the passengers understood. When singing was over and the last of them had gone below to the chapel, they suddenly heard loud cheers on deck and summons to come up quickly. There they beheld the crew pointing dramatically to a column of fire rising from the sea, perhaps a hundred yards distant, and heard their exultant shouts, "Neptune's fire! Neptune's fire!" During the day the men had produced this ancient portent by soaking a barrel of peas in pitch. When the passengers left the deck that night, the crew dragged the barrel from its hiding place, set fire to it and cast it overboard. As the flames leaped up, a ghostly voice was heard in the rigging above, addressing itself to the captain who calmly answered it.

"Captain," asked the voice, "have you any passengers on board?"

"Yes, I have twelve passengers."

"Do they hope to cross the line?"

"Yes, they do."

"Well, tomorrow Neptune will baptize them in person," the ghost announced.

"This is necessary to all who pass the line."

Enjoying the fun, the twelve passengers stayed on deck for the crossing of the line at ten o'clock that night, and were rewarded by the sight of a tremendous light that flared up from the topmast to signal the crossing.

At exactly ten next morning, the ship rang with the cry, "Neptune! Neptune!" Then the Fathers and Brother

Francis were told to accompany the captain to the bridge where Neptune was presiding with his court, all arrayed in grotesque and ragged costumes, Neptune himself half-hidden in an immense wig and beard of raveled hemp. More like Pluto, was Sister Mary Aloysia's comment. With his great wooden compass and sextant, the god of the sea entertained his court and audience with very clever mimicry of Captain Moller. At last, after solemnly taking the longitude, he announced that on this their thirty-seventh day at sea, he had come to promise the passengers a happy voyage. But he added that there were certain rites to be performed before this promise could be assured. First of all, he and his court must shave Father DeSmet. At that the courtiers, armed with wooden swords, rose and stood guard around their king and his ludicrous queen, glaring dire warnings at their victim. Somewhat fearful of the lengths to which the sailors might go, Father DeSmet begged off. In vain. The god of the sea insisted on his "inalienable rights" and on the "bounden duty" of all passengers to submit. Captain Moller whispered that the men would not go too far and that this was the only fun they had. So Father DeSmet entered the game with a piece of sailcloth over his chest for a towel. Dipping his brush once or twice in a little tub of soapy water, Neptune "lightly and gracefully" applied it to the priest's chin and then rubbed the lather off with his wooden razor. Now his religious brothers had to sit down with him at the mainmast and submit to the same ceremony. That finished, Neptune ordered the baptism. A deluge of water descended upon the six, much to the merriment of the Sisters who had been gallantly placed at a safe distance to witness the morning's fun. Now satisfied that the Fathers were good sports, the crew indulged in a water-bucket contest among themselves. At last, thoroughly soaked, they gave over for the rest of the morning. But later in the day they reappeared, dressed in their best, to entertain the passengers with a series of dances, "each more ridiculous than the last." Then as a climax to the crossing-the-line celebration, Captain Moller ordered the best dinner possible. Good humor made up for deficiencies, and Father DeSmet's eloquent speech of thanks for the day of merriment supplied the proper finale.

March came gently, with steady wind bearing *l'Infatigable* and her northern passengers into shortening autumn days instead of accustomed spring. Now between hours of prayer and study, the diarists recorded wonderful sights. On the evening of March first, three ships loomed on the horizon, two of them westward bound and etched with black grace on the sun's low-hung disk; "ce qui offrait un coup d'oeil magnifique," wrote Sister Mary Aloysia.[4] And that night, alone on the deck, Father DeSmet witnessed a gorgeous meteoric display of which he set down a lengthy and eloquent description, as well as of the Southern Cross and the Clouds of Magellan. Then suddenly out of all this peaceful splendor came the first ocean storm of the voyage. Thunder growled over the water. In quick succession, torrential rain and battering hail struck terror. As quickly, the storm passed over, leaving the sea so rough that the missionaries thought of their earlier hard days. For a week there was neither studying nor writing. But on the eleventh they were on deck again viewing a terrible battle between a school of porpoises and a flock of sea birds, "the size of a goose," wrote Father DeSmet. In mid-March the ship was readied for another oncoming storm; it passed over, however, and left a very quiet sea for a sportive whale over sixty feet long to play in.

As they approach the Horn, Sister Mary Aloysia's journal becomes quite independent of Father DeSmet's. Each now records incidents omitted by the other, and Father DeSmet's notes are filled with scientific and historic explanations which Sister Mary Aloysia would have included had she had access to his book. It may be that Father DeSmet was often too ill to write as they passed through those rough seas, or that he completed his account later, perhaps with the aid of a library. Concerning the Faulkland Islands, which they sighted on March sixteenth, he tells of the failure of Spanish, French, English, and Americans to remain because they could not endure the harsh climate. Sister merely mentions passing these islands, but tells of a second pirate scare near the South Shetlands three days later, which Father DeSmet omits. The captain was alarmed, she says, and Father DeSmet ex-

horted them all to pray. All the ship's arms—lances, sabers,
and guns—were brought up, and the cannon was primed. But
the Sisters were really not frightened; that very morning they
had made a promise to St. Joseph to be fulfilled on their
arrival in Valparaiso. After that not one of them doubted
a safe and sound arrival, nor did they wonder that a favoring
wind carried *l'Infatigable* swiftly past the cause of worry.
But if Father DeSmet forgot this thrilling escape, he recalled
instead his regret at rounding without seeing it the most
southern point of the Hermit Islands, which another adventurer had named The Horn for its resemblance to his
little hook-shaped Dutch harbor.

Both diarists fill those days with the horrors of huge ice-
bergs and volcanic rocks. Yet Father DeSmet found pleasure
in the sight of the "formless, isolated masses" of the islands
Diego Ramirez and Ildefonso, "being tired of seeing nothing
day after day save the water and the firmament." Certainly
the wild life in this inferno region afforded great satisfaction
to naturalist DeSmet. In his account stand the measurements
of the giant albatross, the habits of the tiny stormy petrel, and
the tameness of the gannet, which once aboard refuses to
leave the ship.

When *l'Infatigable* at last made away from this dangerous
coast line, she ran into the worst storm of even Father
DeSmet's varied experience. For an entire week the hatches
were battened down, and the bravest feared to creep on deck
to witness "the terrifying spectacle." The sails were "torn to
shreds," and the ship became "the sport of wind and waves";
all on board spent hours "in mortal agony," wrote Sister
Mary Aloysia.[5] Catching up later with his story, Father
DeSmet set down these exact phrases as a start for his
dramatic telling. When at last they breathed again, he says,
a terrific gale drove the ship toward the awful coast. Now
with two sails spread she had to make head against a wild
hurricane or be dashed on the rocks. The wind tore away
at the pyramids of water around her, casting great masses
from their summits in foam on her deck. Even with his
megaphone, the captain could not make his orders heard
over the roar. Storms, as a rule, were "sublime," but if this

one were a bit "less frightful" Father DeSmet would have enjoyed it more.

All except the Sisters were on deck now, their eyes fixed on the frightful cliffs which line the wild and barbarous coasts of Patagonia. This was the end! Unable to endure the "gloomy silence" any longer, Father DeSmet went below to warn the Sisters, who were praying together in the chapel. Did they wish to receive final absolution? They answered in "unalterable calm" that they were not really disturbed. When he had gone, Sister Mary Cornelia remarked dryly, "I do believe the Reverend Fathers are easily alarmed, *un peu trop alarmés.*" And she was the most timid in the band, was Sister Mary Aloysia's comment.[6]

Father DeSmet had no more than reached the deck again when the wind changed suddenly and carried *l'Infatigable* out to sea. The Sisters' faith, of course, had done it. Where he might have expected lamentations and groans, he said, he found perfect tranquillity.[7] This peace of soul in dangerous moments established the Sisters forever in Father DeSmet's high esteem. But one at least of his religious brothers refused to accede to this perfect balance of resignation and trust in the Sisters, at any rate in all of them. If the terrors of the storm had struck fear into the Fathers themselves, it was reasonable to suppose that the Sisters had been apprehensive, too. So this doubting Thomas accosted Sister Marie Catherine next day, conjuring her to tell him the truth. Hadn't she been at all perturbed during that terrible night? Laughing, she assured him she had not. And why should she have feared? She had been sent by her Superiors to do God's work in Oregon, not to be the food of fishes. It was really quite simple. Sister Marie Catherine laughed as she told this story in her grand old age, but she always added that humble Sister Mary Cornelia's spirit of faith was a great source of strength to her and the other Sisters in all the dangers of the voyage.

After the storm, *l'Infatigable* was borne tossing and plunging up the Chilean coast in constant danger of drifting too close to the shore line. Movement about the ship was again almost impossible; classes were unthinkable; Mass was cele-

brated only on Easter Sunday, April seventh. The journalists made only the briefest entries; they were very close to
Cape Tres Montes on April third, they skirted the long island
of Chiloe on the eighth and ninth, on the tenth they were in
full sight of the Island of Mocha, the greatest danger of all by
reason of extensive shoals hidden by shallow water.

On the twelfth, toward evening, *l'Infatigable* entered the
lovely bay of Valparaiso at last, out of Antwerp ninety-three
days. Captain Moller cast anchor at five. Then patience!
They are not to go ashore until morning. But there were
preparations to make, and there was this enchanting city
rising from the crescent line of the bay, the sunset reflected
in its windows, a lighted amphitheater at the base of the
mountains. After their long captivity, wrote Sister Mary
Aloysia, they were "capable of appreciating the sight." And
Father DeSmet, who hastily copied from her notes for the
last troubled two weeks, added with feeling, "and were very
well disposed to do so."

CHAPTER 5

Pacific Cities

Father DeSmet was a stranger in Valparaiso. He had heard bright stories of wealth and opportunity about this attractive city, and also harsh stories of oppression and revolution. He had never known of a Jesuit foundation there. He was not sure that he would find any religious communities; revolution might have driven them all out. There might be a few contemplative monasteries left, and the people would surely still love their old faith. He would thus find some sort of lodging for his companions, but the search might be long and difficult. He must get an early start in the morning, and go ashore in the first boat that would come out to *l'Infatigable*.[1]

It was a happy surprise to him, then, to discover that the Jesuits from Buenos Aires had founded a house in Valparaiso some time before. He learned, too, that the Picpus Fathers (Fathers of the Sacred Heart) had a college there, and that the Picpus nuns directed a boarding school.

Busy as they were with the approaching end of the school year, these good French nuns assured Father DeSmet they would be happy to receive his six missionary Sisters. And the Jesuit Provincial, Father Verdugo, extended the same welcome to him and his five companions. Relieved by his unexpected successes, he hurried back to the ship, taking little notice of the mid-morning earthquake. But on board he found Sisters and Jesuits in a state of consternation. The ship, they told him, had shuddered from prow to stern with sharp twitches quite unlike the effects of a storm. While it lasted, people on the wharves knelt praying with extended

79

arms. Did the land really move about? To the Sisters that
prospect seemed more alarming than the roughest sea. Captain Moller explained that though earthquakes were frequent in this region, they were themselves not so dangerous;
the fatalities were caused by falling buildings. When they
felt a tremor, he cautioned them, they must run from the
house and take refuge under a tree. But Father DeSmet
made light of earthquakes in general, and announced that
the two boats waiting alongside would take them all ashore.
There was instant action. Down into the boats went the
Sisters' bulky bundles of brownish-gray linen, Sister Mary
Albine smiling at the thought of seeing it white again, if
that were possible. She didn't know about these Picpus
nuns, but all Sisters had laundries; one could be sure of that.

At last they stood on the soil of the new world. Two-
thirds of their travels already memories, observed Sister
Loyola, and really pleasant ones! Her Sisters agreed; it was
easy now to make this light-hearted review, looking out on
the blue-green, feather-tipped waves and long combers breaking pearly in the afternoon light. Valparaiso! Sea, strand,
snow-peaked mountains close-folding but pillaring the sky!
Again they look out at the bay. Their ship, all the ships,
riding the waves so gracefully! But Captain Moller has told
them the bay will soon be empty, for May will bring fierce
northwesters that make anchorage in the open harbor a
hazard. Now Father DeSmet is explaining that those same
strong winds will be a blessing on the last lap of their
voyage.

As he was speaking, a carriage sent by the Picpus Sisters
arrived for the Sisters of Notre Dame. Fortunately a commodious vehicle, observed Sister Loyola gratefully as the
last of the bundles and valises were tucked in. She looked a
little sadly at those valises which the good captain had so
kindly lent her to replace the Sisters' strong Belgian valises
which the rats had nibbled to pieces in the hold. And the
trunks! Between storms and rats, there was little left of some
of them. Sister Loyola found it easy to forget her own past
discomfort, but those fine trunks! The sturdy gifts for which
Mère Constantine and the Belgian Superiors had made

sacrifices! And those valises! "Les grandes et pesantes caisses d'Anvers."

Father DeSmet led his brothers to the newly founded Jesuit college, where they found abundant good will together with an apportunity to share extreme poverty; the community was on the point of starvation, but they were "true brothers and friends, *corde et animo*." At the Picpus convent, the Sisters of Notre Dame fared much better. Care, rest, and strengthening food soon restored their good health. When Father DeSmet called, he found them quite overcome by the kindness of the Ladies of the Sacred Heart. They could never forget such goodness, they told him. Certainly Sister Loyola could never forget the response of these generous nuns to her request for the use of the convent laundry. The almost ruined linen was whisked away and restored to lovely whiteness while the Lady Superior kept her guests hospitalized for a few days. This was the story Sister Marie Catherine liked best to tell about these white-robed nuns who wore the insignia of two hearts surrounded by thorns.

On their side, the Sisters of Notre Dame were not going to be outdone in charity. As soon as they recovered from the "little indispositions" caused by three months of sailing, they freed their hostesses for their intensified school duties by doing up the housework and replacing them at their hours of adoration. Between times, they enjoyed the beautiful enclosed garden in which they found a large tree suitable for shelter in case of earthquake. A place where the earth could move about under one's feet was not to be trusted, however lovely to the eye. And even though the Picpus Sisters seemed to take the matter of earthquakes quite casually, Captain Moller could hardly be wrong about the danger of falling buildings. So when a rumbling and shaking awakened the Sisters of Notre Dame one night, they rushed out to their tree without waiting to don their habits; all, that is, but Sister Norbertine, who took her time and dressed. When she finally joined the others, they chided her in chorus. She might have been buried under the ruins, they told her. Then suddenly they all burst into laughter. The convent was still standing. The Picpus Sisters were

safe in their beds. The city was quiet. Next morning they
discovered that such light tremors were common occur-
rences, and that most buildings were constructed to with-
stand shocks.

Adjusted to the possibility of tremors, the Sisters of Notre
Dame turned their attention to the schools taught by their
hostesses. With the revenue of their small boarding school,
these Sisters were financing a day school for three hundred
poor children. Both were so well taught that Sister Loyola
thought it a pity to have closed their new school for middle-
class children for lack of Sisters to staff it. When the Picpus
nuns opened this third school, they expected reinforcements
from their French convents. Eighteen of their French Sisters
had volunteered for the large expedition led by Bishop
Rouchoux to Honolulu and other South Pacific missions in
the winter of 1842. But the brig *Marie-Joseph* in which the
Bishop and his missionaries sailed that December was lost.
None of them survived.[3] And in Valparaiso there were no
local vocations to make up for this terrible loss. In this
city of churches and Catholic tradition, leaders were anticlerical and citizens were apathetic; pride and selfishness
were choking out dedication. All this seemed very sad to
Sister Loyola and her community. Saddest of all was the
thought of the closed day school. These children, the future
leaders of the people, would grow up without instruction in
faith and morals. Yet the Picpus nuns numbered twenty;
with fifteen, Sister Loyola would have staffed all three
schools.

But it was different with these nuns whose first duty was
perpetual adoration, a duty that might not be set aside to
allow for more teaching hours. It seemed clear to Sister
Loyola that stress on contemplative and cloistered life tended
to separate these religious too completely from the people,
a fact that alone would explain failure of indigenous growth
of their congregation. The Picpus Fathers, it would seem,
were also of this view; at least they considered there was
work in Valparaiso for another order of Sisters. When some
of them came to call on the Sisters of Notre Dame, they tried
to dissuade them from going on to Oregon. Why not stay

in an established mission field instead of going to the wilderness? Sister Marie Catherine was annoyed. To yield to this invitation would have seemed to her a betrayal. She "thought less" of these good Fathers as she listened to their arguments.

But Sister Loyola at once began to envision a foundation of Notre Dame in Valparaiso, and that dream grew clearer as she listened to the still more persuasive invitation of Father Verdugo. Satisfied by the Sisters' replies to his questions about their congregation, he declared he believed the Sisters of Notre Dame had all the qualities needed for the South American mission. He "overwhelmed" them with attention, Sister Marie Catherine recalled, urging them to ask their Mother General for foundations in Rio de Janeiro and Montevideo, and thus prepare the way for his own request. Sister Loyola was quite impressed by the Jesuit Provincial's description of Montevideo. The need of Sisters there was very great, she wrote to Mère Constantine. The climate was healthful, and the cost of living reasonable. And there were wealthy persons in Valparaiso who would help a foundation there; in fact, these persons had already "signified their intention" to make up a purse for the Sisters of Notre Dame before their departure for Oregon.[4] That is the last heard of the intended purse, though Sister Mary Aloysia, who was also somewhat impressed by South American possibilities, tells of two ladies sent by Father Verdugo to help the Sisters, as well as of a supply of provisions from him for the voyage to Willamette. The wonder is that Father Verdugo's wealthy friends failed to assist his own almost starving house in Valparaiso. At any rate, the city abounded in good intentions.

Mère Constantine might well have been perplexed by Sister Loyola's letter from Valparaiso. The suddenness of the writer's transition from her brief account of the storm in the South Pacific to arguments for foundations in South America indicates a mind quite taken with a new idea. And after reporting her gratitude to the Picpus nuns, she returns again to the project. As their chapel is very poorly furnished, she has decided to give them an alb which she re-

ceived in Antwerp. Then she mentions candlesticks and
other needs in case the Mother General would like to send
a gift to these nuns, "should Providence destine our Sisters
to come here later."

While Sister Loyola was not tempted to give up the Oregon mission and remain in Chile as the Picpus Fathers
advised, still she saw one or more South American foundations as possible. Certainly she encouraged Father Verdugo
to ask Mère Constantine for two foundations. Just as certainly, it would have been more consistent with reality to
tell him that the still small Belgian Province could hardly
spare six Sisters for the Willamette venture; that it would
be several decades at least before the congregation could
support two such widely separated missions on the Pacific
Coast.

Though the Reverend Fathers and other persons called
on the Sisters of Notre Dame at the Picpus Convent, it seems
not to have occurred to any of them to show them their fair
city and its beautiful churches. Apparently they spent their
eighteen days in Valparaiso in the strict cloister of their
hostesses. The visiting Jesuits, of course, managed to get
about. With bilingual Father Gomila, Superior of the Jesuit
Missions in Chile, and Father Landau, a local Jesuit, as
guides, Fathers DeSmet and Vercruysse managed to include
in their sight-seeing a somewhat dangerous trip to Santiago.
Father DeSmet thought such travel worth while when he
saw the wide streets and fine public buildings of Chile's
capital. He was gratified, too, as he always was on meeting
important persons, that visits to the President, General
Vulnes, and to other government officials, were included in
his tour of the city. He returned to Valparaiso filled with
admiration for Chile with its seven hundred copper mines
and delicious climate, and for its friendly and progressive
chief city. As proof of this friendliness, he brought back
with him the gift of the Museum of Santiago, a fine mineral
collection, which he sent in a nice public-relations gesture
to the Museum of Brussels. But when Father DeSmet related his account of his trip to the Sisters of Notre Dame
and their hostesses in the Picpus Convent, he added one

sad observation. In Santiago there were eight monasteries of nuns, but only that of the "Picpus Ladies" had a school attached. And in this the capital reflected other South American cities. Schools closed by revolutions had not been reopened even when new governments became more lenient. Catholic education seemed paralyzed. Parents were calling in vain for religious teachers for their children. But Sister Marie Catherine thought of Indian and half-breed mothers waiting her coming along the Willamette. Let others reclaim these old Spanish cities. She would have her "dear savages" on the fringes of wilderness.

And now with sails mended or renewed, *l'Infatigable* was ready for the sea again and the rising trade winds. She would next put in at Callao as she had cargo for Lima, and at Callao Captain Moller would have his ship fumigated and be rid of the loathsome rats. With that announcement to cheer them, Sister Loyola and her Sisters bade farewell to their kind hostesses on the first of May. "Nous nous séparâmes en nous donnant rendez-vous au ciel." And every letter and memoir of these Sisters of Notre Dame mentions the gratitude they tried to express as they were hurried away to their ship, with neatly packaged delicacies and perfectly ironed white linen to remind them en route of their new-found friends.

It was fortunate that Father Gomila had business in Lima; besides being a fine interpreter, he was on friendly terms, it seems, with everyone there. And he enjoyed this short stage of the voyage, slightly over a week, with the missionaries. He liked the way in which they all returned at once to their daily routine. Captain Moller liked it, too. There were the Fathers walking back and forth reciting Divine Office and holding down the pages of their breviaries when they faced the wind. There were the Sisters saying their Rosary together in the chapel. There was Sister Mary Aloysia setting out the English books for Father DeSmet's class and marking the hymnals for singing practice. And between classes and religious exercises, there was Sister Marie Catherine in her nook under the cannon, enjoying the immediacy of God granted by the sea.

For Sister Marie Catherine, the thought of Lima was thrilling. The city of St. Rose! And Father Gomila would take them to see the very home of this American saint, whom she had to thank for her mission to Oregon. Sister Marie Catherine thought she had reason to be the most grateful person in the world. For one thing there was this fine, swift sailing, this almost constant clear sky and refreshing wind. A beautiful run, Father DeSmet called it, as he listened to the sailors singing. No wonder they sang. Not once did *l'Infatigable* have to deviate from her course; right up to Callao her sails remained just as they had been set in Valparaiso. This "smooth and beautiful" ocean, said Father DeSmet, had a right to be called *Mare Pacificum*. For once he was satisfied with sameness, "agreeable monotony" he called it.

In the late afternoon of May eighth, Captain Moller cast anchor in the Bay of Callao. Immediately Fathers DeSmet and Gomila went ashore in the little port town, where they boarded an omnibus for Lima, there to secure lodgings. Approaching this capital, Father DeSmet was impressed by its magnificence; the long tree-bordered avenue lined with stone benches, the entry under a triumphal arch, the very extent of the city, all spoke of past importance and strength, which were now ebbing away by reason of civil wars. But Lima presented a picture of lovely peace that evening, a gently rising expanse of flat, pink-tiled roofs, pearly gold in the sunset, from which an array of church towers tapered up to golden crosses.

As in every place that Father DeSmet visited, Lima was soon aware of his presence. By dint of his own initiative and Father Gomila's friendly Spanish conversation, he made a number of valuable contacts that very evening. Among these was Father Mateo d'Aguilar, who gave the two Jesuits hospitality that night and presented them the next morning to a group of Catholic women for whom he was conducting a retreat. Hearing that there were Sisters in the mission party, these ladies were "in a marked state of impatience, mingled with joy and curiosity," said Father DeSmet. So was everyone else before long, both in Lima and at the port.

When the two Fathers returned to Callao, they found an excited crowd gathered on the wharf, emotionally welcoming the missionaries who had just come ashore and understood not a word of the welcome. Some of the women were weeping, others were raising their hands to heaven, all talking together. Father Gomila made his way through the crowd and interpreted the din as best he could. And it went on and on, since the five-horse omnibus that Father DeSmet had hired was half an hour late. When it did arrive, the crowd was so large that the missionaries could not get near it.

In the city the travelers were stopped all along the way, their five-horse equipage notwithstanding. Spaniards, Negroes, Indians crowded around and stopped their progress. One old man, Sister Mary Aloysia relates, cried out that these were the first Jesuits he had seen since the suppression, and that at last his desire had been granted. But Father DeSmet was impressed most by the ovation everywhere accorded the Sisters. Mothers held up their children, kissed the Sisters' hands and veils, begged them to stay with them. No wonder, Sister Mary Aloysia remarked; of the twenty-five religious communities in Lima, not one was engaged in teaching. When at last the Sisters made their way through the crowd at the gate of the old Carmelite Convent where they were to lodge, they found the building occupied by a number of little orphans with only one lay woman to teach and care for them. As a second surprise, the Sisters turned to find that the crowd had surged in after them. And for the next four or five days they had visitors from morning till night, some of these distinguished Spanish ladies who brought their own interpreters along, and insisted that the Sisters accept their carriages for tours about the city. Father DeSmet remarks that "the humble Sisters" received "these homages" reluctantly, yet with "heart-felt consolation." Everyone in Lima, it seemed, wanted religious teachers for their children, even the wives of Peruvian leaders, men who played the anticlerical game, an instance of the Latin-American paradox familiar to registrars of North American Catholic schools and colleges for many decades.

Despite all the well-wishing, Father DeSmet and his

companion Jesuits were not at all well cared for in Lima.
Though Archbishop Pizarro received them "with affection"
and seemed filled with good will for Jesuits far and near, he
entrusted them apparently to a somewhat careless official.
So the poor missionaries found themselves assigned to a
single room in St. Paul's, the former college of their Society,
a group of four large buildings that occupied an entire city
block. The Oratorians and some other Fathers now had
quarters there in the portion not used by the government
for barracks and stables. So now the first Oregon Jesuits,
huddled in one small room of their once famous college,
discussed the effects of suppression and revolution and the
chances of finding greater stability in the Northwest. Yet,
said Father DeSmet, "there seemed but a single voice in
the whole city—all demanded the return of the Jesuits."

Of course the visiting Jesuits did not allow a failure in
hospitality to prevent their making the most of their stay
in the capital. As always, Father DeSmet insisted on the
educational aspects of travel, and it is plain from the memoir
which he later wrote up on Peru that he and his companions
neglected no opportunities. The reader of that memoir
sees Lima of 1844 almost as in a modern movie. But of much
greater importance is his interpretation of his picture. Here
in the midst of natural wealth, he saw a terrible lack of
initiative and energy; the people of Peru "walk on gold and
silver and lack for bread." Buildings, especially churches,
speak of opulence, but the Peruvians have failed to construct "the first essentials of internal commerce; roads, canals,
bridges." Merchandise was being transported on the backs
of mules. Agriculture was so far neglected that they had to
import most of their grain. In the hundreds of mines started
in the past, there was fabulous wealth still untouched for
want of proper mining methods. Lima was an "unhappy
city," paralyzed by revolution and counterrevolution, with
the people trusting little to the leaders of any faction.

And Lima was a city of religious contradiction; its inhabitants wept and cried out for religious teachers, but their
lives and lack of respect in their churches were out of step
with their emotional protestations. Sister Loyola and her

Sisters were shocked at the carelessness of the local clergy in celebrating Holy Mass, as well as at the bad behavior of the congregations. She asked her community to join her in a great novena to St. Rose that missionaries might be sent to Lima. But on the whole, she was in no great haste to make a foundation there. Sister Mary Aloysia wrote to Mère Constantine that His Excellency and certain of the clergy thought the Sisters of Notre Dame could work wonders in Peru, but these made no definite request as did the clergy of Valparaiso. On both sides, the matter ended with wishing. "Would that we were twelve instead of only six!" But there was no great desire on the part of the six Belgians to choose Lima even if they could. It was not their atmosphere, despite all the "dates, pillas, chilomoya, and pignas" with which the ladies regaled them, the toothsome breakfasts sent in to them each morning when they returned from Mass, and the beautiful chapel gifts including a tabernacle "de fort bon goût." Even Señora Riverodero herself, with all her elaborate kindness, failed to impress them deeply.

The Señora was one of the ladies who prevented the Sisters from "spending some days in silence and prayer" by driving them about to church after church and chatting endlessly. She could not understand that daily excursions in her elegant carriage were not quite to their taste. Seeing that they admired the opulently ornate interiors (Sister Mary Aloysia was in ecstasy over them), the Señora and her friends insisted they visit every church and monastery chapel in the city. And when the possibilities of pilgrimage had been exhausted, the Señora invited the Sisters to spend a day at her country villa.

Thus one morning in her stately carriages, they enjoyed the gorgeous Peruvian mountains in meditative quiet. But at her estate they found her waiting to entertain them with her steady flow of French through the length of a delicious dinner. There was no end to the good they might do in Lima, she told them, and unlike His Excellency and the clergy, she offered them an inducement. Her "good and virtuous daughter," she confided, had a great desire to become a religious. The Carmelites had refused to receive the young lady, but now the Señora had thought things over and had come to the conclusion that the Señorita would make an excellent Sister of Notre Dame. So if the Sisters would consider founding a house in Lima, the Señora would be happy to allow her daughter to enter their congregation. For some reason, she failed to present the Señorita to the Sisters; more strangely, she said nothing of her daughter's willingness. Sister Loyola's response to such generosity on the mother's part was probably discreet but certainly final. At any rate, Señora Riverodero and her good and virtuous though unseen daughter were always subjects of mirth for Sister Marie Catherine.

At last Sister Marie Catherine knelt in the cell where the American Saint Rose had prayed. She loved that little room, but found the opulent shrine in which the Limans venerated their heroine little to her liking. She wanted her saints to take Heaven by violence and she liked their shrines to remind her that they had struggled. So she studied the details of this stark room, treasuring the more gruesome for future meditation. She could not associate with sanctity the artistic extremes of "massive gold and silver" which delighted Sister Mary Aloysia; she was really more deeply impressed by the poverty in which her saint had lived there in the heart of that very materialistic city. To the citizens of Lima, religion meant the possession of the relics of their saint, by which they hoped to be saved, not by the acceptance of her spirit.

Not given to analyzing situations so deeply, Sister Mary Aloysia set down notes about the smallness of the saint's little room, in which a fairly tall person could not stand upright, the solid silver reliquary that enshrined her remains, and the murals that depicted her life. So with the usual platitudes of "deep emotion" and "hallowed spot," she brings her account to Sunday, May twenty-sixth, when the Captain announced that *l'Infatigable* would sail next day. That morning Mr. Bosch, the Belgian Consul, and his wife called on the Sisters. His Excellency, Archbishop Pizarro, bestowed a final blessing on the missionaries, and of course, crowds gathered to say farewell. And their visitors were genuinely sad to leave them, for their hospitality, though a bit excited, was charming as it was generous.

Aboard their ship once more, the passengers heard a piece of welcome news from the sailors and the cook. The rats were gone! The railing was repaired, too, of course; in fact, a good deal of mending was done on that battered little ship at Callao. But the rats made the headlines. The fumigators had reached the remotest corners of the hold with their poisonous gas. Fifteen hundred was Sister Marie Catherine's more conservative estimate. And the sailors showed her a plank that had been replaced in the side of the ship. The rats had gnawed it almost through! They had been saved by nothing short of a miracle, she insisted. It proved again, the missionaries assured one another, that God wanted them to do His work in Oregon.

Up to the moment of sailing, the Sisters hoped for a letter from Namur. Hadn't Mère Constantine promised to be ahead of them all along their route? They knew her plan to send letters by every possible carrier to Valparaiso and Lima. Letters by way of Panama, for instance, should have reached those points long before *l'Infatigable*. One letter from home would lessen their feeling of complete separation as they started for Oregon. Sister Loyola reminded the others that Mère Constantine and the Sisters in Belgium had certainly written, and that they must take comfort in knowing it. They must set their minds now on their "beautiful mission." They tried, but as they felt the familiar roll of the ship riding at anchor, each read in the eyes of the others her own nostalgia and the finality of this last setting to sea. The remedy was to keep as busy as possible, to arrange their cabins and their altar, to store away the kind gifts of their admirers in Lima with quick little prayers for the donors as they worked. In the midst of these arrangements, the Sisters were summoned to the deck where they found Father DeSmet pointing happily to the pile of boxes that Madame Bosch had sent aboard for them. All sorts of provisions for the rest of the voyage, Sister Mary Aloysia wrote in the letter she hurried off to Mère Constantine that very evening. And how practical as well as generous the good lady was!

At this proof of such great kindness, joy shone again in the Sisters' eyes. Their homeland fitted into its niche of shining memory; their call to the Willamette was again their cloud and pillar of light. How white the altar linen gleamed on Sister Mary Aloysia's piano, and how tall and straight the candles! Red flowers for Pentecost, artificial but so lovely! As though there had been no interruption in their routine, Fathers and Sisters sang Vespers on the deck. And as the stars came out, *Ave Maris Stella* floated over the Bay of Callao, Sister Marie Catherine looked at the darkening city. She would pray always for those people, spoiled but friendly and generous. Her people were the poor but unspoiled children of forest edge and river bank. Her savages! Soon she would be with them.

CHAPTER 6

Last Hazard

From Lima to the Columbia, Father DeSmet leaves the precisions to Sister Mary Aloysia, who now seems to be consulting the ship's log daily herself. He writes occasionally, his account marked by the omissions and reversals of retrospect; she pinpoints the voyage, giving latitude and longitude with date, weather, and wind. But both paint a charming picture of life aboard ship through the first few weeks of fine sailing, and both relate the grim weeks of calm and storm that harassed the little brig after she left the southern trades.[1]

Father DeSmet kept his band in spiritual and scholastic high key through those earlier days when the Pacific seemed justly named. Most of his students were doing well in English, accenting it, of course, in their instructor's manner, but at least understanding one another's more or less prolonged Anglo-Saxon flights. The Italian Fathers were loping through French grammar and making rapid strides, of necessity, in the speech that surrounded them. Everyone helped them; Sister Marie Catherine dedicated an hour each day to them in addition to their class with Father Vercruysse. And often through those lovely days, there were spiritual conferences by one or other of the Fathers after the morning Masses.

The Sisters, of course, had to add little devotions of their own, small extras like their novena of gratitude to St. Joseph. Hadn't he saved them twice from pirates? Beyond a doubt, too, his intercession was obtaining this steady wind that modified the heat as they approached the line for the second time. And for the last day of May, their floating chapel had to resemble their church at the Mother House as closely as

possible. Every candlestick they had appeared on the piano
with Murillo's Madonna in the center. Before this shrine
they sang their "belles litanies" to honor Mary, "cette étoile
si chère aux missionnaires voyageurs." There was some sadness, though, in this likeness to the elaborate display of their
Belgian chapels. When Sister Mary Aloysia had set her final
touch in preparation for Corpus Christi, she turned around
and found her companions on the verge of tears. They were
thinking of beautiful garden processions, of lights and
flowers, of white-veiled girls with high, sweet voices and
reverent eyes. Quickly Sister Loyola knelt. As the others
joined her in prayer, the fair, white-veiled children became
black-eyed natives walking with equal reverence and singing
the same sweet words:

> Le Seigneur est mon Berger,
> Je ne manque de rien.

Thank God, there wouldn't be time for nostalgia in Oregon, Sister Marie Catherine told herself as she attacked the
same English exercise for the fourth or fifth time. How did
Sister Mary Aloysia master it so quickly? Perhaps one should
turn her back to the ocean to study. How long would the
Pacific remain so utterly beautiful?

The steady breeze was still with them when they crossed
the line June thirteenth, at 110 degrees longitude. Sister
Mary Aloysia entered the fact briefly, adding that to honor
the event, the cook produced "une petite fête." That evening
the Sisters prepared the chapel for the Feast of the Sacred
Heart, another day of special solemnity in their home convents. Whether all the candlesticks came out or not, the
homesickness was more acute this time. Noticing the tears,
Father DeSmet asked Father Vercruysse to give a little
sermon about the ill effects of sadness. The resulting return
to heroism was fortunate; mid-June brought trying days
of alternating weather, long hours of calm in the blistering
tropic sun and relieving hours of wind that swept *l'Infatigable* northward toward her port. The missionaries had
come to expect these periods of relief and so were not prepared for the constant bad weather of the last days of June
when calm was succeeded by contrary wind and *l'Infatigable*

made almost no headway. Prolonged delay caused worry over the food supply, and at the end of June when they were still well south of the Tropic of Cancer, the cook announced there were no more vegetables. Rice would now be the principal article of food. Over a month out from Lima, *l'Infatigable* had covered roughly only half the distance to Vancouver. Her passengers began to ration carefully what was left of the provisions sent them by good Madame Bosch.

Weather, delay, and the food problem caused Father DeSmet to suffer more than usual. Preoccupied and worried, he began to talk about the dangers awaiting at the Columbia Bar. His intention, Sister Mary Aloysia said, "was to inspire us with courage." But they were understandably depressed, especially Sister Marie Catherine, who knew more about this danger than the other Sisters. According to her story, Father DeSmet entrusted her with a troublesome secret shortly after they left Lima. The captain, he told her, had lost his chart of the treacherous bar. She must pray daily for a safe passage, he enjoined her, but she must not tell the other Sisters about the lost chart. Perhaps he had noticed her hours of contemplation under the cannon, but for whatever reason, he seemed to think her strong enough to share his worry.

In his own account, Father DeSmet says that the captain had not been able to obtain a chart of the Columbia at Antwerp.[2] This may have been the case since the first official survey was not made until Lieutenant Wilkes lost one of his ships, the *Peacock,* in the Columbia in 1841, at a point subsequently known as Peacock Spit.[3] As the survey must have required some time, it may be that the chart was only in preparation when *l'Infatigable* sailed. Still, the shipowners must have possessed some information based on the experience of skippers, and they would have certainly furnished Captain Moller with available directives. In any case, the captain, Father DeSmet, and Sister Marie Catherine shared a great worry about the Columbia sandbanks, as to some extent did all the passengers and crew.

Captain Moller's health was another cause of general worry through the last part of the voyage, for all could see the poor man was playing a losing game with tuberculosis. When he sank into spells of deep gloom, Father DeSmet was the only one who could raise his spirits. But Sister Marie Catherine prayed incessantly for Father DeSmet as well as for the captain; she saw that neither of them had the disposition to endure prolonged trouble. She had often observed Father DeSmet playing games on the deck with one or other of the Jesuits, but now he walked back and forth alone, the games forgotten. And this preoccupation of his was not good for the others; even Father Accolti was beginning to look gloomy. So Sister Marie Catherine was careful to place the dominoes and lotto on the table in sight of all. If none of the Fathers took the hint, she feigned a great need of distraction and challenged Father DeSmet to a game herself. He appreciated her thoughtfulness as well as her prayers; devoting hours of both day and night to the captain's morale, he stood in need of both.

They all stood in need of help through those early July days in the retarding northern trades. On the second, "the Pacific was as turbulent as the waters around Cape Horn," and that stormy weather continued as they crossed the Tropic of Cancer on the fifth. Then, with the wind against them, they looked at their rations of salt meat and ship biscuit at the captain's almost silent dinner table. How long would these last? Huddled together, the Sisters decided not to consider this fear. Sister Mary Aloysia wrote their trust into her journal. God sustained them by the trust He inspired, she said.

But the second week of July nearly drained their spiritual resources. Protracted calm with its accompanying heat was less tolerable than a storm. How Father DeSmet dreaded it! The storm might drive the ship out of its course, but at least it was movement; a calm fastened it to one spot on the sea, hemmed it around with somber sky and clouds that seemed "impenetrable obstacles." A calm set a glum discouragement on the faces of the most experienced seamen. But at last rough weather broke the monotony. That was a relief until the sea worked itself to frenzy and touched the Sisters one by one with fear of its angry might. On July eleventh, Sister Mary Aloysia recorded that they said among themselves:

"Our Sisters in Belgium have ceased to pray for us. They believe we have reached our destination, and here we are tossed about on the sea, driven on by contrary winds and by waves that threaten to engulf us." Yet there was no hysteria in these complaints. The Sisters knew *l'Infatigable* was making headway. They would reach Oregon. Their trust runs through their little outbursts of frustration like a golden thread. Except perhaps Sister Mary Cornelia, each of them complained a little and thus rested her burden on the composite strength of the group. But not even Sister Norbertine, who was certainly the most brittle, broke under the strain. Day by day, it grew more saddening for each to see the effects of poor and insufficient nourishment in the haggard faces of all the others. Still, little Sister Mary Albine, who had come to feel responsible for the health of all on board, managed to bestow her smile with her remedies. That kind and solicitous smile was her way of dealing with her own natural impatience. Her exasperation withered up as she dispensed advice, medicine, and smile, just as Sister Marie Catherine's was dissipated in prayer under her cannon.

Sister Mary Aloysia continued bravely to enter their daily calamities. July twelfth brought such continual changing of wind "that we did not sail in one direction for an hour at a time." Next day only two words: "Encore calme." Then after the respite of "une brise légère," more contrary wind, "mauvais," followed by the dismal "Continuation." On the seventeenth, the temperature dropped so low that the passengers had to get out the heavy wraps they had packed away so carefully in the tropics. While they were about it, Sister Loyola said briskly, they might as well pack their trunks for landing. The mate had just reported they were nearing the latitude of Fort Vancouver.

Landing? Alas, no! Three days of stillness. ". . . une situation toujours plus critique." But one must not be troubled; one must "take patience," the Sisters translated, even now struggling with English conversation.

On the twenty-first they needed more patience than ever. Now in the very latitude of the Columbia, *l'Infatigable* was driven far to sea by a wild east wind. Next day, with wind reversed, she was carried back toward port again. Very soon her voyage would be over, on the twenty-fifth at latest. But the twenty-fourth brought a furious northeaster. No one could speak now. "Un morne silence!"

Food was running very low. There was no more salt meat. They had finished the last treasured bit of smoked ham; how they managed it, they couldn't tell, for both smell and taste were insupportable. They had used up the last of the carefully rationed Lima provisions. Lima! And kind, good Madame Bosch! Really, the people there were so kind. Should they have stayed in Lima? Or in Valparaiso? They might have done so much good in either place. Sister Marie Catherine knew the answer. So did Sister Mary Cornelia. They had been sent to the Willamette. But it did seem as though Heaven had forgotten them. The water supply was low, too; on the twenty-fifth the cook said there was not enough left to make soup from the sorry ham bone. The Fathers brought up the altar wine, to mix with what was left.

"Le ciel paraissait sourd," wrote Sister Mary Aloysia, as she filled out the story of that day later for Mère Constantine's reading. But her elaborate protestation of trust at the end was all very well in retrospect. On that black day itself, even she could scarcely have composed that little sermon.

Through those days Captain Moller's occasional appearances accentuated the gloom. His stooped shoulders, his despondent expression were frightening. He was getting no sleep, Father DeSmet told Sister Marie Catherine, adding that he himself was staying near him as much as possible. Sister was terrified. Suppose the captain should lose his mind. With his unseeing, dispirited eyes, he seemed to her scarcely rational. Through the second morning of that wild northeaster, he sat on deck, his head in his hands, heeding nothing. That was bad enough; but when the Fathers, with looks of new concern, began to urge the Sisters to pray more earnestly, Sister Marie Catherine's anxiety mounted. It would be better to know the worst; one would then face the danger prepared. But the Fathers thought otherwise and told the Sisters their story only after their landing. By that time, Father DeSmet, at least, completely discredited the warning of a friendly but excited sailor which had quite terrified the Fathers for the time. Some of the men, he told them, were urging Captain Moller to make directly for Manila under the persisting gale. The ship could not get near the coast, they said, so why not throw the missionaries overboard and forget about the Columbia.[4] The poor man based his story on a conversation and refused to consider the suggestion a joke.

For the moment, at least, Father DeSmet was equally credulous. It was this new peril, Sister Marie Catherine insisted, that prompted him to suggest the vow made by each of the twelve after Mass next morning. He himself composed the somewhat lengthy formula promising extra prayer and fasting for three years.[5] That done, he spent the rest of that day and all of the night gently "diverting" the distraught captain, said Sister Marie Catherine. Father DeSmet, she always insisted, in this way prevented the tragedy.

But Sister Marie Catherine forgot the "plot" in the hurricane that next drove *l'Infatigable* back toward the coast, ripping off her main topsail and lashing up waves twelve to fifteen feet high. But they had made their vow, she told herself, and at once found it possible to "take patience." The gale would subside before they reached the rocks. It did die down early on the twenty-seventh but left a strong reminder in the swell of the ocean until late afternoon. That evening they were still too far out to see the coast. Perhaps the next day! The wind was just right for entering the Columbia.

At ten next morning, all were on deck awaiting their first sight of Oregon, "cette terre si ardemment désirée." Suddenly there it stretched before their eyes. At once the Sisters recalled their promise to the Bishop of Namur to sing the *Te Deum* together at their first sight of their mission land. Long afterwards they recalled the joy of that singing. They had escaped "comme par miracle" danger after danger. What if the most dangerous part of the voyage lay only fifteen leagues ahead? That was nothing. How Good He is, the Good God!

A dense fog hid the mouth of the Columbia from view next morning, but the river made its presence felt by the fury of its onset as it met the sea. Then as the fog lifted a

little, the Sisters huddled in a group on deck, looked with
horror at the breakers, "un aspect affreux." [6] Abandonment,
Sister Mary Aloysia discovered, did not prevent "an impulse
of terror." And the terrible banks beneath the wild water!
If the visibility were only better so that the sight of other
craft might indicate the channel. After hours of indecision,
Captain Moller ordered a boat to go ahead and take soundings. Then he suddenly revoked his order; it was too late
in the day, he said.

Sister Loyola lost patience. It was clear, she thought, that
God was opposing their entrance to the Columbia. They
should have stayed at Lima. Why not return there now?
It was a wild idea, of course, with the food so low and the
water almost gone. When she suggested it to Father DeSmet,
he understood the anguish of her mind and managed to quiet
her. If they must turn back, he said, it had better be to San
Francisco. From there they could reach Oregon by land.
Her calm restored by that gleam of hope, Sister Loyola shared
her reassurance with her Sisters, whereupon they went to
rest, "malgré les angoisses de cette journée."

As the next morning was fairly clear and the wind good,
Captain Moller decided to make a second attempt, but
presently observations from the topmast again changed his
mind. The river, he declared, was a labyrinth of dangers,
and at this word depression settled icily around the hearts of
his passengers. But suddenly a seaward-bound ship appeared
up the river. Then the moment of exaltation died as the
vessel veered around and vanished. For nearly two hours
l'Infatigable's crew and passengers searched the river with
glasses. Again the ship came into view advancing in slow,
spiritless fashion. Captain Moller ordered the cannon fired.
But there was no answer; instead, the ship turned again and
sailed up the river out of sight. It could not have been a
friendly ship, the Sisters concluded, since it failed to return
the salute. And at that they all recalled what they had heard
in Valparaiso; a man-of-war would block their entrance to
the Columbia since the territory was disputed. No, it was not
a man-of-war, Father DeSmet explained, or it would have
three masts instead of two. It was a symbol of *l'Infatigable*

sailing securely up the river. "Tomorrow is the feast of St. Ignatius. He is telling us that we shall cross the bar."

Next morning, the second mate tried to persuade Captain Moller to let him explore the bar in a boat. That, as they both knew, would be a terrible risk since the boat would require five men in that seething torrent, and if these should not return, the ship would be left undermanned for the crossing. But at last the captain reluctantly consented. The boat was lowered and was soon lost to sight in the surging waves. With it, wrote Father DeSmet, went "our last gleam of hope." Sister Marie Catherine thought it utter folly, but seeing that the other Sisters did not realize the new danger, she left them in ignorance and went below with them to make preparations for Sister Loyola's feast day.

All five crowded into the little cabin to wrap a few gifts that they had thus far successfully hidden from their Superior. As Sister Mary Aloysia daintily tied the packages, she thought of the contrast; they had planned to celebrate this feast of Saint Ignatius Loyola, with special honors for the first Superior in the West, in the new house on the Willamette. But she started to hum their greeting song and in a moment they were singing together. Father DeSmet stood listening. What courage! Then he thought of the Jesuits' gift for Sister Loyola. They ought to be getting it out.

That night the lookout reported a fire flaming high on the north side of the river. Was someone trying to signal *l'Infatigable?* Captain Moller considered the matter and then decided to pay no attention to the beacon. Indians, he said, were known to lure ships to their destruction in this way. That might be true, Father DeSmet thought, though he felt inclined to agree with Father Accolti that it would be a relief to hear Captain Moller express a positive attitude for once. If that poor man could only share the spirit that made the Sisters sing in that dangerous hour!

The keeping of that feast of Saint Ignatius is a monument to heroism. All the priests celebrated Mass in turn, their weakened condition and the tossing of the ship combining against their efforts to stand. And the Sisters sang as though they knew neither hunger nor fear. Then after the last Mass the Jesuits brought in a large, gold-framed painting of Christ and presented it to Sister Loyola for her new convent chapel. That beautiful gift and Father DeSmet's eloquent little speech set up a new hope. Then they went on deck to pray and watch for the returning boat. Surely it would bring back good news.

Up to eleven, Father DeSmet paced restlessly to and fro between Captain Moller and the watchers on deck. Then one of the crew spied the boat, now rising on a wave, now hidden by another. Five men! That was it. Breathlessly they waited for the sign of good news the mate had agreed on. But he gave no sign. He seemed not to look at the ship, not at all concerned with those on her deck. No one spoke as the five men climbed aboard, their expressions inscrutable. The officer went directly to Captain Moller.

A few tense minutes and then the report. The boat had crossed the bar about eleven the night before; the mate had found no less than thirty feet of water anywhere; there were no insurmountable obstacles. Thirty feet! The ship's minimum was eighteen. The word was on every tongue. Captain Moller was smiling. The crew sprang into action. Presently all sails were spread, and under an easy wind *l'Infatigable* made slowly for the mouth of the river.

Warm sun and cloudless sky. A safe and happy landing. For the moment all the tired faces relaxed. But as they approached the bar, a silent seriousness descended. At a nod from Sister Loyola, the Sisters went below to say their rosary together. When they had finished they joined all the others on the bridge and learned that the ship was above the sand, riding the breakers that marked its presence. A boat had been launched to take soundings and had just reported forty-two feet. Then at short, horror-filled intervals the measurements decreased.

"Thirty-six feet."

"Thirty."

"Eighteen."

"We are between life and death," the mate cried.[7]

But now, "Twenty-four," and hope is reborn.

Again, "Eighteen," and Father Accolti's voice raised in prayer.

"Fifteen!" And the mate telling the captain they are in the wrong channel; that the second officer lied when he claimed he had crossed the bar. Father DeSmet expected they would cast anchor. There would be a wild scramble for the boats. But at that moment the captain was a man of might.

"Bah!" he cried to the terrified mate, "vous voyez bien que *l'Infatigable* passe partout; avancez." His ship! She must make it! In five minutes they were in the deep channel with horror behind them.

"Le Tout-Puissant nous conduisit."

PART III

THEIR LOVELY LAND

CHAPTER 7

Trader and Blackrobe

To understand conditions in which the missionaries found themselves in Oregon, one must be acquainted with the character and work of the great Hudson's Bay Company leader, Doctor John McLoughlin, with the apostolate of the Quebec Mission, and with the characteristic American settlement pattern which even then was beginning to work a solution of long-standing international claims.

The missionaries' interest was the Quebec apostolate. That was Oregon to them, the framework in which their own zeal would function. The Honorable Company meant forts and farms, centers of civilization in which they would find sympathetic assistance. They did not see that its day was almost over. Most of them, certainly the Sisters, knew little of the international claims to the territory, though Father DeSmet soon became deeply interested in the outcome, his steadfast contention being that no nation had the right to take the land from the Indians.[1]

While explorers—Spanish, Russian, English, and American—came and went, making reports to their governments without significant local consequences, fur traders were building their forts and outposts. Thus the real struggle for supremacy was between fur companies, rather than nations. In the last decade of the eighteenth century, the Russian-American Fur Company and the "Boston Men" were the strongest competitors, with the latter in the lead by 1800. These New Englanders made quick and easy fortunes in the fantastically priced markets of China until in their eagerness they oversupplied them. Their consequent decline and Russia's withdrawal to territory north of 54′ 40″ in 1824 left an almost open field to HBC, recently strengthened by its union with Canada's Northwesters, a merger accomplished chiefly through the efforts of John McLoughlin, a loyal Northwester, but shrewd enough to see that without it both companies would die.

The Northwesters had organized as a protest. In 1784 a group of bitter East Canadians had banded together, with the Frobisher brothers and Simon McTavish as leaders, to break the power of HBC. They resented its having headquarters in London; they resented its wide field, which they considered unjustly acquired. For the Honorable Company had interpreted its grant from King Charles II very generously. To its founders, Rupert's Land meant from Labrador to the Rockies and from the watershed of the St. Lawrence to Hudson Straits. This was all too much for East Canadians, who nourished their bitterness, pointless though it was after the Treaty of Paris in 1763. And the year that brought the Northwesters into existence also saw the birth of the company's future leader, John McLoughlin, in the little village of Rivière du Loup some twenty miles below Quebec.

The father of this famous child was John McLoughlin, a

farmer of Scottish-Irish parentage who, according to his neighbors, married above his station when he won the hand of Angélique Fraser, daughter of Malcolm Fraser, the "Seigneur" of Murray Bay, and Marie Allaire, a French-Canadian. The fine stone Fraser mansion stood across the river from the McLoughlin farmhouse, and neighbors shook their heads and questioned Angélique's ability to make the adjustment. To their surprise, she made it with ease and no regret. Her life was one of deep contentment.

As John and Angélique McLoughlin were both Catholics, their sons John and David were baptized in the local parish church. When they reached school age, their grandfather began, as a matter of course, to look after their education. Certainly he was in a position to do so, especially as his son, Simon Fraser, was able and willing to teach the boys the elements of science and medicine. This meant that young John and David would spend most of their time in the Fraser mansion.

The McLoughlin boys received a somewhat broader education than Grandfather Fraser had intended. His son Alexander, the family adventurer, often spent weeks between treks at the Fraser house, as ready to talk as the boys were to listen. He held them spellbound with tales of the fur trade and the Northwesters, of enterprise as far off as the northern shore of Lake Superior. As he talked, the name Northwester became a symbol of noble courage. Hudson's Bay became a synonym for evil, especially when Uncle Alexander related how the great explorer, David Thompson, had been won over to it from the Northwesters. Both boys enjoyed the stories, both thought their uncle's vehemence wonderful, but John was always the more deeply impressed. Even when, as his grandfather hoped, he decided to become a doctor, his mind was still on the fur trade. In his early teens he was almost as eloquent on this subject as Uncle Alexander. His most willing hearer was his mother and he repaid her interest by respecting her advice which was, of course, to follow out his grandfather's plan for the present, though she certainly did not discourage adventure.

Malcolm Fraser arranged for a four-year medical apprenticeship with a certain Doctor James Fisher, who accepted fourteen-year-old John McLoughlin, planned his studies, and, for his internship, took him on his sick calls. At nineteen he was received in Montreal as a practicing physician, well liked because he was compassionate, and trusted because he knew at least what was then generally known about his profession. But before long the young doctor decided to combine his profession with fur trading. He joined the Northwesters and was sent to Fort William on the north shore of Lake Superior. Some seven years later he became a wintering partner in the company and about the same time he married Marguerite Wadin McKay at Sault Ste. Marie, Ontario. Marguerite was the widow of Alexander McKay, a Northwester who had lost his life on the Astor Expedition. She was thirty-four, McLoughlin's senior by perhaps six or seven years, the mother of four children, but she had not lost the handsome charm of a young French-Indian woman. Her mother was perhaps pure Indian, probably Chippewa, her father a French fur trader who valued education enough to send his intelligent daughter to the Ursuline school in Quebec, where she must have known McLoughlin's sister, Marie Louise. The marriage was a very happy one. McLoughlin was completely devoted to Marguerite, even when age had accented the Indian characteristics that mark her photo in the McLoughlin House in Oregon City.

It was McLoughlin's initiative in the Northwester-Hudson's Bay merger that brought him to Oregon. When the two companies faced their struggle for survival over the rich Athabasca country, McLoughlin saw the folly of his youthful loyalty to the die-hard Northwesters. He took the stand that the cause of bitterness had passed; that merging was for the greater good of all. Whether he took part in the merging negotiations in London or not, he made a point of being present when the meetings began. In fact, he crossed on the same ship with HBC's Colin Robertson, whose purpose was to block the merger by attempting to prove it unnecessary. He claimed that the Northwesters had already died a natural death, while their die-hards were boasting that all was well with their organization, that it needed no assistance from HBC. McLoughlin's persuasive lobbying was needed to steer a course between these extremists. When at last they yielded, McLoughlin's maturity of judgment and ability as public relations expert were clearly recognized. HBC now looked on him as the very man to develop the Oregon country.

But as a rising HBC leader, McLoughlin was now a subordinate of Sir George Simpson, the company's governor in America, whose unquestioned ability to organize was too often counteracted by his fear of ability in others. Simpson made McLoughlin's appointment rather grudgingly; it would be difficult to control this promising leader in so distant an area. Yet there should have been no problem in Simpson's mind as he outlined plans with McLoughlin; their common ability made the two men see almost eye to eye, and the governor realized that his new deputy could be trusted to do what was best regardless of personal interests. Yet Simpson made his feelings plain in the guarded hesitancy that marked his future dealings with McLoughlin, an abiding distrust that often prompted him to keep his subordinate waiting quite unreasonably for permission to act.

At least their general agreement in plans was a good starting point. Posts accessible by water should be contacted by small boats which would carry pelts to deep-water ships bound for China and England.[2] The Columbia Valley's agricultural possibilities should be exploited. Farming around HBC posts was usually limited to the needs of the posts, a policy intended to discourage permanent settlement. The plan for the Columbia Valley included large grain areas and sale of grain to lighten the company's expense, the areas, of course, belonging to the company, not to individuals, though McLoughlin realized that in Oregon's fertile valleys settlement would be the outcome. Uncontrolled exploitation would work the fur industry to death.[3] Its decline would find the fur men older and anxious to settle; it would then be only fair to let them use the company's agricultural holdings for their start as farmers.⁴ In fact, the lasting good of the HBC farms would be easy transition of its workers to settled life. To McLoughlin, humanity was always more important than business; because it was, his business was always the better served. In 1844 the Belgian missionaries found McLoughlin's agricultural policy a blessing; the presence of ex-HBC workers as settled farmers furnished them with a sense of security. These people shared their faith and language and they were permanent dwellers.

Chief Factor McLoughlin quickly built a reputation for firmness as well as for humanity, and thus was soon accorded complete respect. In dealing with natives especially, iron will had to be as much in evidence as kindness, and after the Clatsop incident no native doubted the McLoughlin iron will. He may have been mistaken in believing the Clatsops murdered the crew of the HBC ship, *William and Anne,* when she was wrecked on the bar in the late 1820's, but there was no doubt that they stole the ship's cargo; when he went to their village to demand restoration of the goods, they mocked him insolently, throwing a tin dipper in his direction. As his force was small, he waited until the next HBC brigade arrived; then he sent the ship *Cadboro* with a hundred men against the Clatsop village. Apparently expecting this to happen, the Clatsops fired on the men as they landed. No one was injured in this attack, but McLoughlin ordered their village to be bombarded. The Clatsops fled, leaving the stolen cargo behind them. The lesson went home; when another HBC ship was wrecked in the same spot a year later, her cargo was unmolested. McLoughlin's control was established, and the Belgian missionaries thus had another cause for gratitude.

After this one punitive example, McLoughlin's authority could rest on his administrative order and success. According to Simpson's report to London headquarters in 1824, HBC affairs in the Northwest were then in chaos; in fact, the company was operating at too small a profit to justify its existence there. Soon the new chief factor's tremendous ability in planning and capacity for detail proved the wisdom of his appointment. Now supplies reached posts on time,

Above: Sister Alphonse Marie came to Oregon with the second group of Sisters of Notre Dame de Namur.

Above: The first school and convent at St. Paul. The right wing was begun by Vicar-General Blanchet in 1843 and completed after the arrival of the Sisters. The chapel seems more pretentious than its description in the memoirs which perhaps refer to its unfinished interior. The statue above the entrance was a wood carving brought from Namur.

Lower right: St. Paul's Church, successor to F. N. Blanchet's little church of 1838, and intended to be his cathedral. It still serves as the parish church at St. Paul.

Below: Sister Mary Stephana, S.N.J.M., of the present St. Paul's School, reads Sister Renilde's name among those of Holy Names pioneers. The monument stands in the Catholic Cemetery at St. Paul.

An act to incorporate the "St. Pauls Mission Female Seminary"

Sec 1 Be it enacted by the legislative Assembly of the Territory of Oregon, That Cornelia Neugan, Marie Cathrine Colareau, and Odelie Colarde, their associates and successors be and they are hereby created a body corporate and politic, by the name of the "St. Pauls Mission Seminary." in Marion County, and as such shall have perpetual succession, and be entitled to all the rights and priviledges granted by, and be subject to all the liabilities and restrictions defined in the act entitled "An act to regulate incorporated literarys and religious societies passed one thousand eight hundred and fifty one

Sec 2 This act to take effect and be in force from and after its passage.

Passed the House of Representatives Jan. 29th 1851

Passed the Council February 1st 1851

Ralph Wilcox
Speaker. H. R.

Wm Buck
President of Council

Sister Mary Cornelia, Cornelia Neujean in the Act of Incorporation of St. Paul's Mission Seminary.

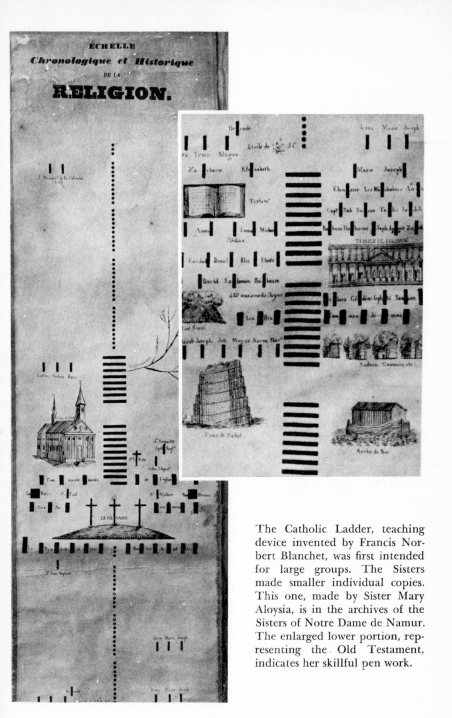

The Catholic Ladder, teaching device invented by Francis Norbert Blanchet, was first intended for large groups. The Sisters made smaller individual copies. This one, made by Sister Mary Aloysia, is in the archives of the Sisters of Notre Dame de Namur. The enlarged lower portion, representing the Old Testament, indicates her skillful pen work.

Above: Letter written by Sister Loyola to Governor Joseph Lane. *Below:* Signatures of Amory Holbrook; Francis S. Holland; Aloyse Vermuylen (Sister Alphonse Marie); Robert Caufield; John McLoughlin; Archbishop Blanchet.

consignments moved on schedule, all with consequent good will and satisfaction. The company could not have been other than pleased with his work; he was as diligent in its interests as though he were building up a private fortune. Visitors like Father DeSmet praised the thriving order of farms as well as posts, and reports of such business deals as the HBC contract to supply the Russians with butter indicated loyalty to the company as well as thrift.[5]

McLoughlin's dedication of his powers to HBC and his insistence that the company's authority should be supreme in in the Northwest, stemmed from his belief that the Northwesters had possessed prior rights there, and that HBC had succeeded to these rights. Besides, HBC was the only organization powerful enough to push its interests in that territory. And HBC had placed its power in his hands, a fact which tended in time to give his outlook a somewhat paternal and autocratic slant. But McLoughlin's altruism made him acceptable as he built up his HBC empire, though there were occasional objections against trials in the company's courts.[6] To some that seemed like British control in an open territory. Yet McLoughlin's generosity, hospitality, and sense of justice made a modus vivendi possible for the early American settler. The American found himself on a footing of equality with the British subject and the recipient of liberal aid if needed. Of course, non-HBC fur traders could expect severe competition.

Before 1843, most American emigrants to Oregon were Methodist or Presbyterian missionaries and, according to their own statements, they received a kind welcome and generous aid from McLoughlin, who felt that any sincere minister of God would be a helpful influence. Though he had long since drifted away from his childhood faith, he had always maintained respect for religion in general. Strictly moral, he insisted on his subordinates living up to his code; he expected them, for instance, to be faithful to their native wives even in cases of marriage without benefit of clergy. But up to the time of his conversion in 1842, McLoughlin left religious practices to his devout wife, though occasionally, in the absence of clergy, he led Sunday prayers in the chapel at Fort Vancouver. When occasion presented itself, he attended High Mass sung by the Vicar-General and he never failed to show his appreciation of the Catholic clergy, but his actual conversion marked the period of anguish over the murder of his son and the treachery of those he had helped.

Against McLoughlin's wishes, Sir George Simpson had appointed hotheaded young John McLoughlin to the difficult post at Fort Stikine. Visiting that remote post, Eloisa McLoughlin remarked the excessive drinking of the Indians there. To make matters worse, Sir George then removed the only other commissioned officer from the fort as an economy measure. Young McLoughlin lost respect and control and was finally shot by a French-Canadian during a drunken brawl at the fort. Then, since neither Canada nor Russia had a criminal court in that northern territory, Sir George allowed the murderer to go free. McLoughlin's resentment of years against Sir George now broke out in a furious complaint to the company which foreshadows his complete withdrawal three years later.

Ingratitude of those to whom he had been most open-handed was another source of annoyance to McLoughlin through these years after 1840, and worst of all it struck at his favorite project, his Oregon City claim. Seeing that the fur trade was falling off as he had expected, McLoughlin had decided to provide for his family's future by staking a claim. In his choice of location, however, he was thinking of more than a home for his old age and property for his children. He saw the falls on the Willamette as a source of power; settlers were bound to come in, and a site at the falls would develop in time into a distribution and purchasing center for farmers. The project merely needed someone to give it direction. He mapped out his claim in the future Oregon City, including Abernethy Island, on which in 1829 he began to build a sawmill. Other HBC men were staking claims at the same time. There was Etienne Lucier, whose term had expired, plotting a farm claim in French Prairie that same year.

To these claim holders, security of tenure was a matter of good will among themselves. They worried little about international settlements and joint occupation, vague concepts which seemed more unstable than the Golden Rule which they respected. The process was simply to assert one's claim to hitherto unclaimed land. McLoughlin took pains to assert his claim, especially in the late thirties when the rights of the United States in Oregon began to be pressed in Congress.[7] He felt sure the Linn Bill would pass, in which case his being a British subject would not jeopadize his claim, since the bill offered 640 acres to any male citizen regardless of nationality, providing he cultivated it for five years. Its failure to pass the House in 1839 was followed by the first challenge to his claim in 1840. The challenge was made by Rev. Alvin Waller of the Methodist Mission, who had received great kindness from McLoughlin at the request of Jason Lee.

When Jason and Daniel Lee made their foundation in the Willamette Valley in the name of the Methodist Board of Foreign Missions, McLoughlin treated them hospitably at Fort Vancouver, gave them the use of horses and cattle belonging to HBC, just as he was doing in the case of retiring HBC men. Jason Lee was impressed by this generosity.[8] But when the *Lausanne* arrived in the summer of 1840, bringing the "great enforcement" to the now fairly numerous Methodist Mission, Jason Lee assigned Alvin Waller to work with the Indians at the Falls. Waller took a claim of 640 acres north of McLoughlin's claim for his mission, selecting as headquarters for himselt a site opposite Oregon City. Soon Waller wanted to build a store on the McLoughlin claim, and at Lee's request McLoughlin granted the permission and furnished Waller with a "loan" of timbers squared and ready for use. Presently McLoughlin heard that his beneficiaries were planning to jump his claim. At once he notified Jason Lee that he had taken possession in 1829 and that he meant to maintain his right, but on receiving a satisfactory answer from Lee he permitted Waller to go ahead with the store. Soon, however, an employee of the mission began to erect a house on Abernethy Island without asking permission, but at McLoughlin's protest, Waller called off the building. In order to forestall further attempts, McLoughlin began rapid improvements on his claim, his most conclusive step being a survey in 1843. His "Oregon City" project was now laid out in city blocks, and he began to sell lots and in some cases to give them away.

At these developments, the Reverend Waller threw off his disguise. Through his attorney, John Ricord, he protested his right, by a posted proclamation early in 1844, to the entire McLoughlin claim, on the ground of having built there. He excepted the island since the Oregon Milling Company laid claim to that.

Unfortunately McLoughlin had not joined the Provisional Government the year before because of its unfair Article 4, which required American citizenship as a basis for landholding, and which had been inserted at the instigation of such men as Lee and Waller and was plainly intended to invalidate McLoughlin's claim and turn it over to the Methodist Mission. Realizing that he was for this reason at Waller's mercy, he compromised. He paid Waller $500 and surrendered one block and six lots in Oregon City to the Methodist Mission. Waller withdrew all other claim to McLoughlin's property. But this was not the end of the matter, though that same year saw the end of the Methodist Mission in the Willamette Valley.

Although the Board of Foreign Missions had spent thousands on its Oregon project, up to $42,000 one year, the mission was not prospering. In utter poverty, two Canadian priests had reached many more natives and whites. Perhaps the desire to establish themselves and their families had hindered the Methodists' missionary work. When Farnham visited their missions, he found them doing little for the natives; they were chiefly engaged, he recorded, in cultivation of mission farms and care of their own livestock. At any rate, shortly before the arrival of the Belgian missionaries, the Methodists decided to withdraw, but before leaving, some of them made another attempt on McLoughlin. This time Reverend George Gary approached him with an offer to sell him back his lots with their recent improvements for $6,000. McLoughlin refused. He would pay $3,800 for the improvements, he said, but they must give him back the lots.

Furthermore, he wished the whole matter to be referred

to their Mission Board. Gary would not hear of this; undoubtedly he knew that the Mission Board would want an honest settlement with McLoughlin, and perhaps he realized that the standing of several of the missionaries with the Board was not as high as formerly.[9] It must have gratified McLoughlin to know that some of the Methodists at the Falls considered Gary's action unjust. His argument, they knew, was that as a British subject and head of a British concern, McLoughlin could not hope his claim would be honored by the United States Government when, as everyone expected, it would assume undisputed control in Oregon. But some of the Methodist missionaries, Jason Lee for one, were not American citizens themselves. And it must be said in fairness to some of the Methodists that they still thought McLoughlin was holding the claim for HBC; they could not believe that HBC leaders had lost interest in holdings south of the Columbia since 1825, when it became clear that England did not intend to press her claim in that area.

Gary's demand was plain extortion, but it was futile for McLoughlin to tell him so or to remind him that the compromise with Waller of three months before was a final agreement. There was nothing for McLoughlin to do except pay the $6,000 and save his claim at least for the present; with the departure of the Methodists it might be possible to delete Article 4 from the Provisional Constitution. When it was taken out, in 1845, McLoughlin wisely joined the Provisional Government and faced the annoying necessity of explaining his action to HBC leaders and winning them to a compromise. It was difficult for them to understand that Americans would soon greatly outnumber British subjects in the territory and that the movement started by American settlers in the "wolf meetings" could not be checked. McLoughlin had seen for some time the inevitability of Americanization and recognized that local meetings and provisional government were steps in a usual pattern. He saw that even HBC men with land claims were joining in these moves for the protection they afforded. But Sir George Simpson and other company leaders could hardly be expected to take McLoughlin's view of the matter. To them any move toward Americanization would jeopardize company interests, especially after they heard that the Provisional Government's plan was to extend its control north of the Columbia. The leaders were losing patience with McLoughlin. They had long been annoyed at his goodness to American missionaries and settlers, and they could scarcely have been mollified by his caustic defense of his views. For when he felt that wisdom and justice were violated, he was quite the opposite of the fatherly official who sent boats up the Columbia to meet penniless immigrants, and bade them stand in line in his office so that each in turn might tell him his needs.[10]

When the Belgian missionaries first saw McLoughlin in early August, 1844, he had just paid Gary's extorted $6,000. He could rejoice to have seen the last of Lee and Waller and Gary, but he knew he still had enemies who at any time might try to dispossess him and that the gap between his thinking and the company's was widening every day. Still, the newcomers found him planning enthusiastically for his city on the Willamette, willing to help them in every way, unwilling to burden them with his troubles. The Sisters at least knew nothing about the $6,000 or Article 4, matters which would have left them bewildered. They knew they had a friend in Dr. McLoughlin, that the Methodist missionaries had withdrawn and left them a clear coast, and that they had a tremendous work to do.

The ground for that work had been broken by four priests of the Quebec Diocese, the Vicar-General and Father Demers, rugged pioneers of six years' service, and the later comers, Fathers Langlois and Boldoc. To their accomplishment the new missionaries must look for patterns for their labors, admirable patterns cut in strenuous outline and drafted in joyous letters for Bishop Joseph Signay of Quebec. That prelate had been burdened with this new and far-distant mission when Bishop J. N. Provencher of Red River, Manitoba, unable to grant Dr. McLoughlin's request for priests for his French-Canadian Catholics, referred the matter to him.

Oregon, it is true, was not the responsibility of either of these bishops. When Canada passed under British control in 1763, the Catholic Church there was left under the jurisdiction of the Diocese of Quebec, and when the Red River area became a vicariate British Columbia formed a part of it; but Oregon, as disputed territory, was not included in British Columbia.[11] It was thus left quite unshepherded, and life among both traders and settlers was consequently often far from angelic. Their request for priests was perhaps partly by way of apology to McLoughlin, who insisted on good conduct on the part of HBC men, retired or not.

But there were staid and settled French farmers along the Willamette and in French Prairie whose way of life did not worry Dr. McLoughlin.[12] Some of these were past servants of the company; some had come in with one or other of the great expeditions. In French Prairie, for instance, were the families of LaFramboise, Lucier, LaBonté, Gervais, and others, men who had come in with the Astor expedition and settled there. Dr. McLoughlin respected their wishes as he did those of all good men. So whatever truth there may be in reported wordy requests by natives of the Northwest for missionaries to minister to their people, action on the part of Bishop Signay was in response to Dr. McLoughlin's requests, especially in view of his promised help when the first priests should arrive at Fort Vancouver.

Forty-one-year-old Father Francis Norbert Blanchet was pastor of Les Cèdres in the district of Montreal when Bishop Signay selected him for the Oregon Mission. He was thus under the authority of Bishop Lartigue, who consented to part with so competent a member of his clergy only on condition that he be replaced by another equally capable.

Francis Norbert Blanchet was the son of a representative French-Canadian family. With his younger brother, Augustine Magloire, he attended the parish school in their village of St. Pierre, Rivière du Sud, in Lower Canada. Together they entered the seminary in Quebec in 1810, Francis Norbert winning high distinction in theology. He was ordained in 1819 and Augustine two years later. After a year at the cathedral in Quebec, Francis Norbert was assigned to the little village of Richibucto in New Brunswick, as pastor of the Micmic Indians and Acadians who had settled there. His next post was Les Cèdres, some thirty miles west of Montreal on the north bank of the St. Lawrence, a point at which river boats stopped and travelers talked of the fur trade and easy money. But seven years at Les Cèdres had turned Father Blanchet into a settled parish priest with no thought of far western missions in his busy mind, happy to reflect on his experience among the Micmics as one proper to youth. His acceptance of his mission in Oregon was qualified; a shocked surprise runs through the lines. For one thing, the loneliness of a priest's life on the Columbia would call for heights of sanctity which he was convinced he lacked.

It was certainly not want of courage that caused Father Blanchet to demur, as his heroism during the cholera epidemic of 1832 amply testified. Through the worst of it, young Father Blanchet was everywhere, ministering to body and soul regardless of creed. When the scourge had passed, the non-Catholics of the place presented him with two beautiful silver cups in token of gratitude. So whatever reluctance accompanied his acceptance of his new appointment was due to an understandable satisfaction with his success as a pastor as well as to his very genuine humility. At any rate, Bishop Signay held to his decision. Father Blanchet's zeal would adapt itself to Chinooks as well as to farmers at Les Cèdres; his meticulous sternness would prevent a *laisser faire* attitude; he would be bound to raise the level of living from the low standard accepted hopelessly by settlers with native wives. As head of the mission, he would be as exacting with his clergy as with himself, and a bit of rigor would not be amiss in a land where "wicked Christians" had taken over the "vices of Indians," and were living "in licentiousness and forgetfulness of their duties." [13] And from his New Brunswick days, Father Blanchet had displayed rare physical endurance. In his far-flung mission there, he used to go on sick calls over a hundred miles from the village, by dog train or on snowshoes or skates, in thirty-five below zero weather. The Acadian farmers told how he would return to the village cheerful and uncomplaining after battling the blizzards for days, and his Indian and Acadian guides admired his strength and courage. This was just the man for the Oregon mission.

So in April, 1838, Father Norbert Blanchet received his appointment as Vicar-General to the Bishop of Quebec, his jurisdiction reaching from the Rocky Mountains to the Pacific, and from the Russian possessions on the north to the territory of the United States on the south. And in this vast area, his only assistant for the time would be twenty-nine-year-old Father Modeste Demers.

Father Demers, son of a middle-class French family of St. Nicholas, Quebec, was ordained by Bishop Signay in Quebec some fourteen months before his assignment to Oregon. Shortly after his ordination he was sent out to the Red River Diocese, where he heard about the impending Oregon mission and decided to volunteer for it. His acceptance was fortunate for the new Vicar-General, who liked him from the start, and described him as very pious and so agreeable and filled with good will that "even the most peevish" would be quite won by his manner. The admiration was mutual; Father Demers considered himself fortunate to have such a "guide and model."

It had taken three years to set the Oregon mission enterprise in motion, despite the strong desire of both Bishop Signay and Bishop Provencher to grant the request of the Willamette Catholics as soon as possible. The delay was due to hesitation on the part of HBC executives in London to grant passage in the company's overland brigade to missionaries destined to make foundations south of the Columbia, and at this time there was no other safe communication between East Canada and the far West. At first the committee refused the permission flatly, but finally Sir George Simpson gave a conditioned consent; he suggested the Cowlitz River as the site of the mission headquarters and required assurance that it would be located on the north side of the Columbia. Bishop Signay accepted the condition, and Vicar-General Blanchet joined the brigade early in May, 1838. In light bark canoes and by portage the brigade covered the distance from Lachine to Red River, over two thousand miles, in thirty-three days. There the two missionaries met, discussed plans, and meditated on Bishop Signay's instructions through thirty-five days of impatient waiting to leave for the West.

Father Demers found Bishop Signay's first directive much to his liking. The missionary's first duty must be to the Indians, the Bishop said. From the start, Father Demers wanted to work among the "lowlies" as a means of maintaining humility and becoming Christlike. With these ideals, together with his aptitude for Indian dialects and his ability to lead a crowd in singing hymns, it was no wonder that Father Demers met with his new Superior's approval.

The arduous two thousand miles to the Rockies required eighty-four days, including stopovers. On October tenth, the Vicar-General's red-letter day, they reached the summit; and there, after he and Father Demers had celebrated Mass, he consecrated "these sublime Rocky Mountains" to God. It was a grandly pious gesture, the kind that appealed strongly to Blanchet, but the pleasure he derived from that solemn ceremony was not to be compared with his joy when the brigade halted and trappers gathered around him and Father Demers, men who had not seen priests for years. And when Indians gathered in crowds, smiling and gesticulating, it was hard not to believe that the conversion of all the western nations would be fairly simple. At the sight of these poor creatures, Father Demers recalled Bishop Signay's instructions about reaching the Indian through his language. That was right; in Oregon he would master the dialects; he would reduce each to linguistic principles and have a grammar published for it as the Bishop wished. These accomplishments might perhaps have to wait a little; the first step would be prayers and hymns in the native tongues, with Chinook as the first native tongue for mastery. Thus Father Demers airily constructed the unconditioned plans of the inexperienced, while his Superior dotted the valleys of Oregon with carefully organized parishes like Les Cèdres, parishes in which pious Canadians offered shining example to newly baptized natives. It would be very arduous work, but with God's help it could be done.

As the journey progressed, the Vicar-General's enthusiasm mounted so that he had to share it with his Bishop. His letters are a researcher's delight; he furnishes every event with names and dates, like one who never puts off the writing for another day.[14] And touches of vivid beauty adorn his meticulous accounts, as for instance his first impressions of the Columbia; with his marked tragic sense, he highlights the mighty and the dangerous. With the dalles and falls of the great river as material, he becomes Homeric. Through his letters runs a thread of strong feeling for others, as when he relates briefly the loss of twelve lives at the Dalles of the Dead, or tells of his "beautiful and happy day" with the family of Peter Pambrun, head of the HBC fort at Walla Walla.

Flags were flying at Fort Vancouver when the brigade arrived. At Dr. McLoughlin's orders, a grand reception awaited the missionaries, though he himself could not be present to greet them. Acting in his absence, James Douglas showed them the traditional hospitality of the fort, insisting on a two-day rest and a tour of the place before they plunged into the conversion of the Northwest.

Among the delegations that came to greet the missionaries at Fort Vancouver was one from the Willamette settlements, but as the flotilla was delayed so long by the Dalles accident, only three of these men could wait there for its arrival. These three, Joseph Gervais, Stephen Lucier, and Peter Lebèque, knelt with retired HBC settlers from points along the Columbia and men still in the company's service, to assist at the first Mass offered in western Oregon. Some wept; they had not assisted at Mass for up to twenty years. In the afternoon they chanted Vespers as they had been taught in boyhood in Quebec churches. Then the Vicar-General preached to them, kind and encouraging words strengthened by some of the sterner admonitions of their distant Bishop.

The sermon over, the Willamette men came to present their petition. It was the people of their valley who had sent the requests for priests; encouraged by Dr. McLoughlin, they had built a church at Willamette two years ago. It seemed only right that the mission center should be there, they thought, and they were ready to escort the Vicar-General to his little church up the river beyond the falls, and to build a house for him. They had heard something about the Cowlitz, but surely that must be a mistake. A little sadly, the Vicar-

General explained his obligation to the Honorable Company. He must go to Cowlitz first and establish a central station there. After that, other missions would be started, but if they would return for him early in January, he would be happy to visit Willamette.

As the fort was thronged with traders during the sojourn of the brigade, the two priests began a long and intensive mission there with gratifying results. Then in December, the Vicar-General left the fort to Father Demers and went to Cowlitz. Here he found the white farmers eager to carry out his wishes, and Indians docile to his teaching. He selected a 640-acre tract for a mission site, and started plans for buildings. Christmas found him again at the fort, happily listening to Father Demers' men's choir practicing a Gregorian Mass and French carols. In the evenings everyone gathered to sing hymns, or at least to join in the chorus. The rosary devotion had become so popular that Father Demers could not make rosaries fast enough. The chief difficulty was catechism; it was hard enough, with all Father Demers' skill, to find words for the prayers in Chinook; it was quite impossible to translate the theological phrases of the catechism. So that was taught in French and learned by rote as always in those days. Father Demers repeated it again and again, hoping for recognition of words here and there and helping his class along with Chinook words by way of explanation.

The Vicar-General was at Willamette for the Feast of the Epiphany, offered Mass in the destitute little church of which his parishioners were so proud, and started a second mission on its way. At once, he liked those sociable Canadians, leading their comparatively quiet lives after more adventuresome years. He was so charmed with Indian good will, too, as not to suspect the surly resistance to change which the natives of the valley could offer on occasion, the difficult strain in them which was breaking down the determination of the most earnest Protestant missionaries in the valley.

Though the Protestants, especially in the Willamette area, were certainly inimical to this burst of Catholic energy in what seemed to them their private preserve, it is still quite likely that the Vicar-General's worry was not all necessary. The difficult Reverend Beaver, who had annoyed Dr. McLoughlin at the fort, had withdrawn before the priests' arrival. The really troublesome members of the Methodist group were becoming a source of worry to their own generous sponsors. Actually the Canadian priests had only to ignore their acrimony and await their departure. But the Vicar-General could not foresee this outcome; instead, the fretful vein in his nature made him overaware of criticism and injustice.

If the Vicar-General's critics could have observed his austere life and his intense devotion to his people, they might have understood his annoying success where they were failing. Together he and Father Demers worked at reaching the mentality of both savage and illiterate settler. While his assistant wrung meaning for children's hymns from the scanty jargon, the Vicar-General invented the *Catholic Ladder,* a device which Father DeSmet declared should be used throughout the missionary world, presenting as it did the entire scheme of Christian instruction in picture and symbol. For his first *Ladder,* the Vicar-General used wrapping paper pasted on thin white cloth. A strip two yards long and eighteen inches wide, it presented the story of revelation, the figures and lettering done with brush and India ink. The Vicar-General would explain it to a selected group, and these would carry it proudly off to their village, there to take turns displaying it, mimicking their pastor's words and gestures.[15] These children of the Oregon forest required unlimited understanding, for oftener than not such initial zeal proved ephemeral. They lacked the docility of the Flathead Indian, and the missionary had to be prepared for casual returns to renounced practices.

Through nearly four years of lonely hardship, these two priests labored among unpredictable Indians and sometimes more unpredictable half-breeds. From the missions at Cowlitz, Fort Vancouver, and St. Paul of Willamette, they made incredible journeys to establish missions and revisit them, keeping their deeds and their needs all the while before

the eyes of Bishop Signay and hoping that the Jesuits would
soon find their way to the far West. Their greatest comfort
was Father DeSmet's promise to come himself to Oregon.

When at last he arrived, and Father Demers saw his
Superior and the great Jesuit both drop to their knees and
each claim the other's blessing, he knew the Northwest mission must flourish. Through that June of 1842 the three
made their plans. Father DeSmet would try to secure Jesuits.
These and the priests who were hopefully awaited from
Quebec would free Father Demers to go to British Columbia.
But everything, Father DeSmet said, depended on having
Sisters to teach the women and children. There were Sisters
of Notre Dame now in Cincinnati, Belgian Sisters who had
expected a more truly missionary life in America. He might
secure some of these. He would ask the Superior to write
to their Mother General about it. Better still, if he should
go to Europe as he hoped, he would ask her himself. And
the Vicar-General at once began plans for a convent at St.
Paul, which he was coming to consider the center of mission
activity, a logical arrangement in view of Dr. McLoughlin's
plan for developing the valley. There should be a boys' school
at St. Paul, too, the nucleus of a native seminary.

At the end of June Father DeSmet and Father Demers set
out to journey together as far as Walla Walla. From there
Father DeSmet went on to St. Louis and Father Demers disappeared into British Columbia on an almost year-long
mission tour, leaving the Vicar-General alone with his bright
dreams among his far-flung missions. Through the summer
his dreams dimmed out; no Canadian priests as yet and much
annoyance from the Methodists. But just as he was settling
down to a winter of impossible labor alone, Fathers Anthony
Langlois and John Baptist Boldoc arrived from Quebec; they
had been over a year on their way to Oregon.

Another blessing came in the form of a donation of 4,800
francs from a certain Joseph Larocque of Paris, who stipu-
lated its use for a boys' school. The Vicar-General hurried to
completion the building intended for a convent school,
secured a certain Mr. King as principal and English teacher
and a Mr. Bilodeau to teach French, and made Father

Langlois director. To commemorate the donor, he gave the school the ambitious title of St. Joseph's College, and blessed it though still quite unfinished, in October, 1843. Twenty-nine young half-breeds, sons of valley farmers, and one son of an Indian chief were enrolled. As it was a boys' school, no one thought of finishing it; mostly no one thought of sweeping it. All the parishioners were proud of it and happy to see that the Vicar-General was starting another building for Sisters; a smaller building, it was true, but everyone knew that funds were very hard to come by. The poor Vicar-General certainly knew it; when the Sisters arrived ten months later, their house was still unfinished.

As the months wore on, it began to look as though Father DeSmet had forgotten Oregon.[16] To the anxious Vicar-General, the Jesuit's voyage to Europe seemed improbable. It was over two years since his visit, in any case. The lonely priest in Oregon had no picture of the brave little bark doing battle with the sea to reach the Columbia.

Quite alone for the most part, he worried over the unfinished convent and over the first wave of migration into Eastern Oregon. How would that affect his missions? Would it be a multiplication of Lee and Waller troubles? Still, he often reflected on Father Boldoc's zeal, Father Demers' strong loyalty, the tower of strength he possessed in Dr. McLoughlin, and Father Langlois' persuasive manner that drew people to the missions. These were blessings to be counted. But if only Father DeSmet would come!

CHAPTER 8

Fort, Falls, and Forest

Moving east with slow dignity in the Columbia's south channel, *l'Infatigable* was a seven years' wonder for loitering natives, to whom any unusual movement on the river furnished cause for abandoning village corn plots for a few hours. But this incredible entrance over high sand banks called for a much longer period of aimless speculation best carried on in an easy, squatting position. Two mounted HBC servants riding down from Fort Astoria watched the brig with more purposeful curiosity. Whatever port she sailed from, she bore a charmed life on two counts; last night their chief had given her up for lost as her officers failed to understand his signals from the north side. He and his men had watched the fog banks close around her in the churning billows outside the bar, and had abandoned hope of her survival. And besides surviving those thunderous waters, this little vessel had crossed the bar at its most dangerous point. They were running up the flag of Belgium on her mainmast now; she would be out of Antwerp, apparently an unexpected visitor in the Columbia. And the riders returned to the fort at a brisk trot to give the news to Chief Birnie.[1]

Meantime, *l'Infatigable*'s passengers had passed quickly from the dread of almost certain destruction to realization of their physical miseries, the worst of which was the parched weakness that became visible pain in the leathery dryness of their skin. Sister Marie Catherine noted Sister Loyola's drawn mouth, sharp nose, and outlined jawbone. And big, hearty Sister Norbertine! The Sisters in Belgium would not know her. But the tension was slipping away from all their

126

faces as they watched the sailors bringing up fresh river water in wooden buckets.[2] Tin dipper in hand, Sister Mary Albine filled the waiting goblets, which the other Sisters passed quickly around to passengers and crew. The cook carried down a bucket to his kitchen, emptied the remaining coffee into a big pot, and poured in the water as though witnessing a miracle. Now if some good soul would row out to the ship with fresh food for one good meal before his famished passengers went ashore!

Weak as they were, the passengers forgot their wrechedness at the sight of the luxuriant forests that lined the river. This country, they assured Father DeSmet, was quite as wonderful as he had described it. At that he made a stirring little exhortation about their privilege to spread the kingdom of God in this beautiful land and their debt to St. Ignatius. They had escaped certain death that day, he insisted. St. Ignatius had heard their prayer, and in grateful memory of their miraculous entrance into the south channel they would name it *Le canal Saint Ignace*.[3] Like true pioneers, they were ready to bestow names on land and waterway. Sister Mary Aloysia wrote the name down solemnly. How grand it would sound read out in the community room in Namur!

As she entered that historic note, she heard cries of surprise and looked up to see Father Accolti pointing to a strange boat with still stranger occupants making toward the ship, now coming to a standstill as the breeze fell off. As the shapeless craft drew near, Father DeSmet explained that it was a hollowed-out tree trunk fitted with oars, and that, except for one, its occupants were natives. The visitors looked up to the group on the deck with friendly smiles, though their throaty cries of "Catche, Catche!" alarmed the Sisters. Worse still, after a few words with the white man, Captain Moller invited them all on board. What an uproar! All talking and gesturing together, these Clatsops delivered a welcome of undoubted friendliness. At last their American leader quieted them down and explained in English that he had seen *l'Infatigable* in the breakers. Certain that she would be wrecked, he had tried to coax these Indians to go with him to the rescue, but could not overcome their fear. As he spoke, the Indians enacted in anguished signs the terror they had experienced. Then they left with such ear-splitting assurances of friendliness that no one except the captain heard the American's promise to send a dinner of fresh fish and potatoes. If one just didn't notice the noise, it would be easy enough to get on with the Clatsops, Sister Marie Catherine observed, and Sister Mary Aloysia wrote quaintly ". . . ils nous firent beaucoup d'amitiés." [4] And these Clatsops were quite in character; their tribesmen had good will toward all except their dreaded enemy north of the river, the Chinooks.

About four that afternoon a boatload of these dour and self-assured savages came aboard, silent and curious. Unlike the earlier visitors, these Chinooks had made no compromise with white man's attire. Their tunics and blankets were stiff with dirt; their long hair added to their general repulsiveness. This, reflected Sister Loyola, is the obdurate and sullen type of native, or else they have had unfortunate contacts with whites. At that thought she beckoned to Sister Marie Catherine, and the two went to the dining room where they found a large pitcher of steaming coffee.

Staring suspiciously at it, the Indians watched until one of the Fathers took some with evident satisfaction. Then they accepted it, grunting their enjoyment, and showed approval of their reception by scrambling down into their boat and paddling off to tell their friends about it. For the rest of that day band after band of curious but friendly Chinooks climbed up to the deck. When there was no more coffee, the Sisters gave them pictures which they received with childish delight. These people, Father DeSmet said, would be much harder to civilize than the gentle Clatsops. Nature spoiled them; hunting and fishing supplied them with an easy living, leaving them free to bask their lives away in the sun. The only effort they made was to beat the Clatsops back from their favorite haunts.

Between these Chinook visits, a Clatsop dugout came alongside with the promised fresh salmon and potatoes sent by the chief himself, and the passengers prayed for this first Indian benefactor as their dizziness and feverish lassitude began to leave them.[5]

They were singing the *Te Deum* together at nine o'clock when Mr. Birnie came aboard with the owner of the ship they had watched with such frustration the evening before. Now they learned how that ship had been forced back by the wind and how Mr. Birnie had taken a band of Indians to Cape Disappointment, where they had lighted fires, waved flags, and fired guns and cannon to attract *l'Infatigable* in that direction.[6] Certainly God had saved them, Mr. Birnie agreed, but in order that a second miracle might not be necessary he would come aboard again very early in the morning to guide them through the banks that lay between them and the fort. He added that Mrs. Birnie would be expecting all the passengers as soon as they landed.

Father DeSmet declared the next day a holiday and that, by common consent, meant a walk in the forest, Such a forest as none of them had ever seen, its giant trees shining rain-clean in the morning sun! To walk again on land, and under those glorious trees! All the world was bright for the Sisters as they stepped ashore and found Mrs. Birnie and her seven fine-looking daughters waiting to receive them. One and all, the girls were quite captivated by the Sisters, who in turn were delighted with the cordiality of this Protestant family. A school at St. Paul? The three oldest daughters at once announced their desire to go there with the Sisters. No, they didn't mind if things were not ready. Such eagerness should be rewarded, said Sister Loyola, producing a little gift for each.

Strolling under the giant trees, the Sisters chatted about the hospitable Scotch captain, his equally hospitable Canadian wife, whose French was "very good," and their well-trained children. Sister Marie Catherine thought mostly of the Chinooks, and how they would one day come to be clean in soul and body and kneel down to pray together with the Clatsops. And Captain Birnie was explaining to Father DeSmet that the fir before them was forty-two feet in circumference, and that the blackberries growing on all sides under the big trees made excellent pie.

What an exuberant country! Everything, including the fine dinner at the fort, spoke of a gracious land. But the Sisters were somewhat astonished at certain customs. Here was

Father DeSmet requested by the staunch Protestant head of
the house to ask a blessing before dinner. And what was
really disconcerting, the women of the house declined wine.
Unwilling to offend, the Sisters had to forego this strengthening concomitant of a Belgian meal.

Governor Birnie advised Captain Moller to wait for high
tide late next day to return his ship to the channel. The passengers, he insisted, must come ashore for dinner again, and
Mrs. Birnie would have blackberry pie for them. Besides, he
said, they had not had time to explore the fort on their first
visit. They accepted with delight, all except Father DeSmet,
who insisted he must go ahead to Fort Vancouver to announce the ship's arrival and to arrange for lodgings for the
Sisters.

As they sat in the lovely fort garden enjoying the Birnie
children's friendliness and their mother's "very good French,"
Sister Loyola marveled at how quickly her Sisters were throwing off the haggard look that had so distressed her. Good food
and security were gentle restoratives, she thought, but this
first kind and friendly reception in their new land was more
efficacious than either.

At five that evening, *l'Infatigable* passed safely over the
banks, slipped into the channel, and started up the river with
a good breeze. Then, as if a last trial of patience, the wind
fell off and for three full days the eager missionaries followed
their sea routine within sight of their field of labor. But one
couldn't really feel depressed by the delay, Sister Mary
Aloysia thought, as she jotted down her impressions of the
Columbia's majestic beauty, fitting magnificence into her cir-
cumscribed phrasing. For her, the river islands are "garlanded
with verdure and festooned with flowers." For Father De-
Smet, they are "handsome little islands . . . thrown as it
were like groups of flowers . . ." Still, the reader sees that
she was genuinely captivated. If she had seen Multnomah
Falls, she might perhaps have escaped for once the tyranny of
her proper diction. The pity is that, being so near it, the
Sisters never saw it.

At one of the surprising turns in the river, *l'Infatigable*
passed a sea-going vessel preparing to sail. To Europe, of

course, the Sisters told one another, and at once began letters to Namur to tell of their safe arrival, of the Birnie family, and of the breath-taking beauty of the cascade they were passing. But no, the captain apologized, his run was to points on the American coasts. It seemed unbelievable that a ship should not return to some European port at the end of a voyage, that lines sending vessels out of Boston, for instance, should find it profitable to ignore Old World ports! Presently the Sisters forgot their disappointment when a boat with Father DeSmet and two of the crew rounded a bend in the river.

All was in readiness for the missionaries at the fort, Father DeSmet told them. The Vicar-General was at Willamette, but they had got word to him and expected him to come at once for the Sisters. The next item of news the speaker cushioned as tactfully as possible; the dream house at St. Paul had been used for a boys' school, St. Joseph's College for Boys, but the Sisters must not worry as another house was being built for them. It would mean merely a delay in getting started. The Sisters' detached response was a relief to Father DeSmet. He had expected Sister Loyola to resent this setback. Instead, she was quite taken with the idea of a future native seminary; that seemed to her a progressive step.

Father DeSmet hurried on with his news from the fort. His arrival there was just in time; Father Demers would have set out for Canada in another day or two. Everyone had given up hope of Father DeSmet's return, and the Vicar-General had decided to appeal to Quebec for Sisters. Having no mind for this journey to Canada, Father Demers hailed the arrival of the Notre Dame Sisters with joy. His one desire was to return to British Columbia, where he had already converted so many. And Father DeSmet had two wonderful reports from the mountains. Father Peter DeVoss and others, who had gone to the western tribes after his plea on their behalf in St. Louis in 1842, had been working among his beloved Flatheads. Best of all, the entire tribe of Coeur d'Alênes had been converted! The missionaries listened with shining eyes; not one of them questioned the thoroughness of such rapid conversion; neither did the speaker. Their work and

days were to be post-Pentecostal. For such things the Good
God had lifted their ship over the sand banks. And elated
Father DeSmet sat for the last time at the weather-beaten
table on the deck and wrote his rich impressions of the
Columbia. Here was a scribe who could do that river justice.

At last, Fort Vancouver! And on the bank below it, a
group waiting to receive the missionaries. The tall, dignified,
white-haired man, Father DeSmet said, was Doctor McLoughlin. Madame McLoughlin stood beside him, and there were
Mr. James Douglas and Doctor Forbes Barclay with their
wives and children. Wonderful people, all of them, Father
DeSmet added. Had he not often told them of the hospitality
they might expect at Fort Vancouver? He had, indeed. Yet
not one of the Sisters had quite expected this gracious scene at
a fort in the forest. Solicitous greetings of the grownups and
admiring smiles of children! Everyone taking their bags and
bundles from them. And now kind Madame McLoughlin
showed them the two spacious rooms prepared for them.
With delicate thoughtfulness, she had arranged their quarters
in quite cloistered fashion so that they would feel at home,
had even planned to have their meals served in a separate dining room. If only Mère Constantine could see them now, they
said, walking about erect in these large and airy rooms after
nearly seven months of crouching in their boxlike, airless
cabins! Comfortable beds, spotless linen, and Madame Mc-
Loughlin happy at the thought of caring for their needs! It
was fortunate, she said, that the Vicar-General was detained at
Willamette. She could thus keep them a few days and see
that they rested properly before going to their mission. And
smiling at that prospect, she left them to enjoy their first night
in a good bed on land.

In a moment she returned to say that Father Demers had
just come in from a visit to an Indian village and, seeing
l'Infatigable in the river, he had hurried to pay his respects
at once. Would they come to the parlor? Of course, it would
be just a few minutes for introduction, Sister Marie Catherine
assured herself, as with a regretful glance at her feather bed
she joined her Sisters and Madame McLoughlin. But the
few minutes lengthened to two hours or more as Father

Demers held the twelve missionaries spellbound with his talk of British Columbia and the possibilities of the Willamette Valley, of Doctor McLoughlin's plans for a city at the Falls, and of the vision which he shared with his much admired Vicar-General of a fine new chapter of church history in the Northwest. All the missionaries forgot their weariness through those two light-winged hours as Father Demers' quiet flow of speech was heightened by Father DeSmet's forceful comment.

Now for a few hours of uncramped, untroubled sleep, Sister Marie Catherine told herself at last. But no! The quiet room was presently loud with buzzing. Mosquitoes, hundreds of them, and no screening of any kind on the open windows! "Quel fléau que ces petites pestes de maringouins!" And to think that Madame had said nothing! One wouldn't sleep a wink, of course. But the six slept too soundly to defend themselves from the onslaught and awoke next morning scarcely able to open their eyes. Like everything else in this tremendous valley, these mosquitoes were giant size, it seemed, and most certainly they found newcomers especially tempting. Madame McLoughlin's sympathy was accompanied by an expressive French-Canadian shrug. In the matter of mosquitoes and certain other details, her attitude was primitive.

But one could quite forget such inconvenience at the sight of Doctor McLoughlin and his family assisting devoutly at Father DeSmet's early Mass.[7] This princely governor who for years had wielded unquesioned power over a great area, knelt in prayerful attention to each word and act. What a blessing to have him as a protector! He was a sort of lay missionary, his good wife told the Sisters proudly; besides leading his people in prayers in the absence of a priest, he had of late been preparing a weekly exhortation for the company's Indian servants. Even before his conversion, she went on, he organized a class for the relogous instruction of the Catholic children of the fort and enlisted her service as teacher of hymns.

With the kind McLoughlins doing everything possible for their comfort, the Sisters spent six quite idyllic days,

despite mosquitoes. Then the Vicar-General arrived with
several of his St. Paul parishioners. He had been called
away from St. Paul, he explained, and thus had not received
Father DeSmet's message at once. His efforts to speed up
work on the Sisters' house had, of course, detained him,
too; for the easy-going habits of the few available workers
made personal supervision necessary after one succeeded in
persuading them to start. But they were much better boats-
men than carpenters. In their desire to meet the missionaries,
they had covered the distance between St. Paul and the fort
in one day and night. Now their canoes were waiting below
the fort for the missionaries and their belongings. Canoes! In
their desire not to offend their new pastor, the Sisters smiled
their approval of canoes, while he stood exclaiming that the
Good God had preserved them from the perils of the sea to
work for his Glory in French Prairie. If canoes were a part of
it all, very well! A long section of a forest tree dug out and
fitted with oars, that was a canoe; they had already seen
one. In a fleet of these they would cross the Columbia and
make the trip up the Willamette to St. Paul. Sister Marie
Catherine whispered her usual, "Courage, my soul," and
glanced at Sister Mary Cornelia, who looked somehow as
though canoes were her accustomed mode of travel. The
others wore inscrutable expressions except Sister Nobertine,
who clutched her crucifix and gazed at it for assurance in
this danger.

Fortunately, at that moment Doctor McLoughlin entered
the room to greet the Vicar-General. He had just met his
good parishioners, he said, on their way to the fort store,
and had told them that he would arrange for a river boat
for the Sisters. Their canoes were well-built and roomy, he
added, but really not comfortable for such a long trip. What
a relief! It would be quite ironical, Sister Marie Catherine
thought, to have escaped the dangers of the Patagonian
coast and the Columbia Bar, only to be drowned in the
Willamette.

Quite unaware of this brief nautical crisis, the Vicar-
General continued his encomiums of such heroism as had

emboldened the Sisters to face the storms of the Horn, while Doctor McLoughlin interrupted to quote Father DeSmet's account of their courage. But the Sisters were not interested in praise. The Good God had brought them through it all, they said, and now they wished to begin His work in Oregon, as soon as possible. This was the spirit for which the Vicar-General had hoped; if only good Mère Constantine had sent twelve such instead of six.

As the Sisters saw their pastor's embarrassment at not having their house ready for them, they protested eagerly that any sort of temporary dwelling would please them. After all, wasn't this a missionary country? And Sister Loyola said they were ready to set out the next morning. That was a little hasty, Sister Marie Catherine thought. Suppose the river boat should not be ready. *Les Canots!* Again she saw herself rising and falling on the billows of the Columbia in a hollow tree. To her relief the Vicar-General explained that business would keep him at the fort a few days; besides, he agreed with Madame McLoughlin that the Sisters ought to remain a little longer.

As the Vicar-General sat with Father DeSmet and Father Demers, mapping out a glorious future for the work of God in the Northwest, Sister Mary Aloysia wrote of the Sisters' appraisal of their pastor. His very appearance, they all agreed, "revealed the goodness of his heart and his tender charity." And if Sister Mary Aloysia had hesitated in her writing, her five Sisters would have prompted her, for they were all standing at the dawn of a golden age since they had talked with their new pastor. They knew he had had his share of troubles and opposition, but now that chapter was closed. He could assure the Sisters gaily that the whole Willamette Valley was theirs, "un champ libre." since the departure of Lee, Gary, and Waller.

But both consultations and rest were cut short next day when a case of the prevailing dysentery epidemic was discovered at the fort.[8] The Vicar-General insisted on taking the missionaries to St. Paul at once. Father DeSmet had as much baggage as possible transferred from *l'Infatigable* to the canoes and river boat, sending the rest to the fort for storage. Then he sat chatting with Captain Moller for the last time.

In late afternoon of the fourteenth the Sisters said goodby to all their new friends at the fort and went with the Fathers to bid a last farewell to Captain Moller. To the surprise of all, this very silent man spoke feelingly of his great respect for them. It was a painful parting, wrote Sister Mary Aloysia later, recalling her sudden tears as he asked to be remembered in their prayers. A good, kind man, Father DeSmet said, as they turned away. They must all pray for him, for certainly this was his last voyage. Sister Mary Aloysia allowed herself one last look at *l'Infatigable*. The others turned, too. *Un dernier regard . . . Anvers . . . Namur . . . Liége . . . Ma Mère . . . Les soeurs. . . .*

But what was Sister Loyola saying? Yes, indeed, it was well the river boat was fairly large; they could take quite a number of their boxes, all the most valuable things, along with them. One couldn't tell about those canoes. But where were the canoes? Near the river boat there were moored four long and very graceful boats, made skillfully of fine oak and well painted. The wood, Brother Francis was explaining to Father Accolti, had been cut and cured in Doctor McLoughlin's mill at the Falls, and the Canadians had learned the art of canoe building in their youth on the St. Lawrence.

So these were canoes! Perhaps after all they would never be expected to make a journey in a dugout tree. But even so, it was assuring to have the solid-looking river boat, and assuring to see the McLoughlins and the other families of the fort coming down laden with provisions for their trip, a little surprise farewell that Madame McLoughlin said must really not be for long. She would come to see them soon. And Doctor McLoughlin said they must open a school at the Falls. They would see for themselves presently what a promising location it was. Father Demers and two Canadians had left for the Falls that morning, he added, and would be waiting there to show them improvements and the property set aside for church and school. Sister Loyola's sudden in-

terest subsided for the time as the Vicar-General and Father
DeSmet turned toward the Sisters and began to explain
their plan for a central mission house for the Jesuits on
French Prairie. All things are possible in America, it seems,
was Sister Marie Catherine's silent comment. Everyone was
talking of building.

The best that man could build would spoil this wonderful
country, thought Father DeSmet as he watched the light
glancing on the water and the canoes slipping easily over the
waves. It was for the natives. If the missionary could just
convert them without breaking up their life pattern, just
teach them to be clean and industrious. But there was the
trouble; any change involved further change. Besides, the
whites would come; some were already there. And they were
not all princes among men, like Doctor McLoughlin.

An hour of rowing on the Willamette brought the little
brigade to the site selected by the Canadians for encampment. Probably wigwams under those big trees, Sister Mary
Aloysia remarked, as the rowers turned to the east bank. But
no. No wigwams. Nothing in sight except rolls of blankets
and boxes and baskets of provisions. And before even Sister
Loyola could quite evaluate this situation, the expert Canadians had a fire started on the bank. That was enough; one
would have thought the Sisters had enjoyed Girl Scout training. What a supper it was! Large, thick pieces of bread,
fine butter and cheese, cold beef, freshly baked cakes, and
rich blackberry preserve! *"La terre pour table . . . et nos
talons pour chaises."* Then as Sister Mary Albine supervised the making of coffee, the Canadians stripped some long
branches, planted them firmly in the ground, stretched
blankets around these, and behold, a tent for the Sisters!
No roof, of course, but will it not sound delightfully idyllic
when read in Namur? They will want to come at once,
n'est-ce pas? And the blankets for the tent, Madame
McLoughlin had thought of that too. How very good! But
now Father DeSmet was beginning night prayer for all, and
the Canadians were balancing themselves a little clumsily
on one knee and bowing their heads very low. They must
sing, of course. Were they not still *en route?* Sister Mary

Aloysia intoned the voyage hymn and found her usual choir augmented by the rich voices of the Canadians. How the old phrases rose in swelling crescendos over the quiet river, with the wind in the mighty branches as accompaniment!

There was still the "great silence" to observe, but who could help laughing rolled up in a blanket on the sand in that topless tent? Moving branches and starlit sky for ceiling, and the sides of their tent billowing out like sails. But thank God for the breeze; it kept the mosquitoes away. What would they sing for Mass? Sister Mary Aloysia had to decide that before going to sleep. There was no sign of an altar, but Father DeSmet had said there would be Mass on the feast, so there would be; but before she could recall the possibilities, she was sound asleep.

At four next morning, Father DeSmet aroused Brother Francis and the sleepy Canadians to help him piece together an altar of split wood and boxes. Soon they were all kneeling on the damp sand, watching Brother Francis light the two little candles for this Mass in the wilderness. But the Vicar-General's grand sermon at the end changed the face of things. Listening to his words, Sister Loyola saw churches and schools, orderly and well organized parishes, things primitive leaping to culture at her controlling touch. But Sister Marie Catherine wondered. Would the savage move so rapidly toward European standards? Building and planning were for white men, but had they not come for the "dear savages?"

Hoping to avoid another night en route, the Canadians rushed the brigade into early action, but as the morning wore on the rowers lagged because their canoes were so heavily laden. They did well to reach the Falls by five o'clock and to get all the baggage as well as their canoes ashore before dark. The more exhausting labor, the portage of all their belongings above the falls, they left to morning. Apparently Father Demers had been called away, and since none of the families at the Falls made any friendly gesture, the travelers spent another night in the open. It was not quite what the Sisters had expected there, the future center of their valley. But tired as they were, they soon lost their disappointment in sound sleep. By noon they were embarking again above the falls, a flat barge replacing the river boat. Another great spurt of energy, and again a decline. Another night! But Sister Loyola said that they must not even look disappointed. As they pulled up on the wet sand at Champoeg, Sister Mary Albine smiled as though entering the Mother House.

There was no breeze now and a heavy fog was settling. Never mind, they still had plenty of good food and the Sisters arranged it appetizingly on the packing boxes. Mosquitoes again and giants they were. But patience! Tonight the missionaries sang their journey hymn for the last time, and responded as Father DeSmet led night prayer and offered a special thanksgiving that not one had succumbed to the epidemic. Silently he prayed that not one would be the worse for the cold fog and wet sand; even wrapped in a blanket, he found it too cold to sleep. Shivering, Sister Mary Aloysia thought about the wonderful falls and what she would write about it. Sister Loyola planned the school she would build within sound of its music. If only those Canadians would row a bit faster tomorrow morning!

A fresh burst of energy carried the boats along the last lap. The men sang as they rowed, hymns learned in boyhood and revived in the little church at St. Paul under Father Demers' direction. Now *Pange Lingua,* now a haunting *Noël.* Suddenly a shout and a returning call from the left bank. There another band of St. Paul settlers stood, waiting for their pastor and the missionaries. And now only five miles to St. Paul, the Vicar-General said, smiling to think that his Canadians had not failed him. Here the settlers were with horses and farm carts, giving up a second day of their harvest time. What a welcome, and especially to the Sisters! In French reminiscent of Quebec village and forest, these farmers were eagerly telling the number and ages of their children. The school might not be ready, but there was no doubt about the pupils.

It would have been easier to walk as the Fathers were doing, Sister Norbertine muttered, as the iron-rimmed wheels lunged suddenly into the deep ruts. Sister Marie Catherine

admitted it was worse in a way than a rough sea; but noticing
Sister Loyola's glance, caught midway between unbelief and
annoyance, she added that the cart had been kindly provided for their comfort. At that, everyone contrived to look
especially pleased with the farm cart as a mode of travel,
so that as the Vicar-General passed them on horseback, he
bowed to a merry group. Then he trotted his horse on ahead
of the carts to see how preparations were faring.

As the party jogged along, Sister Norbertine decided she
liked this broad valley with its fine grain fields ready for
harvest, its boxlike log houses, its groves of giant firs. Here
and there a harvester swinging a scythe told of laborious life.
Now the driver was pointing to a frame house on one side of
the road and a low, log structure on the other. The cross
of St. Paul's! And beyond it the half-boarded-up walls of
their convent!

Sister Loyla led the way into the dim, musty church in
which a lighted lamp was the only sign of care. The six
knelt at the crudely made altar rail, their eyes on the almost
equally crude tabernacle. Their silent prayer could have
been said in unison, their great thanksgiving for being at
last in "la chère mission." At the door Sister Mary Aloysia
turned to her sisters. "L'étable de Bethléem," she said.
"Unthinkably filthy," Sister Marie Catherine sighed. "We
must clean it up," Sister Loyola concluded casually, and the
community knew without asking that the cleaning party
would be that very afternoon.

In St. Joseph's College the Sisters found the two rooms
assigned to them in almost as neglected a state as the church.
The headmaster, Father Langlois, was away. Classes were
over and the place had the air of having been deserted in
haste. As if to add to the disarray, the Canadians were
bringing in the baggage and dropping it in unoccupied
corners, beaming with pleasure as the Sisters thanked them.
Happy enough to sing, the Sisters set about improving their
surroundings. Quickly they located a well and rounded up
buckets and brooms. If they hurried, they might have the
church cleaned up before Father DeSmet and the others arrived.

They swept the piles of dirt from the plank floor; then they scrubbed it. While Sister Loyola went for clean altar linen from their supply and for a statue of the Blessed Virgin that Mère Constantine had give her, her Sisters cut flowers and greens to decorate the sanctuary. Quite a transformation, Sister Marie Catherine commented, as she watched Sister Mary Aloysia hide the ugliest features under branch and spray. Unfortunately, there were hideous paintings on the walls, and the festoons seemed only to emphasize their cheapness. The pastor had perhaps tried to cover the log walls with these murals, but they were ugly; the hewed logs, Sister thought, would really be better without them. She turned to see the Vicar-General standing in the doorway, smiling radiantly. His Sisters had seen their unfinished convent and had found unprepared, disorderly rooms, but with no resentment, had changed this hovel into an attractive little church within two hours of their coming.

The Vicar-General was gone only a few minutes when he returned with the Jesuits. Now, said Father DeSmet, they must sing the *Te Deum* together, and would not the Vicar-General allow them to have Benediction? So this, Sister Mary Aloysia wrote, was altogether "un des plus beaux jours de notre vie," adding that only after all this did the Sisters take "some nourishment of which they had great need."

More than one delight awaited the Sisters on Sunday morning. There was the sound of the church bell from its belfry, set on a platform that served also as porch over the door.[9] At intervals a young Indian boy rang it lustily, smiling at his weekly privilege of filling the valley with music. More unexpected was the crowd that responded to the bell. Canadians, a few Americans, many half-breeds and Indians filled the little church to the door. It was a great day, the feast of the Assumption, which according to Canadian custom was observed on Sunday. But where could all the people come from? There was not even a village in sight, just open fields. Some of the crowd had set out on foot before day break; almost all had walked long distances. Most were fasting; in fact the number of communicants was the Sisters' greatest marvel. But almost as great a wonder was their

reverent behavior. Men on one side of the church and
women and children on the other, they prayed, sang, and followed the Mass with complete attention, outdone in precision
only by the twenty little altar boys in their shabby cassocks
and messy surplices. What angelic faces, thought Sister Mary
Aloysia, as she watched their serious, dark eyes follow the
solemn dignity of the pastor's movements, "avec majesté."
Yes, it might be solemn Mass in a great cathedral. Was this
the wilderness? Or was it rather a tremendous primitive
era in Christianity?

At the sermon, the six Sisters ceased to be a distraction
glimpsed with one eye, for now the Vicar-General spoke
glowingly of the good Bishop and Mother General who had
made so great a sacrifice in parting with them. This could
be no ordinary day that brought "nos chères Soeurs"; its
memory must be perpetuated. In the future, then, the Feast
of the Assumption would be solemnized "avec une double
pompe." It was no wonder that after Mass the Sisters found
themselves surrounded by parents urging their shy, dark-
eyed daughters to welcome them. As native women expended
their few, hesitating words of French, the Sisters won smiles
from their blanket-wrapped babies with easy, sweet syllables.
Standing in the doorway, the Vicar-General saw the picture
through tears.

"Oh! que de bien à faire dans cette délicieuse mission!"
They were scrubbing dishes that had been put away, badly
washed or not at all.

"The boys' cassocks! Did you observe them, Sister
Superior?"

"Yes, of course, but first the Vicar-General. He is in rags.
It's well that Sister Marie Albine brought a cassock pattern."

PART IV

ARDUOUS
NEW WORLD

CHAPTER 9

Hammer, Saw, and Plane

The Jesuits set out at once to look for an appropriate site for their central mission. In their absence, the Sisters scrubbed and cleaned St. Joseph's College from end to end, in an effort to rid the neglected building of its strongly intrenched insect pests. Meanwhile, there were those awful planks in the church floor; the scrubbing on Saturday had only removed the surface, Sister Marie Catherine observed, as she selected the stoutest broom. Only Sister Mary Albine failed to take part in the attack an filth and insects; on the well-scrubbed table in the kitchen, she was cutting out a cassock for the pastor.[1]

Vicar-General Blanchet was troubled when he discovered

143

all this hard labor. His Sisters had not come for this, he scolded kindly. Such labor would break their health and make them unfit for missionary work; life would be hard enough without this excessive scrubbing. But seeing that they failed to understand his acceptance of primitive house-keeping standards, he muttered that time would teach them and walked away. And when they found at the back of the church the little lean-to shed which had been his dwelling before the boys' school was built, they began to realize how hard things could be. No floor! Old bits of canvas covered with fir branches for roof. And here he had slept on a bed of branches; here he had even taught a class of Canadian boys to read. How hard his life had been!

The Vicar-General hoped that many of his people would attend the Mass of Thanksgiving which he had announced for Thursday, thanksgiving for *l'Infatigable*'s safe arrival, but more than all else for the Sisters. The women and chil-dren would certainly come in their desire to meet the Sisters again. And at Mass on Thursday he would announce cate-chism classes to begin at once; that would take the Sisters' minds off scrubbing and washing blankets. He must see Sister Loyola about the classes. Then he saw the fine new cassock, hanging in the corner of his room. How good they were, his Sisters! He went to thank them at once.

He found Sister Loyola in distress; Sister Mary Aloysia was very ill. They had not escaped the epidemic after all.[2] Sister Norbertine and Sister Mary Albine were coming down with it, too. Sister Loyola would care for these three herself and assign Sister Mary Cornelia and Sister Marie Catherine to the catechism classes. Sister Mary Aloysia needed a doctor, and the Sisters would need another place for their pupils because of the danger of contagion. The Vicar-General dis-posed of both problems. He would send for the doctor at the Falls. And the classes? He pointed simply to the field. He had not thought of bringing them into the house in any case. The important thing, he said, was to isolate the stricken Sisters.

As the Vicar-General turned to go, Sister Loyola noticed his troubled look. He was not calm like Father Demers; he

was a worrier. But she noticed, too, that his cassock fitted
perfectly. Good! She liked things to turn out well. She was
happy, too, about the open-air classes, since the school had
just been so thoroughly cleaned; she was beginning to suspect
that the natives themselves were the sources of the ubiquitous
and annoying insect life.

Classes in the field? Why not? The two Sisters were delighted; now this was real missionary work. And hadn't
Mère Julie taught the workers in the harvest field? It was
quite simple, too. A couple of old logs arranged for benches
and a tree stump for the teacher's chair. The pupils were
elderly Indian women with straggling hair and younger
women, mostly half-breeds, proudly displaying their children
again, and complementing their small French vocabularies
with smiles. The Vicar-General expertly divided this ill-as-
sorted school into two groups and assigned the older women
to Sister Mary Cornelia and the younger to Sister Marie
Catherine. Sister Mary Cornelia studied her class, the
youngest over fifty, and they studied their teacher. Here,
she said, was the place for Chinook; all the Indians understood it. From her little store of words she produced fitting
expressions, but there was no response; just stolid, unsmiling
eyes. She made the sign of the cross and, as one, they imitated
her with left hands. The Vicar-General was standing beside
her, smiling. Kindly he took over, signing himself with left
hand, right to left, and uttering the formula in Chinook.
Slowly they repeated it with him, managing their right hands
correctly. Over and over, he repeated it with little explana-
tory phrases, his perseverance rewarded by occasional glints
of comprehension. When the class had mastered a few
prayers in Chinook, he repeated them over and over in French.
He hoped his stolid pupils would thus come to sense a spiritual meaning which Chinook could never convey.

Sister Mary Cornelia learned more than Chinook as she
listened to her pastor's lesson; she was beginning to realize
the childlike qualities of the adult Indian mind. With her
quicker temper, Sister Marie Catherine discovered this fact
less calmly. She found it annoying to repeat the first day's
lesson again and again as though for the first time. Her own

blunders in the jargon irked her, too, and the black-eyed babies distracted her as well as their mothers. But the half-breeds, with their poor and little French, were her comfort as they conveyed her meaning to the savages, employing her facial expression and gestures. And these young women helped her solve the problem of the huge bundles of laundry accumulated between Lima and Oregon.

Before class one morning an Indian boy arrived, gathered a pile of wood, and made an outdoor fire while Sister Marie Catherine brought water from the creek, two buckets at a time, to fill the big iron caldron. Then came her pupils with washboards and wooden tubs. Presently all the altar linens and Sisters' white capes were soaking, as well as a pile gathered in the church sacristy by Sister Mary Cornelia.

Looking from his window, the Vicar-General saw two attentive classes squatted on the logs before their teachers and, nearby, the fire and black caldron, the tubs and washboards. He went down to investigate. Sister Marie Catherine beamed happily as he pointed an inquiring finger toward the fire. They were so good, these native women, she told him; they had promised to do the washing with her after class. And for the next two or three days they brought unaccustomed energy to the task, wide-eyed at Sister Marie Catherine's laundry methods and at the resulting whiteness of the linen.

Meanwhile, Sister Mary Cornelia converted her elderly Indians into a sort of altar society. Following her sign directions, they cleaned up the sacristy, scrubbed the unpainted, pinewood tabernacle, nailed down the unfastened floor boards, all the while learning reverence from her actions, and so coming to a childlike knowing of their pastor's words as he prepared them for First Communion. Now, Sister Loyola observed, as she inspected the rough sacristy press filled with spotless linens, St. Paul's Church is really clean. Next it should have some white paint and Sister Mary Aloysia's skill.

At that thought, Sister Loyola went to kneel before the tabernacle to thank God that the doctor had brought the right medicine with him from the Falls. Without it, they would have lost Sister Mary Aloysia. As it was, she would require weeks to recover fully. That early September day she was sitting up, benefiting by the warm sun, busy with brushes and India ink in making a small copy of the Vicar-General's *Catholic Ladder* from his large original hanging, cracked and worn, on the wall beside her.

Sister Mary Aloysia reproduced the *Ladder* in quite exact proportions, thirty-four by seven inches, on fairly heavy, light-brown paper pasted on close-woven linen. She bound the edges with narrow, blue silk ribbon, sewing it on with a small and even basting stitch. She tacked the lower end to a wooden roll one half inch in diameter, and attached a piece of tanned cowhide to the upper end for protection when the *Ladder* would be rolled up. With fine-pointed pen and tiny paintbrush, she produced an example of artistic perfection. One can almost turn the pages of her New and Old Testaments. The stones of her Tower of Babel can still be counted. Her Star of Bethlehem shines like a little diamond.[3]

Looking up from her brush painting, Sister Mary Aloysia sighed over the very slow progress on the convent. For two weeks or more the work had been almost at a standstill. She picked up a sketch she had made for an antependium to replace the white tablecloth which Sister Mary Cornelia had substituted for the yellowed cotton rag they found sagging from a row of tacks as an altar front. If she had a large piece of canvas she could work in the design in oils. That was Father DeSmet's suggestion. Poor Father DeSmet had been ill for several days, too. Worry always upset him and he would worry until he found his mission site.

But Father DeSmet improved rapidly after the arrival of Father Gregory Mengarini, S. J., who had had to steal away from the Flatheads, as they would have insisted on coming with him, he said, to see Father DeSmet.[4] They were so good, the Flatheads, he declared, "a people of saints." But the goodness of the Flatheads did not prevent Father Mengarini from looking like a tramp, Sister Loyola told her Sisters when they found her washing and mending his wardrobe. And these rags were all he possessed, she added, as

she replaced his old handkerchiefs with new ones. In the
Rockies, it seemed, one lived just as the savages lived. Perhaps that was necessary at first, but Sister Loyola thought
that the sooner civilized standards were presented to the native, the better. That was why she wanted to hurry the
school to completion. Bring the savage into contact with
civilization as soon as possible. At this mention of the school,
Sister Marie Catherine and Sister Mary Cornelia exchanged
glances. Could their Superior's first altercation with their
pastor have anything to do with the lack of progress on the
building?

Out of his 640-acre claim, the Vicar-General had assigned
the Sisters a forty-acre tract for cultivation in support of the
school and community. In his mind this tract was mission
land which he would not think of alienating. The Sisters
might use it as long as they wished, and he hoped that as a
highly esteemed unit of the mission family they would always retain it. But Sister Loyola was not satisfied with this
arrangement. For the sake of security, she demanded a contract that would give the Sisters an outright claim to the
land. When, hurt and perplexed, the pastor demurred, she
held politely to her point. If the community could not be
autonomous, she would have to consider taking the Sisters
elsewhere.[5] With that, she wrote to Mère Constantine, explaining in her convincing manner the necessity of such a
contract.

Sister Loyola's attitude may be attributable to the custom
of the era which made the security of a community depend
on a self-sufficient boarding school. It may have arisen partly
from her own experiences as a Superior, with property and
planning in her own hands. And she may have been acting
under the influence of Father Anthony Langlois, who returned to his directorship of St. Joseph's College in mid-
September, and who was at that time openly critical of the
Vicar-General's administration.[6] Certainly, at a later date,
Sister Loyola was swayed by Father Langlois' judgment.

It is possible, too, that she had herself begun to notice the
worrisome, sensitive strain in her pastor's disposition, a
character weakness which annoyed the restless and change-

able Father Langlois. It may be significant that in December of that year, before departing for his consecration, Bishop-elect Blanchet assigned Father Langlois to Cowlitz, and turned St. Joseph's over to Father Boldoc. Father De-Voss was then appointed chaplain of the Sisters of Notre Dame, certainly with Blanchet's approval.[7]

But Sister Loyola prevailed in the matter of the property. Her pastor yielded because he really admired her zeal and ability. He thought of his fine cassock, of the church transformed from an ugly hovel, of the First Communion classes in the field. Sister Loyola accepted this concession as the result of reflection on his part and turned with her usual energy to the completion of her convent. It was high time.

The hired carpenters, probably Americans from the Falls, seem to have stopped work entirely after mid-September because the pastor could not meet their demands for a raise in their already exorbitant wages.[8] It was just as well; their work could hardly have been more careless. After the harvest a few Canadian farmers would be available, but the Sisters did not wait for them. When Sister Loyola announced the prospect of thirty Canadian boarders, adding that as soon as these began to pay tuition the school could care for Indian children, orphans and otherwise, her Sisters took the tools in hand. Now she found them with yardstick, saw, and hammer, fitting door and window frames, while Sister Marie Catherine puttied in glass panes and delicate Sister Mary Aloysia planed rough floor boards.

In the sadness that he felt over this hard labor, the pastor consoled himself with the fact that nineteen Indian women, between sixteen and sixty, could pass his examination for First Communion. That was the result of six hard hours spent daily by two Sisters at the almost impossible task of memorized answers which he considered necessary. Certainly he had worked zealously, too, so zealously that one poor old woman pointed to her forehead and sadly said, "Look Father, nothing more can enter there." What a shame to worry the poor things with formula! Their simple faith prompted them to bring enough food for days and to sleep in the forest rather than miss class. The Sisters discovered one elderly woman quite famished because a dog had eaten up her two-day food supply. And how grateful they were. On their First Communion Day the Indian women brought the Sisters melons and potatoes and corn; the half-breeds brought butter and eggs.

It was the same with the children when they gathered on Sundays. They talked of nothing but the Sisters. When Sister Mary Aloysia rewarded her Sunday School pupils by taking them to St. Joseph's to see a statue of the Child Jesus, the children gazed enraptured. Afterward, grasping the little prizes Sister had prepared for each, they scampered off to their parents. Presently she heard a noisy concourse at the entrance; a throng of adults wanted to see the statue. As Sister explained the representaion to them, she saw in their eyes the same simple wonder that lightened those of their children. Listening to her words, many of them wept.

As the Sisters' larger boxes were still at the Falls, Sister Loyola set out one morning with Sister Mary Albine and a good old Indian woman whom the Vicar-General sent along as guide. At the Falls she found a grain boat that had brought down a cargo of wheat from French Prairie and bargained shrewdly with its owner for the transfer of some baggage from storage in one of McLoughlin's warehouses to Champoeg. There, too, shutting her eyes to the cost, she engaged a couple of carpenters to put a roof on her convent. Ten francs a day! Robbery!

The journey was otherwise worth while, for at the Falls the two Sisters heard their first item of outside news; a great forest fire had been raging near the fort at a point where several thousand bushels of wheat were stored, but after a week of struggle the men had it under control. It was not pleasant news, but it brought isolated St. Paul's into the course of events.

Home again, the Sisters found more news awaiting them. Father DeSmet had at last chosen a site for his central mission, so near that the Sisters could count on Jesuit Fathers as confessors and retreat masters. It might have been otherwise, since the Jesuits had been offered at a bargain the large and well-built academy which the Methodists were abandoning at the Falls. But this site lacked both wood and arable land, and Father DeSmet thought both necessary. In fact, Father DeSmet was so hard to please that the Vicar-General, after days of futile land-looking with him, offered him any spot he might choose on the St. Paul mission grant. Another period of DeSmet restlessness was ended. Selecting his site, he named it St. Francis Xavier and set down a lyric description of it in his notes. Sloping gently from a slight elevation to the shore of Lake Ignatius, he wrote, this land was ideally situated for a mission residence.[9]

Placing Father DeVoss in charge, Father DeSmet assigned Fathers Accolti, Vercruysse, and Ravalli to assist in starting this central mission. From this point, Father Vercruysse extended Jesuit missionary work to the Canadians at Grand Prairie, where he built a church, "the grandest in Willamette," while Father Ravalli became doctor as well as priest for the sick to be found in almost every Indian hut.[10] Father DeVoss, the only English-speaking Jesuit, devoted his energies to the Americans. With all this activity set afoot, Father DeSmet left for the interior with Father Mengarini, leaving the Sisters of Notre Dame quite saddened. In this new and difficult land it was hard to lose a strong friend. Fortunately, at his departure they were deep in preparations for the children's First Communion.

This time Father Demers was on hand to prepare the boys, leaving the girls to the Sisters. He was present when the Vicar-General began his examination in Chinook, and decided, as was quite evident, that the Sisters needed further training in the jargon. He must give them a few lessons. All very well, Sister Loyola observed, but where would they find time for study? When not cleaning or cooking, they were building their house. However, to the delight of all, the exacting Vicar-General passed thirty-three aspirants as well prepared. How the Sisters longed to pretty up the darlings with veils and wreaths! Instead, they submitted to the Chinook lessons while their Superior urged on the American carpenters. The roof, she insisted, must be finished by October sixteenth.

The roof was finished and the Sisters moved in with their

high hopes and mid-century artistic urges. Though it was at the end of the world, this would be a boarding school, a place of light in the wilderness. It was poor but it must be presentable. Of course, Sister Marie Catherine agreed, but above all, the prevailing forms of insect life must never get a start in it.

Most of the Sisters wrote proudly to Namur about their house, but their letters omitted the fact that upstairs they could see the sky where the carpenters had split the shingles and set the broken edges together unevenly. When the rain dripped in, the very first night, the Sisters brought up tubs and buckets and searched for the leaks by candlelight. Downstairs, the partitions of sun-dried brick, with clay for masonry, were soon dotted with apertures. There were no cupboards, no book presses, no school arrangements. The one of the three "spacious rooms" assigned for the chapel was as unfinished as the rest of the house. Upstairs was a large attic with board partitions and a floor of planks not yet nailed down. Ten to twelve francs a day! They would need six weeks or more to make the place habitable, Sister Loyola remarked; her face had the little frown that was becoming her habitual response to Sister Marie Catherine's comments on the fittingness of accepting primitive conditions.

As Father DeVoss now had two lay brothers from the mountains to work on the new buildings at St. Francis Xavier, he generously sent Brother Francis to help the Sisters. A hard worker, but not a skilled craftsman, Brother Francis looked on in astonishment as Sister Marie Catherine and Sister Mary Aloysia worked with expert inventiveness. They had filled the openings in the roof with rich forest moss. Now they were making shelves and benches out of ends of boards.

Brother Francis set up the stove that the pastor had brought with him from Canada in 1838, placing it, as directed, between dining room and classrooms, and wiring up the long pipe to the ceiling on its way to the chimney. This boxlike stove is treasured today in the Museum at Champoeg, one of the few existing articles used by the Sis-

ters at St. Paul.[11] It required great quantities of short-sawed
wood, but it was such an efficient little heater that Sister
Loyola managed to acquire three others like it. Later on,
when tempting little ads about the new "French stoves" appeared in the first newspapers, she sold these first heaters
and invested in the more modern devices with their ovens
and other advantages. But at best their house was always
cold in winter, standing as it did in the middle of a bare,
forty-acre field. They also planned an outside bakehouse,
as there was no bake oven nor room for one in their temporary lean-to kitchen.

Amid the din of hammers and saws Sister Loyola made
out a prospectus for the good Canadians who wished to enter
their daughters as boarders. These people, she found, had
no money or very little. They bartered their grain at Fort
Vancouver or the Falls for flour and such necessaries as they
could not produce on their farms. Adjusting her bill to this
simple scheme of things, Sister Loyola asked, for a three-
month period, the payment of 100 pounds of flour; 4 pounds
of grease; 3 bags of peas; 1 bag of salt; 3 dozen eggs; 25
pounds of lard (or 36 pounds of beef); 4 pounds of candles;
1 bag of potatoes; 1 pound of tea; and 4 pounds of rice. The
Sisters' "brilliant prospectus," Father DeSmet playfully called
it.

With thirty or forty boarders on this basis, it would be
possible to sustain the destitute and orphaned children of
the area. These latter could be taught to cultivate the land,
to care for the house, to work in the dairy that Sister Loyola
was planning, even to help Sister Norbertine to clear the
acres of brushwood. Thus they would become self-supporting. As Sister Loyola made her plans, she could see poor
Sister Norbertine trying to coax two Indian boys to imitate
her energy, and looking quite disgusted at their tendency
to fatigue. But it would be otherwise with the native child
removed entirely from the native milieu. All the Sisters felt
certain of that. And as adults, what wonders these trained
Indian girls would work among their people!

Sister Loyola glanced again at her prospectus. She hoped
this payment in produce would fairly soon give place, at

least to some extent, to money payment. Until their own land provided their living, it was an acceptable expedient; but she needed money. With money she could send orders to Canadian cities with east-bound brigades, orders for decent clothing material, for articles that would give tone to this prairie school, for proper furnishings for parlors. She thought of poor Sister Mary Aloysia trying to make a rough room look like a chapel.

However she managed to do it, Sister Mary Aloysia produced an effect that charmed even her Superior. Here on an altar made by Brother Francis and the Sisters, she placed Señora Riverodero's gilded tabernacle and the candlesticks that had lighted *l'Infatigable's* gloom. She looped gracefully some soft old drapes that here looked oddly luxurious, and set little adoring angels gazing romantically at the rough ceiling. Beyond a doubt, the chapel in the Mother House was not more beautiful! When Father DeVoss raised the lovely monstrance from Ixelles in first Benediction, the Sisters wept for joy. Surely the Blessed Lord loved this dwelling on the Willamette!

Father DeVoss walked the half-mile from "the Lake" each morning to celebrate Mass in that little chapel. In return the Sisters laundered the Jesuits' altar linens and albs, not in the least an easy task, since for many months the washing continued to require hauling of water from the creek and the building of an outdoor fire. To Sister Marie Catherine's annoyance, the wind often blew the flames away from under the caldron, until an Indian boy, in a passing moment of industry, made a windbreak of boards and branches. Wash day brought many a trial, but at every annoyance Sister Marie Catherine had only to look at Sister Mary Cornelia and Sister Mary Aloysia trudging up from the creek with a huge bucket between them, smiling and reciting short prayers together, or at Sister Norbertine, half Amazon, half desert saint, doing violence with hoe and spade and axe to ancient blackberry bushes.

The labors of that arduous October were broken now and then by a visit from the pastor. Then the Sisters gathered around him in whichever spacious room the few chairs happened to be, to listen to his plans, which seemed always to center around the Falls. With a victorious little smile, he retold the story of Lee, and Waller, and Gary, of Jesse Applegate's survey of "Oregon City." This spot, he said, was in Doctor McLoughlin's seasoned judgment the natural center of the area south of the Columbia. If this territory should fall to the Americans, as it well might, Oregon City would be a state capital. Some nine hundred Americans had reached eastern Oregon that summer, and certainly next year would bring a greater number. These settlers would find their way into the valley, would gravitate to the Falls. So the Sisters really must prepare to accept the good doctor's invitation to his city. At this, Sister Loyola's expression became so concentrated and eager that Sister Marie Catherine and Sister Mary Cornelia exchanged worried glances, and Sister Mary Aloysia looked at her calloused hands and thought of her piano still in storage at the fort. Build another house?

With his sensitive penetration, the pastor read those signs of caution. Of course, he said, they would need more Sisters before beginning another foundation. But had not several more volunteers submitted their names to the Mother General? And if she understood the need, she would consent to send a second band, would she not?

He was, in fact, planning a voyage to Europe, to interest the Propagation of the Faith in the tremendous possibilities of the Pacific Northwest, or rather to confirm interest that Father DeSmet had already aroused, and to secure recruits among young clerics and students in Continental seminaries. The Jesuits were doing fine work in the mission, but they might be recalled at any time. What the country needed was a strong, local clergy. Yet he frowned and sighed as he spoke of a local clergy; and looking at one another, the Sisters recalled Father Accolti's remarks about a bishopric and the Vicar-General's unwillingness to accept it.[12]

The Papal briefs had been almost a year en route when they reached Bishop-elect Blanchet early in November. Even then, in his dread of the responsibility, he kept the communication secret for several days, casting about for means to avoid it. But as other eyes had taken note of the title on the envelope, he soon found himself supported by the encouragement and congratulation that his hesitant nature needed.

Certainly the joy of the Sisters could hardly have been more sincere, with Sister Loyola perhaps the most delighted of all. Their pastor had his faults, she admitted to Sister Mary Cornelia, but he was a man of vision, not afraid to set his hand to the great things of God. He was a holy priest, too, and extremely mortified. And straightway she wrote these opinions to Mère Constantine, relating as an example of his asceticism how he had gently chided the Sisters for sweetening the water that they offered him after his exhausting hours with his Indians. The Savior, he said, had been given gall to drink.

Yet there was the matter of the contract. If Mère Constantine should approve of this measure, as Sister Loyola hoped, she might herself ask Bishop Blanchet for a written statement. She would, at least, discuss the matter with him, and despite his present kind and paternal attitude one could not be perfectly sure what attitude he might then take. With her laudatory letter, Sister Loyola repeated with emphasis her argument for holding property independent of mission control, and hoped her pastor would not revert to his earlier stand.[13] At the Mother House, he would learn of her high esteem and that of her community for him. He would discover that she had prepared the way for his request for a second band of Sisters. Satisfied with these things, he might decide not to make an issue of the acres at St. Paul.

Sister Loyola was in a commending mood that day. The "saintly" Father DeVoss, she wrote, was giving the Sisters a retreat, but at her request he had omitted some of the exercises so that they might also do some letter writing. One and all, those letters bewailed the fact that not a single line from Namur had thus far reached them. That was what it meant to live in one of the outposts of the world. Yet, in their stilted sentences, they all assured Mère Constantine that the Willamette now seemed closer to the heart of things. A Canadian who had acted as guide for some priests, from Cincinnati to the Rockies, had finally reached the Willamette, bringing them letters from their eastern Sisters with bits of news from home. And Father DeSmet had sent back word that His Holiness, Pope Gregory XVI, had approved the Rule of the Congregation in July. Besides, a valley that could boast a Bishop-elect was not a forgotten land.

When Father DeVoss had his retreatants back into line again, he regaled them with accounts of the very dirty but good-hearted savages of the Rockies, accounts that they found credible enough as they looked at the speaker, still haggard after his mountain experiences. How strange it was that some, like the always ailing Father DeSmet, could live through it all and still love it. But Father Accolti was already showing an aversion for work among the natives and was talking of Oregon City and progress in the valley.[14]

After retreat the Sisters resumed activities in an atmosphere of optimism and happy cooperation; even Sister Norbertine gave gracious and smiling assistance at indoor chores. Soon there would be an even more important event than the opening of school, the last visit of the Bishop-elect before embarking on his voyage to Quebec, a circuitous journey, for the ship *Columbia* was scheduled to sail first to Honolulu, from there to Liverpool, and thence to Boston. Such lengthy voyages were common in those days, when the alternative was to wait a year or two for another opportunity. With no other choice at hand, the new prelate accepted Captain Duncan's offer; besides, he was not loath to interest distant peoples in his new bishopric.

The Bishop-elect's own mood was radiant as he estimated apostolic accomplishments since his arrival with Father Demers, at the end of this "most providential year."[15] That inventory included: "9 missions, 5 of these in Lower Oregon; 11 churches and chapels; 6000 pagans converted; 1000 Canadians brought back to their religious duties; 2 educational establishments; 15 missionaries, without speaking of the treasure the mission has in the persons of the good religious of Notre Dame de Namur."[16] To be sure, Bishop-elect Blanchet tended in his enthusiasm to round-number estimates. The 6,000 savages must have included many a gaping Indian, come for a first look but too lazy to pursue further instruction. Among the 1,000 Canadians he must have counted transient brigade men who received the Sacraments at the fort. Yet certainly with his tremendous zeal he alone had reached great numbers. And as he knelt in prayer in the convent chapel after his last visit, Sister Loyola thought that no other could have deserved his new dignity so richly.

CHAPTER 10

Sainte Marie de Willamette

With all the clatter and babel, one would have thought at least a hundred pupils were being enrolled that December second instead of only eleven boarders and a few day pupils who lived within walking distance. These and their three little orphans, that was all. As there is no name list one can only guess that "comfortable" families, like the Béliques, were represented among the boarders.[1]

Comfortable or not, their native or half-breed mothers provided outfits that quite shocked the Sisters. For bed, each brought a coarse mat, "une natte de jonc," a blanket or two thin ones, "bien minces," and a pillow; wardrobes included "an old chemise" and a dress all patched, "une robe toute rapiécée." It was the shortage of European merchandise, Sister Loyola explained to her Sisters; a good blanket cost ten dollars![2] The orphans, of course, brought no blanket, nor anything but the scanty rags they wore.

It was harder to explain the nonchalant attitude of the "comfortable" families toward the splendid prospectus. They offered apparently what was at hand, substituting one article for another without explanation, quite upsetting Sister Loyola's neat bookkeeping scheme. If money was out of fashion, "peu en vogue dans ce pays," so was exactness. In one matter, however, there was unfailing contribution. All brought with them a "prodigious number of certain insects," records the usually reticent Sister Mary Aloysia. On these the Belgian Sisters waged an unceasing though discouraging warfare, for from every holiday spent in cabin or hut, their pupils returned with fresh supplies.

159

Cleanliness first, was Sister Mary Albine's battle cry. So off came the faded old red or yellow ribbons or, as often as not, the hem of an old handkerchief that tied the coarse black hair. Almost every poor scalp was marked with unhealed irritations. Books and classes would have to wait; blankets, mats, and clothing were taken out in the sun while three or four Sisters worked on the surprised young heads. In Belgium they had not foreseen this specific problem; now proximity kept them constantly mindful of it. After one day of it, Sister Mary Albine sat down and wrote a request that she prayed would reach the Mother House; if medical science knew of a remedy for that horrible scalp condition, it would be a mercy to send it, she pleaded. And none prayed more fervently for such help than Sister Marie Catherine. As the children's dormitory was her charge, she slept in all too close proximity to the source of trouble; her bed of planks was attached to four posts in a corner of that room and hidden from the pupils' view by cotton curtains.

Retiring was a simple matter for her primitive charges. When they had got through night prayer, mumbling a little but mostly just listening to Sister Mary Aloysia's gentle voice, they climbed heavily upstairs, unrolled mats and blankets, spread these on the floor according to custom, removed their dresses (in some cases only because Sister insisted on this bit of ritual), settled their pillows, rolled up for the night, and went directly to sleep after their astonishing first day. Sister Marie Catherine slipped downstairs and called Sister Mary Aloysia to come up and survey the scene. Sight and odor brought a realistic simile to the lips of that fastidious lady. Just like a cemetery, she whispered.

Yet even with their faded hairbows these little ladies displayed the vanity that impelled their mothers to wear a pair of manufactured shoes, incongruous with a ragged native costume. In lieu of stockings, they would fasten to their shoe tops pieces of cloth, knee length and ornamented with beads or imitation pearls. Sister Loyola sent one of these curious outfits to Namur. Adornment was everything; a Rosary won for good conduct was at once converted into a necklace.

And with this vanity went a less amusing strain of indocility. Surely Father DeSmet must have had only the Flatheads in mind when he told of lamblike behavior. In an age when European schoolgirls curtsied and mumbled "Oui, ma Soeur," these maidens flashed black-eyed danger signals before Sister could finish her directive and assailed her astonished ears with a determined "Wake, wake" (No, no). If Sister's wish met with approval, the rejoinder was a commendatory "Kloshe" (That's good). Stalling for time, the frequent reaction of the more pliant, was indicated by the blunt "Ekita maika" (What do you want?). Both Sister Loyola and Sister Mary Aloysia quickly learned how to employ this brief interval with tact.

Not so Sister Marie Catherine, who made the sad mistake of showing her astonishment. Yet after many an uproar, she too was accepted as a friend by even the most willful. Such was one little maiden whose sullen resistance one day forced Sister to refer the problem to her Superior. Sister Loyola felt that authority must be upheld. She disapproved of the rod, but in this instance she thought that a slight taste of it was necessary. And with an eye on inducing Sister Marie Catherine to employ changed tactics, she ordered her to inflict the penalty herself. Sister was desperate; she had quite expected to leave the recalcitrant in her Superior's hands. She said a hurried prayer and called the child into a vacant room where she reproached her, not for her misdeed, but for getting her teacher into such a predicament. And with a light twig from the woodbox, Sister gently tapped the culprit's hand. Thus far there was no change in the stolid little face, so Sister spread the little wide skirt over a chair and administered to it a vicarious and dramatic punishment. Straightway repentant, the little half-breed burst into tears and promised complete reform.

With her amused understanding, Sister Mary Aloysia had few of these crises to record. Children of the Willamette, she insisted, were never malicious. One had only to remember that their mothers were savages, and that though in many cases their fathers had had good Canadian training, they were too busy wresting a living from their fields to give their children much attention. The brightest of them must not be confronted with ideas; one and all, they could be impressed only by externals. These children would burst into tears at the sight of a crucifix. At the end of the first month, Sister Mary Aloysia recorded improvement in all of them. As an example, she wrote of a newly baptized seven-year-old who was withdrawn from school to assist her mother. At home her incessant chatter about the Sisters and what they had taught her so delighted her parents that they brought her back at the first opportunity for more training. These children were intelligent, too; in two weeks they mastered "the first two tablets of the alphabet." Some had nice voices and in time would become "good musicians."

On feast days they sang to their hearts' content and entered with zest into Belgian boarding-school customs observed at Christmas and Epiphany. Joyously they passed from the awed wonder of Midnight Mass and Crèche to the fun of drawing lots for the Three Kings, this with an eye on the gaudy costumes that Sister Mary Albine was rigging up for the winners.[3] And the Sisters entered into local customs, too. Hearing that the Canadian custom of Paternal Blessing was observed at New Year's, they practiced their pupils in kneeling respectfully to receive it. Drama came easily. And delighted with the reverent pose and the sweeping curtsy that followed their benediction, some of the fathers demanded a repeat performance; one bestowed a series of blessings for joy at the light Indian grace of his offspring.

January brought reports and prizes in the best Belgian tradition, with everyone winning some accolade on the principle that there is some good in all. Mothers squinted at marks which had to be explained to them. Fathers lectured lengthily on the need of aiming at the heights, while daughters, aware of Sister Loyola's proximity, stood in ramrod attentiveness, hands by their sides. On one of these "Good Notes" occasions, an illiterate half-breed father turned to Sister Mary Albine for enlightenment. Sister handed the card to his daughter, who produced something close to ecstasy in her proud parent by clumsily spelling out the words for him.

As Sister Mary Aloysia explained to Mère Constantine, the

"branches of learning" had to be "more numerous in Oregon than in Belgium." At the outset, their pastor had said they must teach the girls to cook, wash, sweep, even to milk cows and make butter. The daughters in turn would teach these skills to their mothers, who were shiftless chiefly because they were ignorant. So by way of home economics classes the girls were rotated through household and barnyard charges, which in many cases the Sisters were only then learning themselves.

Sister Marie Catherine specialized in the wash and though, as she said, she had "no special training in the function," her pupils in their more active moods regarded her methods with wonder.[4] Living was improved, as well as the domestic "branches" and Sister Marie Catherine's peace of mind, when Brother Francis completed the bakehouse, a separate building in which he constructed a combination bake oven and boiler. With its earth floor, it was more of a shelter than a room, so cold by reason of its wide cracks that Sister Loyola moved one of the four stoves into it. This bakehouse became her special sanctum; being the best cook in the group, she made that branch her contribution to the curriculum. But even she lacked experience in bread making, a skill seemingly overlooked by Mère Constantine when making her selection for Oregon. It must be simple enough, Sister Marie Catherine told Sister Mary Albine, but trying it together, they produced "something more like bricks." It was a long time before any of them mastered this "branch," partly because the oven was not a complete success, partly because the flour they received was often inferior.

Providing food ceased to be such a great problem as the number of boarders increased to twenty at Christmas and thirty-one at Easter. The families of these later comers seem to have been more "comfortable," certainly more generous. At least one was an American, a young Lutheran who was baptized just before Lent. But during the heavy rains, attendance fell off for some weeks as the dirt roads became impassable. Fields lay under water and from those dismal stretches arose the nightly concert of frogs, which Sister Mary Aloysia reported to her European readers as the hissing of serpents. That was nothing! They were often awakened at

night by the "roaring of tigers and the howling of wolves." [5]
These last, she said, boldly carried off chickens and even small
pigs, in which case much pitiful squealing supplemented the
uproar.

These first Sisters never quite mastered the flora and fauna
of the country. To Sister Loyola the deer was a wild cow
that nibbled their plants. One had to be brave, she wrote
dramatically, to walk in the woods of Willamette,* for it was
not rare to meet tigers and wolves in open day. And even
Brother Francis, it would seem, was not sure of his bobcats;
he reported one morning that he had just escaped a tiger
by putting his horse into gallop.

After the rains, spring brought rustic beauty and the consolation of another little First Communion group. It brought
another essential "branch," too, in the shape of gardening.
Some good Canadians plowed, the newly-hired Baptiste
plainted grain, Sister Norbertine set out rows of young apple
trees, saplings from HBC farms,[6] and gave general directions
about the planting of carrots, melons, pumpkins, and cucum-
bers. But alas for the new "branch." Spring languor laid a
heavy hand on the young *Canadiennes* and a still more prostrating one on the young natives. Both now viewed the heavy
work of the Sisters as a matter of course, but not as an activity
to be shared. Coaxing seemed futile and delayed the work.
Still the Sisters hoped that with time they might enkindle a
spark of industry; they failed to see that the Indian would
always resist change, that, with a few exceptions, generations
would be needed to overcome the idle strain in the half-breed.
Inertia followed hard upon action in both.

Certainly it was overambitious to attempt to bring all the
acres under cultivation at once, to care for chickens and six
or eight cows, to make butter and cheese. Without Sister
Norbertine, so strong, energetic, and methodical, it would
have been impossible. Sister Loyola knew that her taciturn
directions about farming were always right; the strenuous
outdoors was her domain. In the kitchen it was quite the
contrary. In vain Sister Loyola entrusted Sister Norbertine

* Through this period the missionaries often referred to the mission at
St. Paul as Willamette.

with the dinner. At noon she would be nervous and bungling, trying to start the fire. In her effort to be on time, she would cook a supply of salt meat for three or four days ahead. If she managed the meat and potatoes, she forgot the dessert. When she set homemade cheese before them instead of the apples she had forgotten to bake, Sister Loyola signed her off and took over that charge again herself.

On his first visit to St. Paul as Vicar-General, Father Demers deplored in his turn the colossal labor performed by the Sisters, with the Superior cooking for both community and pupils. But they were in good health, at any rate. The building program was under way, or at least Father Boldoc was about to start the Sisters' new chapel and farm buildings. That was good, and the Bishop would be pleased. In fact, Father Demers' great concern just then was building; he had his own colossal task to complete before the Bishop's return. At Oregon City he had already begun a church, which he spoke of as "the ornament of our growing city," and a parish house. At Fort Vancouver, HBC had donated land for a chapel and residence. Most important of all was the plan for cathedral and bishop's residence at St. Paul. But workmen were demanding "two or three piasters a day," for which he did not blame them, however, considering the cost of living. Really, the Bishop should return with "a well furnished purse to keep us from bankruptcy." Busy with his building plans and his great desire for the return of his old friend, Father Demers put aside the thought of the Herculean labors of a small group of teaching Sisters at Willamette.[7]

Father Boldoc, too, wrote buoyantly of his own projects, other than the cathedral and the Sisters' chapel, to be eighty by thirty feet. He was about to start an addition to the convent, charged as he was by the Bishop with "the temporal affairs of the Sisters of Notre Dame." Engrossed in these plans and the principalship of the boys' school, he seemed not to notice the spading and planting. In a way, it could not be helped; in a way, it was the price the Sisters were paying for their independent claim on the land. Sister Loyola would have objected to the statement about the "temporal affairs" of the Sisters; she would have said that chapel and extension were part of the original agreement; the Sisters were managing their own temporal affairs.

That same spring Father DeSmet returned to St. Francis Xavier, elated as usual over recent experiences, but most of all over his meeting with Father Nobili at the Fort Vancouver. Father Nobili had been hammering away at native tongues for the last eight months; he was now ready for the wilderness. Besides caring for employees of the fort, he had baptized and prepared for death the numerous victims of a recent epidemic in the area. This was the sort of news Father DeSmet liked to hear. It was better than building, better than trying to Europeanize the savage. He rewarded Father Nobili by sending him into the wilds of British Columbia. Still, he praised Father Vercruysse, too, for the good mission he had just given at St. Paul's to fulfill the Bishop's parting request, and in which he had made an issue of contributing to the cathedral. He was happy to see the Sisters and happy to know their school was progressing. He approved the name they had chosen for it and Sister Loyola's plan to have a niche made above the front door for their large statue of Mary Immaculate. He was pleased with Father Boldoc's success because it meant the reclaiming of the Canadians' half-breed sons.[8]

But for some unaccountable reason Father DeSmet was not pleased with the management of affairs at St. Francis Xavier. He therefore removed Father DeVoss, assigning him to assist Vicar-General Demers at Oregon City. Thus the Sisters lost the chaplain whose saintliness they so much admired.[9] Their loss was the gain of the little city with its growing number of Americans; there he made apostolic use of his English to bring about a number of remarkable conversions, among them that of Peter Burnett, first governor of California. But zealous and successful as he was among the whites, Father DeVoss, like Father Nobili, preserved his pristine dedication to the native. He worked zealously among the Indians around Oregon City and in four years, from 1847 to 1851, he converted almost the entire tribe of Kettle Falls Indians on the upper Columbia. There whites and half-breeds of the local HBC post led exemplary Christian lives

under his influence. His greatest faults were the driving zeal
that at last broke him down and his discouragement when
his converts lapsed into their former evil ways.

Father DeSmet now placed Father Accolti in charge at
St. Francis and appointed him chaplain for the Sisters. He
took up the latter office, it would seem, just in time to encounter Sister Marie Catherine's spiritual crisis, the account
of which she later wrote in her half-humorous and completely
extroverted fashion. Worried over the strenuous work her
Superior was performing, Sister Marie Catherine persuaded
Sister Mary Cornelia and Sister Mary Aloysia to divide her
own teaching duties between them and thus free her to do all
the cooking. They managed to do so and Sister Loyola agreed,
perhaps in view of Sister Marie Catherine's inaptitude as a
teacher of young natives. Yet the Superior had at least a
slight misgiving, for though Sister was now a fairly good cook
she was beginning to exhibit traits of absorbed forgetfulness
which might grow with solitary work in the kitchen, to the
disadvantage of both cook and dinner. The fear seemed
justified. Passing the kitchen door, Sister Loyola often found
the new cook wrapped in prayer and shedding tears of devotion. It was the same at community prayers; midway in a
psalm at Vespers, Sister's voice would die off, a disconcerting circumstance in so small a choir. And do what she would,
she could not follow the formal Ignatian meditation book.

In keeping with her time, Sister Loyola considered this
departure quite unfitting in an active congregation. She
insisted on the common meditation book. When the voice
dropped off, she tapped the ecstatic one gently with her hymnal. She made it a point to visit the kitchen often. She told
poor Sister Marie Catherine bluntly enough that her flights
were evidence of self-occupation, and ought to be abandoned
in the interests of the mission. But Father Accolti was of
another mind. Once and for all he freed his penitent from
the bonds of the formal meditation book. But he advised her,
of course, not to allow her own devotion to distract her from
either work or community prayers.

In view of Sister Marie Catherine's emotional bent, these
states of prayer could well have been an induced escape. On

the other hand, her docility toward her Superior seems to rule out self-centeredness; when Sister Loyola inadvisedly tried the effect of a bit of ridicule, she encountered no resentment. Although the matter of spiritual direction was then not clearly defined, and although most Superiors in that era would have upheld her right, Sister Loyola yielded tactfully to Father Accolti and so maintained his good will. And as Sister Marie Catherine's spiritual ways became more normal, she forgot the whole affair. One thing, however, she did not forget; in a matter of conscience, Sister Marie Catherine could take a courageous stand.

As individualistic as Sister Marie Catherine was, she cooperated heartily with all her Superior's projects, even with those which seemed to her to reach beyond the demands of their primitive setting. And Sister Loyola tended from the start to reach beyond those demands. At their first closing exercises, for instance, their pupils appeared in white uniforms, so that the Sisters "were transported to a boarding school in Belgium." Yet what those white dresses cost that overworked little community may be easily conjectured. And coming gradually to hear these little boasts, Mère Constantine wisely disapproved. They should not attempt, she wrote, to imitate the Continental institutions; they should leave these simple people simple, teach them to keep house well and raise good families. Oregon was not Europe, and the Sisters must remember the difference. It was true that in Europe pupils did not see their teachers working in gardens, but it was well for the mission girls to see the Sisters so employed, even though they failed to assist very much. The sight would give the children a wholesome reverence for the soil; it would be the first step toward gracious living. If maintaining the primitive spirit was a great good in Mère Constantine's eyes, so also was adaptability.[10]

The drawn-out closing exercises would have furnished abundant psychological effect without the white uniforms. As literary and musical events marked the last days of the school term, the walls of Sainte Marie rang with parental praises. In recitation and song, classes and individuals demonstrated varying degrees of progress in French. The highest achievement was a conversation piece entitled "La Création," in which the most advanced pupils glibly explained Genesis to one another. As Sister Loyola's feast day occurred conveniently that week, the group presented this chef-d'oeuvre in her honor, the preview serving also as dress rehearsal before performance as the grand finale on the school's first "Exhibition Day." And in accord with "the usages of American institutions," there had to be a public examination. To be sure, the questions were prepared by the Sisters, not by a school board. Father Demers consented to come and conduct a preliminary test with experienced Father Boldoc beside him.

Both were satisfied, and on the "great event" next day the public was duly astonished at the progress in the three R's, the recitations, and the magnificent Creation piece. Memory was all. Hearing that verbal stroke and parry in Chinook-jointed French, one could only conjecture the comprehension behind the flashing eyes. Failure of one cue might have undone them all. But in his "allocution" to admiring parents and friends, Father Demers declared this eight-month accomplishment nothing short of marvelous. Then he conferred the premiums for all the degrees of honor in the various branches, a lengthy procedure that included every name. It was over. Indian mothers hugged their darlings; Canadian fathers had more than ever to say.

A picnic in the woods gave that wonderful first closing a more fitting note. First a very special breakfast, "à la fourchette," and a hurried doing-up of household and farmyard duties. Then the scramble for the woods, stopping only to gather berries on the way. A shout from older girls on ahead announced the discovery of a fine place for lunch under the tall pines. Sister Mary Aloysia unfolded white tablecloths and the girls spread them on the soft pine needles. Best of all, old Baptiste, with a huge covered basket. Hot cakes! So, after all, Sister Mary Albine and Sister Marie Catherine have not quite succeeded with their secret. On such an occasion, one saw love and gratitude in those noncommital black eyes. No side remarks in Chinook! Of course not, when there was no bell, no class, no definite duty; when the holiday brought back the days of long past generations, pushing heavily against the new forces to order. How good the Sisters were to plan this happy day. One must help them over the rough places in the path and hold back the thorny briar to let them pass.

In their best moments, those forest children, half-breed and pure Indian alike, aspired to throw off the torpor of their race. That was clear from the tears shed by some of them on the eve of vacation. Log house and hut had squalor to offer them; boarding school was order and brightness; Sister Loyola was in some way the cause thereof and so to be admired even though she ordered one about. And there was always Sister Mary Aloysia! How very good! She rarely made one write *Je tâcherai de mieux faire* as did Sister Marie Catherine. *En français, vingt fois, ma chère enfant!* "En français." Always "en français"!

When the farm cart arrived on the last proud morning, proud daughter led wondering mother to the grand sewing display—eighty graceful dresses of wool and cotton brought by the Sisters from Belgium, cut out and fitted by Sister Mary Aloysia and Sister Mary Albine. These two were made by daughter herself, except of course, for the cutting and fitting; next year she will learn that. But she can wash and iron very well, Sister Loyola assures the mother. And of course, father will buy a washboard and flatirons at Oregon City. Little wonder that Sister Loyola had to refuse five applications for the autumn term. *Canadiennes,* little and big, now wanted to be seen at church on Sunday in pretty dresses.

Unfortunately no roster of names comes down from this prairie school. Indian misses would bear such tribal names as Mary Clatsop or Josephine Chinook. But certainly Sister Loyola must have enrolled twelve-year-old Sophie Bélique, whom Vicar-General Blanchet baptized at the age of seven, together with little brother Pierre and baby sister Geneviève, in the log church at St. Paul in 1839. And the old record shows a few weeks later the marriage of their parents, Pierre Bélique and Geneviève Martin, and the legitimatizing of the three children (a very common note in the church records for the late thirties).[11] As both Pierre Bélique and Geneviève Martin's fathers were Canadian traders, the children's native strain descended from their nameless maternal grandmother. It would seem that young Geneviève Martin just grew; on the day of her marriage she could recall neither her father's Christian name nor her mother's tribe, to which the latter had probably returned in a moment of irresponsibility. At any rate, Sophie would represent one of Sister Loyola's "comfortable" families; she would be more *la petite Canadienne* than were most of her contemporaries.

Little Marie McKay, of school age in 1845, would hail from another "comfortable" family. The eldest child of Thomas McKay and Isabelle Montour, she was baptized at St. Paul on Christmas Day, 1839, the record entry following that of the blessing of the church bell.[12] Thomas McKay, the son of Marguerite McLoughlin by her earlier marriage to Alexander McKay, and Isabelle were married at Fort Vancouver on December 31, 1838. On that same day Isabelle was baptized, with John and Marguerite McLoughlin as godparents, but as the bride could not write, her scrawled X appears with their historic names and the frequently recurring initials, F.N.B. In 1839 Thomas McKay retired from HBC service for the second time and again settled at Willamette. Isabelle's father, Nicholas Montour, was the son of Canadian Nicholas Montour and a nameless Indian woman; her mother, Susan Umpreville, was also native. Thus little Marie McKay was a child of preponderantly native strain. Whether that fact shaped her attitudes toward things intellectual is problematic; she may have acquired her father's ambitious and active nature instead.

During the Sisters' summer retreat, Sister Loyola contended with the usual combination of laziness and good will as she guided the eight or ten girls who remained through vacation. On the whole, she said, they were then at their best, awed as they were by the complete silence of the retreatants. Certainly it is a comment on the discipline of the day that they asked Sister Loyola why the Sisters, who had done no wrong, should be thus in penance. However she worded it, they accepted her explanation as very nice, so nice, in fact, that they wanted "to be taken for Sisters" when they grew up. This being the case, why could they not also

have a retreat? Why not, Sister Loyola agreed; a very short
one, of course. Surely good Father DeVoss would come for
three days after school reopened. Good! Good! They washed
up the dishes; they swept the floors, all in self-imposed "penance." But when labor and silence presently lost flavor, the
future nuns gave piety full rein in extended visits of devotion to the statue of the Christ Child. When Sister Loyola
reminded them of a little chore in the garden, they signaled
piously in the direction of the statue. Well, said Sister
Loyola sweetly, there was nothing for it but to erect a shrine
at the scene of desired action, and with agreeable seriousness
she produced table, statuette, and candles.

Sudden zeal swept them into the project. Ma Soeur Su-
périeure was almost as nice as Sister Mary Aloysia, and as she
shifted casually from piety to the weeding project, the darlings went with her, heart and hand. On another occasion
indolence wrapped them round just when a rain threatened
to wet the supply of firewood. The very day for a pilgrimage,
Sister Loyola told them, and led them forth to the woodpile,
two by two, lustily singing a hymn. And as a suitable pil-
grim's sacrifice, each carried an armful of wood to shelter.

Sister Loyola kept her promise about the retreat, too, and
persuaded Father DeVoss to come from Oregon City. For
three days the girls moved about on tiptoe, heads bowed
but not without side glances (so as not to miss approval),
enjoying their own utter goodness as much as the ascetic retreat master's humorous stories told in easy French phrases
with plenteous sprinklings of Chinook. At the end, the most
difficult little half-breed came in tears to Sister Loyola. She
could in nowise stop weeping, she moaned, because of her
past life. But she was certain of one thing: she meant to be
taken for a Sister some day. She had written out her intention in strange French words and she confided the rumpled
paper to Sister Loyola, whom she begged to confront her
with the reminder should she forget her promise.

The Sisters had their doubts about even the best of their
older pupils who, after that retreat, talked about becoming
religious. It was true that some of them had improved. They

no longer sulked days on end, but they still looked furtively at one another when displeased and chattered so rapidly in Chinook that an expert would have found it hard to follow their meaning.

It was English rather than Chinook that worried the Sisters that second autumn, for now Father Demers had changed his mind about language needs. Americans would soon be everywhere. One had to know their language. Even the Indians would pick it up and forget Chinook. In October he wrote regretfully to Mère Constantine that the four teaching Sisters knew no more English than they had learned on the voyage; they always lacked time to study it. The pity was that the English-speaking population admired the school, and requests for classes conducted in English were being made on every side.[13]

A visitor during that first harvest would have realized why the Sisters were not learning English. Taking turns with the scythes, they cut the abundant barley crop. They picked the peas. They dug some fifty sacks of fine potatoes, amazed at the size and varied colors. Vegetables disappointed them a bit, but their pumpkins made up for that. What a place for pumpkins! Parents brought them by the dozens as though the Sisters' crop would not supply an army.

A fine harvest to be sure, despite the labor. Yet without money, the farm and the work were the school's security. How Sister Loyola longed for a little money! Money to add a wing to their overcrowded house; money to clothe the new orphans; money for various cherished plans, among them the erection of a shrine for the statue of Our Lady of Sorrows from Lima, a shrine to face the road so that, as in Belgium, passers would kneel and pray.

What an excellent beggar Sister Loyola becomes in her letters to Namur! How she longs for some of the good " half-cloth of our country." Ma Mère should see the cheap, coarse cotton sold at three dollars a yard in Oregon City. And if that apostolic soul, Sister Mary Xavier, is coming, as she surely will, with the second band of Sisters, will ma Mère just allow her to do a little begging before she departs? In all these needs she trusts in Providence, and thus obliquely associates her Mother General with that most dependable source of all good things.

Mère Constantine must have wondered at the proximity of rosy views to statements of labor and poverty. At the end of 1845, Sister Loyola told her of much progress, of regular mail, a fortnightly paper, of sessions of law and justice under the Provisional Government.[14] Civilization was drawing closer, centering arount Oregon City, where her own interest was centering, too. She would need the Sisters who were " no doubt coming" for her foundation there.

Spring of 1846 found the Sisters on a fairly secure economic basis. Now that there were eighteen cows on the farm, twelve on loan in payment of tuition, Sister Loyola began to sell butter (perhaps in Oregon City), and was thus able to clothe her orphans and of course, to put a penny away for her wayside shrine. The dairy work was in itself a heavy burden, but good food was abundant, health was correspondingly improved, and spirits were high.

Unfortunately, Father Boldoc was a less successful provider. The chapel he had planned so ambitiously turned out "little and humble, not at all like those of our beloved Belgium." Worse still, he abandoned the addition to the convent and concentrated on the making of bricks for a cathedral. Even the interior finishing of the chapel was left to the Sisters, who once more had to seal up cracks to keep out the wind. They covered the sanctuary walls with white muslin, regretting there was not enough for the other walls. They pasted colored paper on the front of the altar. They built a May altar lovely enough to surprise a comparison out of Sister Norbertine; every bit as nice as the one in Ghent, she said.

Yet despite the sawing of wood and the weeding of crops, with young natives "assisting chiefly as spectators," the Sisters considered 1846 a happy year. They rejoiced to see the well-built brick church with its graceful tower, to know that their older girls could knit stockings and jackets, and that some could even help to embroider the grand surplice being made for Bishop Blanchet. They were glad to trudge out in early morning to harvest a wheat crop that had been left to them for their care of two motherless children. They were happy to notice signs of sounder piety and a growing sense of order in their young *Canadiennes*.

They were sanguine, too, about the material future of their work. They listened eagerly as Sister Loyola explained that, though wool was plentiful, yarn and woolen materials were very expensive; wool yarn was four dollars a pound. Settlers would be glad to buy wool products at moderate prices, and, if they could obtain them in Oregon, a great deal of money would cease to flow to Canadian cities with every brigade. The Sisters must begin to teach their pupils both spinning and weaving. And surely the new missionaries would bring looms from Belgium; Sister Loyola had asked ma Mère for two, the second with an eye on Oregon City.

The Sisters' confidence was strengthened also by generous approval of their efforts. They knew, for instance, of the laudatory report that James Douglas had sent to HBC headquarters in London after his visit to the Willamette mission with Captain Baillie, Commander of Her Majesty's Sloop *Modeste*. The Sisters, Douglas wrote, were "displaying a surprising degree of address in the management of their pupils." Their school, he added, was "numerously attended by the daughters of Canadian farmers, who may be considered fortunate in having so munificent provision made for the education of their children." [15]

CHAPTER 11

Return with Honors

In two hurried paragraphs, which read like the concise account of a modern businessman's journey, Bishop Blanchet sets down the story of his remarkable sea voyage, his consecration in Montreal, and his arrival in Paris, where he had "a great task to perform." All his movements led to that great task; his departure early in December in Captain Duncan's ship, the *Columbia,* his twelve-day visit in Honolulu, his rounding of Cape Horn on March fifth, his arrival in Deal, England, in May, are counted off as points reached on schedule. Boston in mid-June and then Quebec, where he learns that he is to be consecrated in Montreal in late July, his companion in dignity being the new coadjutor of that See, Bishop-elect Prince. And though few set such value on ceremony as Bishop Blanchet, he pauses in relating that event only to number the five bishops and one hundred and fifty priests who, besides the great throng of the faithful, honored the occasion with their presence; he also notes that Canada had never before witnessed a festival of such splendor.

With title wisely changed from *Philadelphia* to *Drasa in partibus infidelium,* Bishop Blanchet returned to Quebec to spend a short time with relatives and friends amid the scenes of his earlier life, before sailing again to England. In Paris at last in early September, he established himself with the Brothers of St. John of God and launched his plan, the great task which his episcopal consecration seemed to place in his hands. More missionaries for his vast vicariate, more Sisters, funds for passage, funds for the building of churches and schools. The task was formidable enough. But

Bishop Blanchet's aims, keeping pace with his imagination, went bounding over the limits of possibility, confusing the conditions of his vicariate with its extent. In his mind that great domain was already divided into suffragan bishoprics.[1]

First of all Bishop Blanchet went to Namur. He wanted to meet Mère Constantine, to thank her in person for his "treasures" in Oregon, to give her firsthand news of them, as well as to allow his hoped-for recruits time for preparation. His ring at the Mother House street gate one evening was answered by an overperfect young novice. With the downcast eyes which novices maintain at the most ill-advised moments, she explained that it was past visiting hours, whereupon the prelate handed her a packet of letters and departed. The distressed Mother General tried to make amends by dispatching a messenger to inquire for his Lordship at the city's chief hotels. He had not registered in any of them, but to her intense relief he came again next day, quite unoffended at the ways of novices. He prefaced his request for more missionaries with a glowing account of her Sisters at St. Paul. Acquaintance was off to a very satisfactory start; the Bishop of Drasa and the Mother General of the Sisters of Notre Dame, two of the most disparate characters imaginable, found themselves on common ground in the apostolate.

While a large number of Sisters would find plenty to do in Oregon, Bishop Blanchet told Mère Constantine, he would do well for the present to find passage money for six, or passage itself, for that matter. Mère Constantine had a long list of aspirants, whom letters from Willamette had fired to zeal. Some of these had even been studying English for months, as Sister Loyola so strongly advised. Yes, it would not be difficult to select a second band.

The Bishop of Drasa left Namur with only one little cloud on the sunny memory of that visit, a cloud that formed again and again despite his wish to be rid of it. Mère Constantine had broached the subject of the contract approvingly, though clearly the requested deed of conveyance meant to her security of tenure, not absolute ownership. And thinking of her promised seven missionaries, he had agreed. She was completely zealous toward his mission, and he would not risk a word that might change her attitude.[2] It was not that he objected so strongly to the contract; he was hurt rather by an independence that indicated failure to trust him.

Even before the Bishop's visit, Mère Constantine had selected seven from her many Oregon-minded Sisters, but as her funds were then too low to allow for the passage money of the seventh, she reluctantly withdrew the last name, Sister Laurence, from her list; but Sister's keen disappointment reached the ears of a certain Madame Bivor, who kindly offered the needed sum. Thus the scribe of the new band was saved for the mission. She wrote in an interesting if very simple fashion, quite unlike Sister Mary Aloysia, but ironically she is the one member of the Oregon mission about whom nothing is recorded except that she had spent her girlhood in the Notre Dame boarding school at Dinant. Bits of gay humor enliven her page as a sweet smile does her face in her dim, old photo, and the few references to her in the memoirs point to her love of a little fun, even at her own expense.

With the exceptions of Sister Alphonse Marie and Sister Renilde, the memoirs deal very briefly with this second band. The former deserved the little notebook memoir dedicated to her by managing to live a delicate and unusually painful life to the honored age of eighty-five; it was a strenuous life, too, every day of it, and a most self-effacing one. In view of her origin, she might have been less self-effacing; as little Aloyse Vermuylen, she could boast that her father, Jean Charles Vermuylen, was the leading citizen in their little suburb of Antwerp, a gentleman of means to whom everyone turned in trouble, and whose greatest pride was the priesthood of his eldest son. Little Aloyse received her First Communion from the hand of this elder brother at his first Mass in their parish church.

Like daughters of the best families, she was sent to the boarding school of Notre Dame in Namur where she excelled in music and admired the life of the Sisters. At her mother's early death, she returned home to manage the house, care for her little sister, and acquire a knowledge of affairs that was to be useful in Oregon, as is clear from the lacy tracing of her name on deeds of property as Sister Loyola's secretary. A very practical person, she could and did turn her hand to anything.

It was otherwise with Sister Renilde, whose flowery French memoir was written in Namur when a letter from Oregon City brought the account of her early death.[3] There was some hesitancy about receiving this Flemish girl, Melanie Goemaere, into the novitiate, as her two elder sisters who had entered died very young, and Melanie seemed not too robust. But her insistence won the day; it was only right, she said, that she should come to replace the two whom God had taken. From the start, little Sister Renilde was something of a perfectionist, with something also of the scruples and the tenacity that accompany that characteristic. A mere bit of a novice, the extremes of her silence might have gone for priggishness with the professed of years, had not her sweet little smile disarmed them; at this mark of recognition they had to be edified. But at least one onlooker was not precisely pleased when, like certain young saints in the old books, Sister Renilde threw a letter from home into the fire without reading it, and that at a time when her father was very ill. Of course, her Superior took the matter in hand, and that would seem to be the end of Sister Renilde's indiscretions, if not of her scruples and her way of winning out. Reasonably enough, in view of the Goemaere family tendency to tuberculosis, Mère Constantine demurred when Sister Renilde volunteered for the second Oregon mission but, says her admiring scribe, Sister removed all obstacles with her zeal and her courage. Like her sisters, she died young and to the end she edified, always with a smile.

In that band were the more ordinary individuals, Sisters Odelie and Francisca, Elizabeth Golard from Hodimont, and Colette Gernaey from Denderleeuw, near Ghent. Both lived strenuously in California as well as in Oregon, and both lived to ripe old age. In the days of homemade bread, few could compete with Sister Francisca. Few could wield the needle with Sister Odelie; in the early College of Notre Dame in San José, fussy misses wore with jaunty pride the uniform hats that she conjured up. And like these two, Florentine

Delpire from the Canton of Walcourt, strong young Sister
Aldegonde, brought with her to Oregon that special training
in the crafts that the first Sisters saw as a necessary adjunct
to courage and good will. Last was Sister Mary Bernard,
who, like Sister Renilde, provided the group with promising
teaching ability, but who in more mature years developed
marked administrative qualities. In California she was the
first Superior of Notre Dame's foundation in Marysville,
guiding it with a somewhat stern touch through its first
fifteen years.

These seven form the well-assorted second band, with
whom His Lordship was entirely satisfied as additions to his
overburdened Sisters at St. Paul. They were going to Oregon,
knowing full well the labor and hardship that awaited and
yet going eagerly. They were young, in their late twenties or
early thirties, and for the most part, typical and vigorous
Belgians. Three of them would be well suited to teach in
Oregon City. Two were almost ready to hold classes in
English. Sister Aldegonde was in Verviers learning weaving,
and Mère Constantine was installing a small loom at the
Mother House to insure plenty of practice for her on her
return. And Sister Laurence, to her own delight, was learning how to make and mend shoes. No wonder His Excellency
conceived so high an esteem of Mère Constantine.

Elated over these developments, he spent several weeks of
the fall arousing enthusiasm in Belgian cities. Then he
turned to Southern France before Christmas and reached
Rome, as he had planned, in early January. Thus far, except
for one plaguing financial worry, all went well; as Mère
Constantine remarked, he inspired trust and confidence
wherever he went. The worry had begun in London in the
shape of a reminder of a debt of over thirteen hundred
pounds, a borrowing which may explain the completion of
the churches at St. Paul and Oregon City in the face of local
lack of funds. However, counting on sizable donations from
the Paris and Lyons centers of the Propagation of the Faith,
the Bishop took heart, especially after his audiences with
Pope Gregory XVI, and in view of the encouragement he
met with on all sides.

Rid of his worry at last, he applied himself between journeys to his famous *Memorial* for the guidance of the Sacred Congregation of the Propagation of the Faith in its deliberations on the Northwest.[4] It would have been wiser, before presenting suggestions that could not fail to appear extravagant, to have consulted with the Archbishops of Baltimore and Quebec. He could have at least talked matters over with the latter on his soujourn in eastern Canada, unless perhaps his plans had not as yet assumed such large proportions. With their knowledge of the situation, both Archbishops would surely have opposed his plan for the erection of an ecclesiastical province; certainly both would have been aghast at his request for eight suffragans.

In approving the province, the Sacred Congregation cut the number of dioceses to three for the time, but the approval indicated the deep impression made by Bishop Blanchet's arguments. One of these was based on his cherished hope of a native clergy. Native priests, he held, would have greater need than others of immediate and frequent contact with their bishops. That of course, was true. A second argument was the failure of the California missions which were staffed by regulars and remote from diocesan control, but here, of course, he was overlooking other historical factors. This attitude toward the orders is in keeping with the Bishop's change of heart toward the Jesuits in Oregon, a change seen more specifically in his recommendation of restriction of the privileges of religious communities in the vicariate. In this matter, he strongly advised development of native seminaries in advance of regular novitiates.[5]

Even in the event of continuous progress in the Northwest, some of the Bishop's suggestions were on much too magnified a scale, a fact which certain American members of the hierarchy noted quickly enough.[6] His unhappy tendency was toward overestimation; his figure, for instance, of the number of Indians in the Northwest (200,000) was far above the reality; constant depopulation by epidemic alone kept the number much lower.

July brought the Bishop the hoped-for word; his vicariate was now a province; Father Demers was appointed to the new

See of Vancouver Island; his brother, Augustine Blanchet, to the new See of Walla Walla; he himself, to the Metropolitan See of Oregon City. That status gave him entree to the mighty; great rulers and high church dignitaries received him with sympathy and honor. They were generous, too. Louis Philippe offered him free passage for all his missionaries on a vessel of the royal navy; but as royal plans are sometimes too impulsive, the monarch had to change the gift to three thousand francs on his own part, and orders to the ministers of interior and marine to pay the archbishop seventy-five hundred francs each. Best of all, three students at the seminary in Lyons and five secular priests found his zeal irresistible, and Father General Roothan promised him three more Jesuits. Now he had the problem of suitable passage for nineteen, including himself; not at all an easy thing to find.

Despite all the generosity he had experienced, Bishop Blanchet was still worried about finances, his lot being to regret in dark hours obligations contracted in sanguine moments. He had for one thing to pay for publicity printing ordered in the hope of much larger contributions than his tour netted. Mère Constantine, to whom he confided his troubles, thought he created worries. One had to be practical and not expect the impossible, she said. Times were very hard on the Continent at that point. People might be ever so sympathetic, but if they were out of work what could they do? Her own principle was to do as much as possible and be satisfied with that. When funds failed for the chapel under construction at Namur, she stopped the work rather than borrow on an unsure future. She hated debts; in fact, she was as overcautious as the archbishop was overventuresome. In apostolic work, as in other matters, she thought, one must wait for God; lack of means was an indication of God's will which one should not try to force. To the Archbishop she merely intimated her view of the matter, but to Sister Loyola she set down her principles with emphasis. Her October letter is chiefly a strong warning against "too vehement zeal." For Sister Loyola had grown impatient over Father Boldoc's failure to build the promised two-floor extension; she wanted to proceed with it independently to accommodate waiting applicants. Mère Constantine opposed this measure. On the one hand, the Sisters should not become a cause of notable expenditure to the mission; on the other, they should not too soon withdraw from dependence upon it, since with the combined efforts of all the Belgian Sisters, the purse for Oregon was still very small. Independence (and she agreed with Sister Loyola on its desirability) would come later; for the present, no ambitious flight; the mission situation was humble and would long remain so. Ambition led surely to worry. As she wrote, there was the poor Archbishop, making frantic efforts to obtain passage money and fretting over his troubles.[7]

Actually, however, matters financial turned out fairly well for the Archbishop. He squared off his obligation, secured the passage funds for all, and was cheered by a gift of four thousand florins from the Leopoldine Society of Vienna for his mission. There were other gifts, too, and railroad directors gladly gave free passage to the Sisters of Notre Dame from Namur to Paris. But there was presently worry for all concerned when a native uprising at an unnamed port of call caused a cancellation of passages. And when through the good offices of the Oceanic Maritime Society, the Archbishop secured accommodations on *l'Etoile du Matin,* failure of wind delayed sailing until late in February.[8] That was, of course, very late in the season to begin the voyage around the Horn, though only the Archbishop seems to have worried about the fact. Certainly the good Breton Captain François Menes, with his twenty-six years on the sea, and his record of doubling the Horn four times in the most dangerous of seasons, expressed no anxiety as he welcomed his shipload of missionaries. On the contrary, he dispelled all worry by requesting His Lordship to bless *l'Etoile du Matin,* and a very solemn blessing it was, taking the Sisters' minds away from thoughts inspired by so many vessels making off to the harbors of the world, and by women and children on the wharf waving handkerchiefs and brushing tears away.

As the ship got under way, Captain Menes surprised the Sisters by intoning the *Ave Maris Stella* himself. How pleased he looked as priests, seminarians, and Sisters took up the lovely hymn, singing in parts as though they had practiced it together, while the few lay passengers listened in awed delight. Then he showed them a large chart on which he promised to plot the ship's course daily and explain points of interest. There was an altar for morning Masses, he said, and as the Archbishop wished it there would be singing of hymns on deck every evening in fine weather. In fact, Captain Menes' ship was like a well-organized little parish. Lenten regulations were observed; everyone kept a complete fast on Good Friday. Holy Week services, Sister Laurence wrote, could not have been more impressive in a great city church.

The clergy that performed that Easter Liturgy so perfectly included the three Jesuit Fathers, Gazzoli, Goetz, and Menetrey; the five diocesan priests, Le Bas, McCormack, Pretot, Deleveau, and Veyret; the deacons Delorme and Jayol; a cleric named Mesplie; and three Jesuit lay brothers. The ordinations of the two deacons at St. Paul were the first in the Oregon Mission. Father J. F. Jayol later joined the Oblate Fathers whom Bishop A. M. A. Blanchet brought with him to work in his diocese, and Diocesan priest Francis Veyret later became a Jesuit. Apparently several of these missionaries were good singers, but none of them, it would seem, was given to writing rhapsodic travel notes; of course there was no Father DeSmet on this voyage to set the example. And on the whole they had somewhat less of the dramatic to record than *l'Infatigable*'s passengers.

The two recorded storms were not at all of a tragic nature, though the first, off Rio de Janiero, carried the ship a distance off her course. The second, in the far south, raged for some two weeks, but the Archbishop himself was the only passenger who grew nervous about it, and that because he recalled the loss of the *Marie-Joseph*. The Sisters, one and all, slept soundly through the worst weather. Mère Constantine certainly knew how to choose good sailors.

With *l'Infatigable*'s sleeping quarters in mind, the second band of Sisters was prepared for the worst. But *l'Etoile du Matin* was a larger ship with better planning for passengers. The Sisters were assigned one long, roomy cabin with seven beds and a table at which their meals were served. No one had to sleep on the floor, and there were no rats. As they were not plagued by long periods of seasickness, these very practical Sisters studied English constantly, as did the Fathers and students. Out of the Sisters' boxes came new school texts, readers, science books, and catechisms, all in English. Sister Mary Bernard and Sister Renilde, speaking quite fluently now in the foreign accent that never abandoned them, led the others into English conversation; they were all determined to teach their classes in English. Apparently all of them engaged in this practice whether they intended to teach classes or not; gathered around their table they made merry over blunders, but they learned. In fact, they made merry over everything, the inconveniences, the result of their first washing at sea. Sister Laurence tells how elated they were to possess the latest thing in flatirons, irons with hollow interiors to allow for inserting hot coals, a wonderful invention but quite impracticable on a ship. Laughing, they abandoned the notion of ironing linens at sea. They gave names of places in Oregon to various parts of the ship, and sent hilarious little messages back and forth between St. Paul and Oregon City. There was good nature and very little tension on the voyage of *l'Etoile du Matin*.

Something had to be done to honor His Lordship on the feast of St. Norbert in June. In lieu of flowers, the Sisters made a great bouquet of paper poppies and, regretting their lack of artist and poet, wrote all the pertinent clichés they could recall on an elaborate card. Again the best vestments appeared and the liturgy was "worthy of a great cathedral." Captain Menes ordered a grand dinner, and like all his passengers he shared the Archbishop's great happiness. So passed the weeks and months of this relatively short and easy voyage. There were no delays, though *l'Etoile du Matin* must have stopped at some port of call for water and food supplies; the voyage was almost two months shorter than that of *l'Infatigable*, three years before. When Captain Menes sighted Cape Disappointment on August eighth, his good fortune still held; Pilot Reeves came out and led *l'Etoile du Matin* safely across the bar. She was the first French vessel to enter the Columbia. When Captain Menes cast anchor in Gray's Bay, he and his crew joined His Lordship and passengers on the deck. The hills re-echoed their tremendous *Te Deum.*

At Fort Astoria next morning the Fathers set out at once for a closer look at the giant trees. Captain Menes led the Sisters to the fort, but there was no one in sight to receive them. That was as well, they said; the fort was merely a house; they would really prefer seeing some wigwams with a few Indians about. But there were no convenient wigwams and the few half-naked Indians that sauntered past the fort garden sadly disappointed them. No costume, no feathers, no war paints. Prim Sister Renilde was quite shocked at their nakedness. But presently kind Captain Birnie appeared with a large basket, led them to his thriving kitchen garden, and bade them take what they pleased. Quickly they filled it with garden peas as a surprise for their ship's excellent cook.

L'Etoile du Matin met with her first mishap three days later at the mouth of the Willamette when she grounded on a bank, from which, however, she was dislodged without injury. That was better fortune than she experienced two years later, when she was so badly injured at the bar that she had to be towed to Portland and unloaded. Then they burned the hull of the lovely ship, and Captain Menes left the sea.[9]

The accident caused the missionaries no delay. Archbishop Blanchet dispatched Father Veyret by canoe to St. Paul to advise Sister Loyola and the Jesuits of the missionaries' arrival. Experienced now with river transportation, Sister Loyola summoned a few Canadians and came herself to conduct her seven recruits, and as much as possible of their immense piles of baggage, to St. Paul. Soon the new Sisters were having their fill of primitive life on river-bank stopovers, with an occasional glimpse of a huddle of wigwams. Laughing tears, they rode the last five miles of their journey at night, bumping along in the farm carts that had borne their Sisters to St. Paul, the two in front, Sister Laurence loved to tell, with feet hanging down just behind the horse. On the way, one of the carts lost a wheel and its occupants slipped more or less gracefully to the ground. But none were injured, the wheel was made fast, and the ride merrily resumed. At midnight Sister Mary Cornelia opened the garden gate, and presently thirteen Belgian Sisters wept happy tears together.

By this time preparation was under way along the Willamette for the Archbishop's reception. Bishop-elect Demers had adjusted his mind to giving up his new church of St. John, with its side chapels and Gothic windows, the church that Father DeVoss had dedicated in the Bishop's absence, marking the occasion with oratory that won high praise in the *Oregon Spectator*.[10] But it was not in this little cathedral that the Archbishop made his grand entry; as was fitting, he went to St. Paul, his journey there being something of a progress, for Protestants as well as Catholics accompanied him, so proud was everyone of the honor that had come to their valley. Sister Renilde described the procession: Canadians, Indians, Americans, on horseback and on foot, entering the church so magnificently adorned by the Sisters. Adult Indians with lowered eyes, hands folded like First Communicants, but missing nothing of the episcopal robes and splendor. And the Archbishop telling his people that now the Church in Oregon was complete.

PART V

CREST OF THE WAVE

CHAPTER 12

Work for New Hands

While Sister Renilde was reporting the impressive return
of Archbishop Blanchet to St. Paul, Sister Laurence wrote a
humorous and factual summary of things as she found them.[1]
There was the strip of mattress ticking that Sister Loyola
produced for a tablecloth on the journey up the Willamette.
How practical! The same stout piece protected the food
from dampness in the canoes. And Sister Loyola's teakettle!
No one would think of making a journey in Oregon without
a teakettle. And how odd to see tall, straight Sister Francisca
and dignified Sister Odelie squatting on their heels and hun-
grily enjoying their dinner without forks.

It was no one's fault that the seven arrivals had to sleep

189

on the floor in a classroom; the workman had long before cut pieces for bed frames, but with the pressure of field work, neither he nor the Sisters had time to assemble them. That was the way; each was doing the work of several. Assessing the situation, the seven newcomers remarked to one another that they had come just in time. They were shocked at the work the first six had been doing for three long years. And yet, Sister Laurence hastened to assure the Mother General, they seemed well enough.

There were hops and oats and barley to harvest, twenty-seven cows to be milked, and butter and cheese to be made. There was a large field of potatoes to dig. It was at this task that Captain Menes found his passengers when he came to St. Paul's at the Archbishop's invitation for a few days of country air. From a window in St. Joseph's, he saw the Sisters working with hoes and spades, and carrying away the crop in large wheelbarrows. Peasant women worked in Belgian fields, it was true, but the captain knew that most of these Sisters were middle-class daughters who had entered the novitiate from boarding schools and comfortable homes.

Looking up, Sister Laurence saw the captain standing beside her with tears in his eyes. Was it for this that he had brought them to Oregon? There must be some relief for this situation, he said, and he turned away determined to find it. Sister Loyola knew his failure beforehand. There was nothing to do but to continue the toil; when classes began, the Sisters rose at four and even earlier, harvesting, churning, cooking, and teaching through their long day. Being Belgian women, they did every task thoroughly, drawing bright joy from perfectly laundered altar cloth, or well-kept chicken yard.

Taking inventory, Sister Laurence listed, besides the cows, 23 calves, 2 hogs, "black as wild boars," and 100 chickens. The cattle, she wrote, were no trouble except at milking time, since they spent night and day in the woods. Somewhat appalled, she noted the land under cultivation; 12 *bonniers* (almost forty acres) seemed to her an excessive burden, and perhaps her exact statements and shocked reactions prompted Mère Constantine's first adverse criticism of Sisters performing work that required a man's strength. There were the evening chores, wrote Sister Laurence, in which all participated after the long, hard day; because they had no pump, they carried buckets of water to supply all their needs; even the gardens had to be watered in this way as there had been less rainfall than usual. But with Sister Loyola's way of securing things, surely they would have a little pump soon. Everyone had confidence in Sister Loyola.

The novelty of seven additional Sisters touched off a short burst of endeavor on the part of lazy little natives and pouting half-breeds. Happily in charge of the little Indian orphans, Sister Laurence reported them all of good will. She was deeply impressed by the young *Canadienne* who wept for joy in the chapel; this was the sort of thing she had read of in missionary stories. Of course, disillusionment came swiftly enough to poor Sister Laurence. Yet she could see that at least some of the older girls had been affected by two years of selfless example. Through that very harvest time some of them were rising before daylight of their own accord to help the Sisters with the peas and barley. Still, the new Sisters were to learn sadly that even in the best of their charges, lapses into native passiveness had to be expected.

With the harvest disposed of, there was another moment of youthful fervor occasioned by the unpacking of Sister Aldegonde's two weaving machines, for which Mère Constantine had paid two thousand francs in Brussels. With a roomful of spellbound black eyes following each movement, Sister skillfully assembled the parts, explaining their uses to Sister Loyola's delight as she envisioned yards of lovely soft material made of fine Oregon wool. And the black eyes lighted with happy expectation as Sister Laurence displayed rolls of good, soft leather and her tools for shoe-making and mending, explaining that worn shoes could be made to look just like new. Shoes! Native toes wiggled for joy in ragged moccasins. The shoe was the badge of distinction. Just look at the pairs of smart shoes Sister Laurence had made! And as Sister arranged them with toes pointed primly, a low musical hum of approval rewarded her industry. The piles of readers and notebooks, the boxes of pens, the charts with

big letters, the maps and geographies brought less spontaneous approval.

Presently the show was over; Sister Marie Catherine marshaled the younger generation to bed and left the Sisters
happily clustered around the school supplies. Double sets,
double amounts of everything, Sister Mary Bernard was explaining, on account of Oregon City. That was music to
Sister Loyola's ears. How generous she is, notre chère Mère,
and our Belgian Sisters and friends!

When the recruits arrived, Sister Loyola was hurrying to
completion the large kitchen which Father Boldoc had begun
instead of the new wing ordered by the Archbishop. With
her usual foresight, she added a roomy attic supplied with
windows, to serve as combination workroom and storage
space for the supplies she knew the Sisters would bring. In
this attic they stored the weaving machine and all their treasures for Oregon City, and when a second consignment of
baggage arrived from *l'Etoile du Matin,* they filled the new
kitchen shelves and bins with the unexpected gifts of flour
and sugar and coffee. There were even thirty great loaves
of Belgian beet sugar! Best of all was the fine French stove
with its array of iron and copper pots and pans that fitted
into the round openings on top, and tin baking pans for its
oven. This grand surprise, exactly like the stoves pictured
in the ads of the first weeklies, soon graced the new kitchen
and made the branch of home cooking suddenly attractive.

The Sisters had still another purpose for the kitchen attic.
To make their supply of coffee last longer, they had planted
a crop of chicory in the spring. At harvest time a year's supply of chicory roots could be dried in the new bake oven
and stored in the attic. The combined oven and boiler, built
in the center of the kitchen by a master mason, was a great
relief after Brother Francis' rather unsatisfactory construction. In fact, Sister Loyola was quite happy about her kitchen;
it was roomy and well equipped, and His Lordship had paid
for it.

In those laborious harvest days, gentle Sister Odelie was
suddenly the recipient of Sister Loyola's accolade and every-
body's gratitude. The three-year indoor war with insects had

just burst out in one of its never successful campaigns. Sister Odelie studied the situation and planned a new line of action. Noticing that the boards in the attic-dormitory had never been nailed down, she turned them up and applied a strong solution of potassium and soap in generous amounts to both sides of each. This, said Sister Marie Catherine, was the first decisive victory in that war. From that day, the enemy was under control. Sister Odelie had won her spurs.

Sister Francisca was next to solve a long-standing problem. As no successful cook had emerged in the first group, except herself, Sister Loyola cast about for talent among the newcomers and selected Sister Aldegonde. But except for the weaving in which she was so expert, Sister Aldegonde was not at all domestic. She was a guileless, good-natured soul who hoped to go directly into the forest to tell little savages all about the Good God. Whatever called for planning and present-mindedness bothered her. At last, in her somewhat blunt fashion, she told Sister Loyola that cooking was not her line. Amazed at this unadorned candor, Sister Loyola gave the charge to her first success, Sister Francisca, and included in her next letter to Mère Constantine a rather puzzled account of her experience with Sister Aldegonde. The Mother General understood. Sister Aldegonde was young and hadn't had many trials as yet; she probably expected to climb the hills with the Indians in Oregon. Just leave her at her weaving with her little savages around her and all will be well.

The cooking problem was solved. Sister Francisca became an expert. Canadian mothers were soon knocking at the kitchen door to see the golden loaves their daughters were talking about, and clucking their amazed tongues at sight of the reality. Here at last was the ideal teacher for Sainte Marie's most necessary branch.

Sister Norbertine rejoiced at the arrival of reinforcements, for now at last she could carry out her project of landscaping the area around the house. And on the principle that, to be respected, one must present a respectable appearance, Sister Loyola whole-heartedly approved of her plans. Rather ambitious plans they were, calling for walks eight or ten feet wide, one leading all the way to the church. There must be

trees and shrubs, too, and spaces for flowers. Out came spades
and hoes for extracting earth-bound roots and breaking hard
clumps of soil. All worked together at this project, Sister
Marie Catherine's special task being the line of overgrown
shrubbery planted along the road some years before by the
Canadians. Patiently Sister cut all six hundred feet of it to
a low hedge, two feet wide.

The landscaping well under way, Sister Norbertine began
to advance a second project; she wanted to convert their unused acres into orchards. With Sister Laurence as assistant
and with the occasional help of all the others, she raised the
total number of young trees, apples, pears, plums, and perhaps peaches, to over a thousand. Some were seedlings that
she had started three years before; others were young trees
from Henderson Luelling's new nursery. Dawn often found
the Sisters out clearing the land, digging holes for the trees,
bringing water from the well in a tub placed on a wheelbar-
row. It was reward enough for Sister Laurence to see the
smile of satisfaction on Sister Norbertine's strong face.

While all this activity was going forward at St. Paul, Mère
Constantine was in distress about her second band. From
their sailing, thirteen months had passed with no word from
them, though they wrote to her en route and on arriving.
Worst of all, a report reached Namur that *l'Etoile du Matin*
had been wrecked. Even Father DeSmet, who was now again
in Europe, told the Sisters in Ghent that he thought it must
be true. Rumor followed rumor; one report stated that vestments had been found and even a bishop's mitre. But trying
as the silence was, neither Mère Constantine nor the Sisters
at the Mother House credited the story. *L'Infatigable* had
crossed the terrible bar. Then how could anyone doubt the
good God's care of *l'Etoile du Matin?* They knew what wild
stories spring naturally out of long waiting in ignorance.[2]
And though travel and communication were improving, delays were still common. A box sent from St. Paul to Mère
Constantine late in 1847 was detained two months in customs
in London after its long journey around the Horn.

To the Belgian Sisters, Oregon seemed suddenly much
nearer when that box reached Namur, for it contained pre-

serves made from native fruits and berries, carefully labelled packages of garden seeds, and a wonderful gift from Sister Laurence, a pair of shoes made by her native pupils. It mattered little, Mère Constantine wrote happily, that it was late in the season for planting. The Namur Sisters hurried the Oregon seeds into Belgian soil. In mid-August she wrote that this Oregon garden was a great success; that very important persons had admired the strange flowers and vegetables and had asked for seeds of the excellent melons.

In fact, with the coming of messages from her second band, Mère Constantine began to see a not too distant bright future for the Willamette country. A little time would bring great changes, she told Sister Loyola. If for the present things were a bit difficult at St. Paul, one had only to remember that even in Belgium religious foundations were usually made at immense sacrifice. Cautious as ever, she addressed little lectures to Sister Loyola on the subject of money. She understood its absence in Oregon and she promised to send as soon as possible the four or five hundred dollars that had come in as gifts for the mission; meanwhile she hoped that Sister Loyola would be patient and reasonable. It was a little inconsiderate, for instance, to ask the Mother House to send articles to Oregon simply because they cost less in Europe, when the freight charges multiplied their cost. And as for Oregon City, where they would certainly do great good, they still should wait until the Archbishop had funds for a foundation there, especially since he seemed "disposed to look on the dark side of trifles." [3]

Yet with all the caution with which Mère Constantine surrounded Sister Loyola's movements, she still adopted the principle that at such a distance she must, as a rule, leave final decisions to her. For one thing, circumstances presented in a letter written in Oregon might be quite altered before it reached Belgium. Time and distance made correspondence unsatisfactory on both sides. And to eager Sister Loyola, the hesitant and negative attitude of her Mother General's letters would have been very restricting without the liberty of decision which she granted her. Through the year 1846, Mère Constantine made only one absolute decision. The Jesuits

had been pressing Sister Loyola to found a house in the
Rockies, and here Mère Constantine's refusal was for the
present unqualified.[4]

It would have been difficult for Sister Loyola to refuse the
invitation to Oregon City. For three years she had heard of
the "city" at the Falls. Every success occurred there; mills
were in operation, stores were being built, now a horseboat
was running between it and Vancouver. Everyone advised a
boarding school there. In 1846, Doctor McLoughlin had
given the Sisters an entire block in his claim on which to
build, and when over a year later he came to St. Paul accompanied by certain "leading citizens of Oregon City" with a
formal request and reminder of the land awaiting convent
and school, Sister Loyola agreed to send a community there
to open classes in September. And except in one detail, her
readiness to oblige the leading citizens pleased the Archbishop. She had accepted, and undoubtedly had asked for, a
site four blocks north of the church. His Lordship had hoped
to have the Sisters located nearby on church property; for one
thing, in lieu of a parish choir, he wanted to have them at
hand to sing. On the other hand, with his own financial
difficulties, he was perhaps now willing to accede to Sister
Loyola's wish for independence, much as he disliked to do
so.[5]

But hopes and plans for Oregon City were suddenly interrupted by disaster at St. Paul. Late in January, fire wiped
out the treasures the Sisters were guarding for the new foundation. Roused by a child's terrified cry they looked out to see
fire bursting from the roof of their new kitchen. Sister Marie
Catherine and Sister Francisca forced the double doors open
and rescued the pile of dried chicory that happened to be still
downstairs. Then timid Sister Francisca, heedless of frantic
warning, rushed in again and brought out an armful of stockings. She was just safely outside when the wind slammed the
doors so that they could not be opened. Sister was safe!
Nothing else mattered, Sister Loyola told the others, and as
she said it they heard the attic floor and all their precious
stores go thundering down. But they had reason to be grate-

ful; the cold north wind that slammed the doors also saved the convent and other buildings.

What started the fire? They reviewed the day before. They had done the washing, a big washing, too, and had hung the children's clothing in the attic. Sister Laurence had achieved the greatest soap-making success thus far, using the formula of oak ashes and grease far more successfully than did the Canadian women who shared it with her. And because of the novelty, the girls had helped her zealously, cutting the hardening mass into long bars of uniform yellow and spreading them carefully in the attic to dry. But all recalled extinguishing the fire in boiler and stove. They had been as careful as usual. Suddenly they thought about the mason!

That very strong-headed craftsman had laughed mockingly when Sister Loyola asked him to construct the boiler masonry from the ground instead of on the plank floor. No danger whatever, he insisted, with annoyance. Three layers of brick between boiler and floor were enough, he said. It was futile to plead with him; he only grew more scornful, and as he was the only available mason there was nothing to do but allow him his own way.

"When it burns, come and call me," was his parting shot as he left for his home forty miles away, a fairly safe distance in those days. That was it. Cinders had fallen through and smoldered for hours. School supplies, dry goods, flour, sugar! One has only to think of the prices and lack of money, to estimate the loss.

It was the will of God, said Sister Loyola, thus forestalling useless comments on the mason. They would not starve, she added, since, thank God, the cellar was saved. The cellar was a low shed built over an excavation in which they kept dairy products, meat, potatoes, bread, anything perishable. They would manage. And that unpampered community, without thought of a hot drink or a moment's rest, went to the chapel to wait for early Mass.

At the door they found a huge pot of soup sent by Father Boldoc. Sister Marie Catherine set bowls and spoons, and rang the bell for the children. She found them gathered around the ruins of the kitchen, poking the smouldering ashes with long sticks, searching for their precious tin plates, and bending them back into shape. Breakfast without these was unthinkable. Sister looked sadly at the ruins. Half their dishes and nearly all their cooking utensils were in that debris, but that was a small matter compared with the setback to the Oregon City project. She followed the children, who had rushed to the dining room at the mention of hot soup. There they were at the table, seated on their long benches, their feet doubled under them because of the cold, devouring their soup and casting happy glances at the plates of bread and meat Sister Francisca was setting before them.

It would seem that no one, not even the leading citizens of Oregon City, helped the Sisters to replace their losses. Perhaps they could not; perhaps they thought that the Sisters could always manage. When Doctor McLoughlin and Archbishop Blanchet came to view the ruins, both were deeply distressed; both were also greatly relieved to find the disaster would not prevent the new foundation. Neither knew that for the next six months the Sisters' coffee was made of roasted barley.

Now all the Sisters' resources must be channeled to the new boarding school. For the time they must be content with a little unused horse barn as kitchen and with their original laundry day procedure. The small sum now available at Namur must be used for the new foundation; and they must find a temporary house in Oregon City for a few paying boarders until the building was finished. There was only one answer to the problem of a temporary dwelling. That was the new "episcopal palace," which Archbishop Blanchet generously offered, saying it was well he had not yet taken up permanent residence and that he could easily find a room in some good friend's house. The palace was only a two-story house with four average-sized rooms on the ground floor, and they were planning to accommodate a few boarders and teach classes! But they had had wonderful experience in conserving space.

Sister Loyola planned to head the new community herself, leaving Sister Mary Cornelia in charge at St. Paul. For several reasons Sister Mary Aloysia was her first selection. She was the best educated, she had showed herself extremely adaptable in all circumstances, she was now doing well with English, she was always genial; besides, she was expert at mixing house paint and putting in window panes. Sister Mary Bernard and Sister Renilde were, of course, on the list as teachers of young Americans. Good, gentle Sister Francisca was appointed cook, to the sorrow of all at St. Paul. Sister Norbertine was chosen because Sister Loyola knew that the spacious boarding school she would build should be surrounded by beautiful grounds. This would not be another Sainte Marie de Willamette, where Mère Constantine's warning to keep it a simple school for primitive people would certainly apply. Things would shape up to importance in Oregon City, and Mère Constantine would come to realize the fact.

CHAPTER 13

Spacious Halls

In September, 1848, school opened in Oregon City with only four paying boarders, three of them transfers from Sainte Marie. These were the two Cosgrove girls, Margaret and Elizabeth, Mary Cod, a ward of HBC, and Mary McIntosh, who was directed to the Sisters by Father Delevau.[1] The Cosgroves were daughters of Hugh Cosgrove, who had recently brought his family from Indiana and settled at St. Paul, where he straightway became a leader. On every occasion, it seems, he helped the Sisters, both at St. Paul and in Oregon City.

With these four and a couple of orphans to bring blessing on the enterprise by the Sisters' charity to them, the Archbishop's little house was, of course, quite crowded. In fact, from the beginning, the downstairs rooms were used for household purposes at one hour and for educational ends at another. Sister Mary Aloysia's piano, which had been in storage at the fort all this time, was crowded into a corner.

Classes began at once, tiny groups composed chiefly of the few "externs," with hesitant piano beginnings in one room distracting Sister Renilde's English pupils in the next. But Sister Loyola cheerfully reminded the Sisters of Mère Constantine's advice; even the Belgian boarding schools had begun very modestly; if their numbers increased even slowly, all was well. And everyone said she was right when a few months later two more Cosgrove sisters, Suzanne and Caroline, were enrolled with another American, Elizabeth McLean, and Doctor McLoughlin's two granddaughters, Margaret and Maria Louisa Rae.[2]

With further applications and with the building in Block 12 little more than started, Sister Loyola found herself facing an acute problem. She solved it by renting a vacant house of sorts on the river, several blocks north of the church, a window-rattling, door-slamming, drafty structure with creaking floors and stairs, approached in rainy weather through ankle-deep mud. For the time this would serve as a school and leave the episcopal palace for living quarters; the walk back and forth would be healthful exercise.

This arrangement enabled Sister Loyola to enroll two more of the many Cosgrove sisters, Mary and Ann, together with a certain Emma Burton and Harriet Ogden. Harriet was the granddaughter of the famous Peter Skene Ogden and the ward of the just elected Governor Joseph Lane, a connection of potential advantage for a school beginning under the new Territorial Government.

In general, Sister Loyola was pleased with the solid establishment of American control, especially as Doctor McLoughlin was strongly abetting it. Surely now Oregon City would flourish and with it the academy, as she now called it. As if in assurance, the Archbishop took up residence in his metropolitan city toward the close of the year, first as guest in the McKinley home, then in a rented house; and in March Governor Lane also made Oregon City his home. Stores and homes were under construction; the walls of the academy were rising. Yet in the spring of 1849 there was a feeling of unrest in that little capital.

When Captain Newell loaded the brig *Honolulu* with mining supplies in the Columbia, he satisfied the inquisitive by saying it was for coal mining. On sailing, however, he paid for the cargo in the only way he could, from a sack of gold dust.[3] The secret was out; he had sold a cargo in San Francisco and had been paid in gold; he was returning there with the mining implements. Now the thought of wealth disrupted the "almost Arcadian" simplicity of the land; "speculation displaced contentment."[4] For even though this news pointed to ultimate improvement, it was bound for a time to bring darkness. California gold was soon luring the flow of immigration southward. Many who had

taken the relatively easy and safe Oregon Trail made only
a short pause in Oregon, and then followed the gleam to
California. But for the time, this great movement failed to
affect the Sisters and their academy other than to hurry it
to completion. Americans in Oregon City needed a boarding
school for their daughters while they themselves went to make
quick and easy fortunes. Heads of families would soon return with money to pay their bills, to start profitable business ventures, or invest in prosperous farm lands.

A number of Oregon City prospectors did return and with
a bit of wealth, too, though as Sister Marie Catherine remarked, money acquired quickly and easily is likely to be
spent foolishly. But the brigade of French-Canadians that
left French Prairie in May accompanied by Father Delorme,
met tragedy in the land of gold. There the epidemic of
yellow fever attacked it with violence, carried off forty of
its members, twenty of these heads of families, and barely
spared the life of Father Delorme. The disaster so de-
populated the area around St. Paul that the Archbishop
ordered the boys' school closed.[5]

From that time on, Sainte Marie de Willamette might be
classed a home for orphans, children whose fathers died on
the mining expedition and whose mothers returned to their
native villages when they found themselves without support.
Sister Mary Cornelia and her community worked harder than
ever at dairy and farm chores to maintain this shelter for
sad-eyed, hungry, half-breed waifs found by one or other
of the missionaries on their rounds. And as always there
were the poor little abandoned Indians whose parents had
succumbed to disease. Sister Mary Cornelia opened the door
one day to four little Kalispel maidens whose entire wardrobe was the one-piece deerskin tunics they wore.

After the establishment in Oregon City, the Willamette
farm performed the second function of supplying the academy with dairy and farm products, as well as grain and cattle
for which Sister Loyola found sale. Without this good office
on the part of the Willamette Sisters, the Oregon City venture would have been impossible. As it was, Sister Loyola
must have borrowed money from both the Archbishop and

Captain Menes, for within the next two years she paid them unexplained sums which were too large for ordinary expenditure. What the actual cost of the building was remains an unsolved problem, since the contract, if there was one, was drawn up before Sister Loyola got around to bookkeeping. Mystery also shrouds the contractor or carpenter. He was probably Walter Pomeroy, one of Archbishop Blanchet's converts, and the "architect" of the first church. Whoever he was, he must have suffered a good deal of urging from Sister Loyola as crowded conditions in the episcopal residence became daily more unbearable. Both Sisters and pupils slept with beds so close that they had to turn sideways to move between them. They were even forced to use the dining room and kitchen as sleeping quarters; the Sisters, rising at four-thirty instead of five, rolled up their beds and carried them to the little room behind the church, reclaiming them in reverse procession in the evening.

Crowded quarters or shortened rest, or just the general hardness of things, undermined the health of delicate, determined Sister Renilde. She had insisted on fasting throughout Lent. She never admitted fatigue. But in Holy Week, as she carried on her extra duties as sacristan in her usual smiling and brisk manner, she suddenly succumbed. Noticing her seated when the others were kneeling, Sister Mary Aloysia knew she must be very sick; otherwise strict Sister Renilde would never permit herself this indulgence.

In a few minutes, Sister Loyola had her in bed, the only real bed in the house, it would seem, and sent for the doctor. But the disease, probably pneumonia, had run its course, and there were no miracle drugs. In a few days she ended her brief but ardent missionary career in the scrupulously precise manner of her life, her examen book under her pillow, and with contrition on her lips for a minute lapse in duty. Perfect in every detail, she had probably never in her little span known the wholesome humiliation of walking in late for morning prayer. But with her generous ways, her vital presence, and her head-on attack on all difficulties, she had made herself loved by all to an extent surprising in the case of so meticulous an individual.

Sister Loyola decided on a corner of the garden at Sainte Marie de Willamette for Sister Renilde's resting place, a little space next to the shrine of Our Lady of Sorrows. Around this little plot Sister Mary Cornelia had a wooden fence built, which the Sisters themselves painted black and white. And through the narrow gate naughty little Kalispels and Chinooks stole in of an evening to ask the good Sister who was with God to help them measure up.

After the Sisters and orphans had left St. Paul, Archbishop Blanchet thought Sister Renilde's little burial ground too lonely. He had her remains transferred from the neglected garden to the church, and in many a sermon he told her story. She was their apostle, he said, and their pledge that Sisters would come again to St. Paul. And when the Sisters of the Holy Names did come, in 1861, they chose the corner plot of the present Catholic Cemetery as the resting place of their departed. In kind thoughtfulness they laid Sister Renilde among their own pioneers, setting her name with theirs on the tall monument beneath the giant firs.

Sister Loyola now transferred Sister Alphonse Marie to Oregon City to teach music and thus free Sister Mary Aloysia to take over Sister Renilde's classes. At some point during early summer, she also transferred Sister Marie Catherine as a temporary measure, undoubtedly to benefit by the remarkable building sense that Sister had acquired at St. Paul. At the same time, she tried the expedient of converting a couple of second-floor rooms in the rented house into dormitories. From then on a strange procession set out each evening at nine from Tenth and Main and wended its way north on the present State Highway. But the highway those Sisters trod was a narrow path through bushes and weeds. Sister Francisca led the line valiantly, lantern in one hand and house key in the other. Sister Norbertine brought up the rear with a bucket of water "for ablutions." Sister Alphonse, with her extraordinary fear of snakes and wild animals, walked close behind Sister Mary Aloysia, to whom she clung in terror at every movement of a branch or rustle in the grass.

In that new town, without lights and with no police department, the nightly trip to the rented house was sometimes a bit nerve-racking for all. None of them ever forgot the occasion when Sister Mary Aloysia left the key in the door after she unlocked it in the morning. During classtime it disappeared, and the most thorough search failed to locate it. Fearing it had been stolen, Sister Loyola had the lock changed. But that precaution was not enough to relieve the Sisters' anxiety. For a few nights their fear of a prowler kept them awake, their terror increased by the fact that the back door fastening was only a wooden hasp. At last one dark night the thief arrived with the key, and in complete panic the Sisters heard him trying to fit it in the new lock. Finally he gave up further attempt, and from an upper window they watched his shadowy figure cross to the path and disappear.

When the Sisters could forget their fears, they enjoyed this isolated location where often the only sound was the music of the falls. But some nights forest discords troubled the liquid cadences, as coyotes joined their mournful howl to wildcats' protesting wail, and the racket of roused chicken yards told of the conflict between wilderness and settler. It was some little help to know now that these mountain cats were not tigers, though to the end Sister Alphonse Marie held in equal horror any that she could not stroke as a fireside tabby. There was little use in telling her of the mountain cat's preference for plump chicken or choice piglet.

It is quite easy to imagine the Sisters stopping on their way home from their school by the river to note the progress on their academy, counting the days to a contractor's deadline. But there was no contractor in the modern sense, and little time to stand noting progress. Instead, they kept work aprons in the new house, and before and after school they wielded with skill the tools they had learned to use at St. Paul. While Sister Alphonse Marie marshaled the resident pupils two by two along Main Street from the ramshackle school to the Bishop's palace, the others stopped at their academy, donned aprons and worked until dark, fitting door and window frames and planing boards for shelves with a little advice from the carpenter if he happened to be there.

Sister Francisca became the best painter in the group, though she lacked confidence to mix the paint herself. She and Sister Mary Aloysia used to rise at four while the interior painting was under way; between them they finished all the rooms of that big building, Sister Mary Aloysia mixing enough for the day before she left for class each morning. In midmorning Sister Francisca went home to start the dinner and give an eye to housekeeping in general, but this plan had sometimes to be set aside in the interests of building progress.

One morning, for instance, they found the mason at the academy waiting to begin work on the chimney, a bit upset because there was no one there to carry bricks to him as he worked. Rather than have him abandon the job, Sister Loyola called on Sister Francisca. Masons would seem to have been a little difficult along the Willamette; this one was irritable, or demanding, or both. It was not enough to pile the bricks within easy reach; they had to be handed to him as he worked, well but hurriedly, right up to noon. Then Sister Loyola arrived and found Sister Francisca in distress. What would the Sisters and children do for dinner? Quite simple, her Superior told her. Cold meat and bread and milk. And it needed only ten minutes to make a little coffee. To Belgians this was a strange substitute for a hot dinner. But anything could be endured for the sake of their academy. Sister Loyola herself had frequently to abandon all other duties and devote her time to supervising the work and securing materials.

Without any form of refrigeration, there was the usual need of a cellar, an exigency which the Sisters met in the usual manner, with shovels in their hands. One Saturday morning, the Sisters started an excavation for a cooling room like the quite satisfactory one at Sainte Marie. Archbishop Blanchet was horrified to find them so occupied, but as usual the Sisters completed the task themselves. With all the money in the world, they could not have secured labor. White men preferred digging for gold or performing more pleasant tasks made easily available by so many departures to the mines. Willamette Indians had an even greater distaste than most of their race for the sight of a shovel. Over this excavation, the carpenter built a roof resting on low

Above: Archbishop Francis Norbert Blanchet.
Upper left: Memorial Cross erected at St. Paul in honor of Archbishop Blanchet and his brother, Bishop Augustine Magloire Blanchet.
Below: The original Church of St. John the Evangelist in Oregon City was completed and dedicated in 1846.

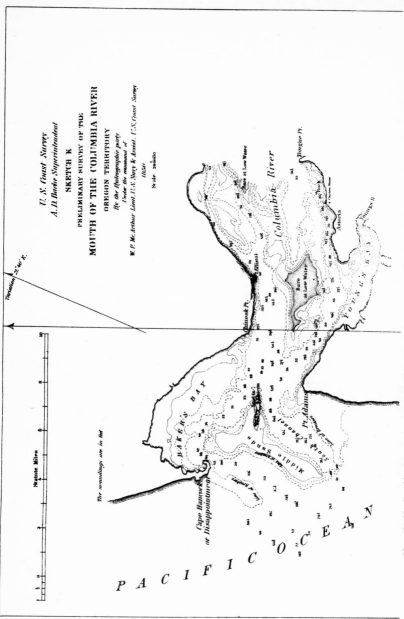

Sketch K, Preliminary Survey of the Mouth of the Columbia River made in 1850 by the U. S. Coast survey.

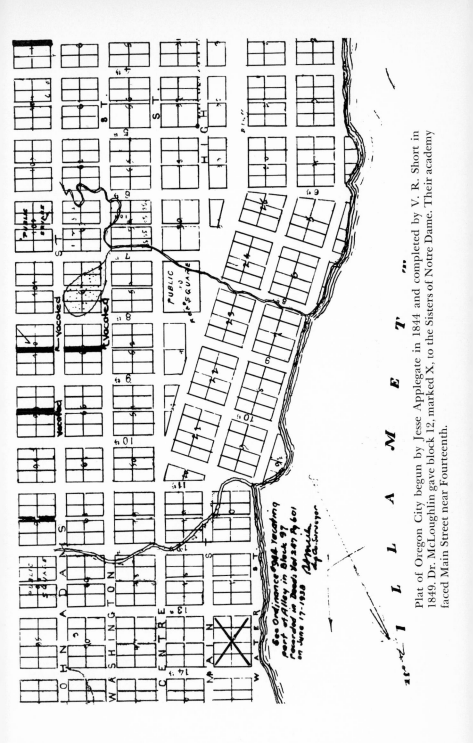

Plat of Oregon City begun by Jesse Applegate in 1844 and completed by V. R. Short in 1849. Dr. McLoughlin gave block 12, marked X, to the Sisters of Notre Dame. Their academy faced Main Street near Fourteenth.

Above: Stove brought to Oregon by Vicar-General Blanchet in 1838 and used by the Sisters of Notre Dame at St. Paul.

Below: Names of the five Indians convicted in the Whitman murder trial, Oregon City, May 24, 1850.

Lower right: Ad in the *Oregon Statesman,* March 12, 1853, p. 3, col. 2, announcing Sister Loyola's auction sale.

Top above: Basket made by the Willamette Indians in 1844 and presented to the Sisters of Notre Dame.

Above: Nail made in Hudson's Bay Company's forge at Fort Vancouver.

The Sisters of Notre Dame

Being about to leave the Territory offer for sale at Public Auction,

AT the Young Ladies Academy, Oregon City, on the 17th inst., all moveable articles, consisting of dining tables, chairs, and all sorts of kitchen and house furniture, linen clothing, linen table cloths, toweling, carpets, (1 Turkey) dinner and tea services, pewter plate. Musical instruments, consisting of two pianos, one harp and one guitar.

Stationery and numerous miscellaneous articles suitable for ladies boudoirs.

Garden and flower seeds of every kind.

Paints for ladies; lamp oil.

Stock, consisting of eight cows with their calves; five at St. Paul's Mission, 3 at the place of sale; all of American blood but three which have 1-4th Spanish.

Any person wishing to inspect the articles offered for sale will be afforded every facility.

The building and gardens are for sale or rent. The garden is under the most perfect cultivation, well stocked with fruit-bearing trees of various kinds, garden vegetables, &c., &c.

March 12, 1853.

52

walls, and a stairs down to the floor level. It must have been a dirt floor with planks to stand on, but the cellar was furnished with roomy shelves, above ground level as well as below, as a precaution against flooding in the rainy season.

In the memoirs there are divergent accounts of this first academy. In the section which the Annals devoted to the second colony of Notre Dame Sisters, Sister Laurence describes it as poorly built, the chapel being "no better protected than other parts of the house." Sister tells of "benches and a few pieces of furniture," and of "the delights of poverty" that the community experienced. But as Sister Laurence never lived in Oregon City, and as she wrote her account at least twenty-five years later, she may have confused the academy with the poorly built Sainte Marie de Willamette; certainly her description fits that house exactly.

Sister Marie Catherine wrote of the academy as spacious and well appointed. Her description is in agreement with that of Sister Mary Alphonsus, a Sister of the Holy Names and Superior of their first mission in Portland, who visited the house with Mother Joseph of the Providence Sisters in 1860, some seven years after the Sisters of Notre Dame had left Oregon. They found "this once elegant convent" in a state of neglect. The orchard and outhouses presented "a sad picture." Sister Mary Alphonsus says that Mother Joseph wept "in passing through these large apartments that had given hospitality to the Sisters of Providence, who sojourned three months in Oregon . . ." One must have visited this place, she said, to realize the amount expended in the erection of this school by the Sisters of Notre Dame.[6]

Sister Mary Alphonsus was, no doubt, comparing the academy with other buildings which she found in the dark decade that brought her to Oregon; the academy must have been a little less than elegant. But certainly Sister Loyola would have wanted the very best building possible and would have bent every bit of energy to the production of an impressive boarding school. All the Sisters' academies of the last century on the Pacific Coast have the look of fine mansions, even though pioneer workers' miscalculations allowed for breezes around window casings and under doors.

That Sister Loyola aimed at a certain air of propriety seems clear from the improvements made and the furnishings purchased during the first two years. She had prie-dieus made for the chapel at the cost of $58.50. She purchased some sort of finish paneling for its walls and apparently for other rooms, perhaps parlors. The little organ which the Sisters brought to San José would have graced any academy chapel of the period. There were good carpets, one of them Turkish, in the house. There were dinner and tea services, and good pewter ware. The furnishings of the sleeping apartments, "suitable for ladies' boudoirs," were a far call from Sainte Marie de Willamette's mattresses on the floor. And now Sister Loyola purchased a second piano and a harp, as well as smaller instruments. She may have purchased accoutrements from Captain Menes when *l'Etoile du Matin* was scuttled in 1849, but the point is that she did acquire them and thus made her academy one of the best.[7]

In construction, the academy must have been more or less like the McLoughlin House.[8] The doctor himself would certainly have taken as great an interest in its planning as he did in that of St. John's Church a little earlier. And while he seems not to have aided the academy beyond the donation of the block on which it stood, he must have helped Sister Loyola to obtain materials not produced in the local mill. But even door and window frames, floor boards and siding, made in the local mill were properly finished. Here Sister Loyola was not making the best of a house already badly begun. This was her carefully meditated plan. She was one to build well, a little on the grand side if possible, and she had the experience of the house in rue l'Arbre Bénit. With her own desire to have things right, and with the exact and intelligent assistance at her disposal, there would be few mistakes in measurements in the building of the academy. In fact, with at least two Sisters present through most of the time of construction, the workmen must have found the atmosphere of exactness at times depressing.

But the supervision resulted in an institution sufficiently imposing to be known as a Young Ladies' Boarding and Day School, one in which "the system of instruction" embraced, "in addition to the ordinary courses of English studies, all the branches usually taught in the best female academies." [9] Here the heart, as well as the mind, was to be formed and "adorned with all those qualities which beautify the manners and render virtue attractive and amiable." Here "moral advancement" would receive "most assiduous care." The very location of the academy, "on the banks of the Wilamet, and remote from the business part of the city," was "advantageous and beautiful." The building was "spacious and airy, and the pleasure grounds dry and extensive." Health and neatness were cared for "with most minute attention," and the pupil fortunate enough to be out of classes a few days with the measles would "experience the most affectionate and constant attention." Those less fortunate would find in the classroom "incentive proper to inspire a laudable emulation."

All this, of course, called for an advance over the barter economy of Sainte Marie de Willamette's "brilliant prospectus." Board and tuition of the privileged young academy ladies was $175 a session, which meant a school year. For a day boarder, it was $75, and in both cases payment was asked a half-session in advance. Day pupils paid according to age and by the quarter, the rate running from $4.50 in the "infant class" to $9.50 in the "more advanced." Rates for piano, vocal lessons, drawing, and painting could be "ascertained" at the academy, or by writing to the "Lady Superior." As was fitting, there was an entrance fee of $10.

But the boarders' account book, begun in 1848, makes it clear that the prospectus was somewhat elastic, that it was not too difficult to make special arrangements with the Lady Superior. A frequent cause of variation seems to have been the fact that a pupil could be enrolled at any time of year, an arrangement that must have been slightly distressing to teachers. And there is evidence that Sister Loyola met, with Christian charity, the always present inability to pay the full amount. But fees for art and music were fairly constant. Art was $24 a session and piano $36, with the full quota of lessons. "Guitare" was also $36 a session, but the lone guitarist of the school, Elizabeth McLean, whose bills were paid by HBC, mastered that instrument in a half session, after which she passed on to the conquest of the piano. Washing and mending, done presumably by the Sisters, was an extra $36 a year. In a very few instances, a bill was paid partly in produce. Sister Loyola accepted 3,000 bricks (valued at $45) on the Pambrun girls' account and a consignment of beef and pork on Emma Burton's; but these perhaps represent purchases which she would have made in any case from the same sources.

Through late 1849 and 1850, the boarders' account book (and there is no other register) shows a roster rising to thirty-six, with several paying in full. There were also a few complete charity cases, abandoned natives whom the Sisters hoped to train in housewifely ways, but who presented problems when, in fishing season, clusters of wigwams appeared on the river banks. These few children, eight or ten at most, came to the Sisters knowing no English. They were probably enrolled in the Infant Class, and learned slowly to read through an English primer. These and the day pupils, who must not have exceeded fifty or sixty, brought the total enrollment to perhaps eighty or ninety during the academy's best days.

We have no description of life in that Young Ladies' Boarding and Day School during its brief time of success, but it is easy enough to visualize it in the light furnished by other Notre Dame schools of the time. The monastic silence in the dormitories after night prayer, the peal of suppressed laughter after the presiding Sister finished the blessing before meals, the round of entertainments at which Governor Lane and Doctor McLoughlin, and perhaps Captain Menes and other worthies, attended with Archbishop Blanchet as distinguished guests.

The academy songbirds, the Cosgroves, Elizabeth McLean, Mary Cod, Eveline Chapman, Frances Powell, Angélique Black, and Charlotte Seymour, would sing the sweetly sentimental numbers that the same teachers taught young vocalists a few years later in San José. The Rae sisters would curtsy as one, seat themselves at the two pianos, and challenge the closest-fitting windows with a marching duo, in a unison that thrilled their white-haired grandfather and, for the time, wiped the Donation Law from his harried mind. And

one, and two, and three, and four! How perfect! But they
do not move their lips or heads. No, No, Sister Mary
Aloysia says that is not done. Besides, the perfect unison of
two well-synchronized metronomes can be achieved without
such aid.

Through the little program all the students, from infants
to young ladies, sit on rows of benches facing each other
across a wide aisle, a sort of mall with His Lordship seated
centrally at one end, opposite the performers' platform.
When not performing, one sits erect, gloved hands neatly
folded, spine rigid, as much on exhibit as when playing one's
solo. How sadly they realize the fact. Now there is Sister
Loyola herself looking squarely at one. The feet! Third
position!

But it is over now, and from the corner comes the muffled
sound of Sister Mary Aloysia's wooden signal. As one, all
stand, noiselessly as a roomful of angels. And the curtsy!
One, two, three down. One, two, three up. At last Sister
Superior has taken His Lordship and the other guests to the
big parlor with the Turkish carpet. One can relax now with
even Sister Mary Bernard smiling her satisfaction. *Très bien,
mes enfants!*

With no movie, no soft-drink counter in corner drugstore,
nor even a school candy store, girlish distractions must have
consisted chiefly in frills. Clothing, bonnets, gloves, shawls,
shoes are the recurring items in the old Boarders' Account
Book. But the young ladies were pleased with it all. The
sight of a row of teen-agers, elbows on the counter, sipping
their cokes, would have set the Cosgrove tongues a-clucking.
Nor did they mind being marched along the river for off-
ground recreation, two by two, with two Sisters bringing up
the rear.

No one expected the purchase of shoes, or gloves, or bonnets to constitute just reason for sallying forth to the business
section. Instead, some wise and trusted friend of the Sisters
would bring samples of the desired articles from the store,
and the academy miss would make her selection in the parlor
under the approving eye of Sister Mary Aloysia or of Sister
Superior herself. Nevertheless, excitement ran high when

the four older Cosgroves displayed new "schalls crepe de Chine," at $8 apiece, and when all six were tricked out with fichus and colets, and with four and three-fourths yards of ribbon each for the sum of $12.50. It was a big day, too, when the ladies of the crepe de Chine "schalls" stepped out with new plaid gowns that cost their proud father $23 in yardage. The gowns were quite likely a major sewing-class project, for though weaving never came to the academy, plain and fancy sewing were required subjects, as testified by frequent entries of yardage, twisted thread, silk, and wool. What delightful scenes reward the perusal of those old pages, worn with daily entries of the needs and whims of academy girls, whose fathers were gathering nuggets in Sonora or scooping up smaller fragments on the banks of the Feather River!

The spendthrift of the school was Charlotte Ann Seymour, whose account runs far over the space allotted her and occupies the unfinished page of one less fortunate. Charlotte must have been a sort of star boarder, perhaps older than the other girls; her buying has the unfettered look of one who could go into the shops and fend for herself. And money was not a problem for Charlotte. On one foray she acquired a splendid shawl, silk and pearls for a fancy bag, and calico for "robes." Her "chapeau de paille," with its "monture" to keep it shapely, cost her $5.60, a price which gives the elegant straw a place with the crepe de Chine shawl. But her real fondness was for footgear; she purchased three pairs of shoes on one occasion and five on another. Space for Charlotte's shoes must have presented a problem, unless perhaps she gave them, slightly worn, to the native girls. Perhaps Charlotte was bargain minded. A nice pair of shoes cost her $2.75 or $3 in Caufield's store. The five pairs cost $12.25. And having a sweet tooth, she spent the gain on "melon confits."

As sisters were entered on one page, it is hard to tell whether it was Margaret or Maria Louisa Rae who caused distress to Sister Alphonse Marie's gentle Muse with her "Accordeum," a noble instrument, which must have been at its best in a canoe on the river, and which she purchased from the Cosgrove sisters for the sum of $3.50. But on the same page, the Muse is consoled by the purchase of piano selections under the tempting entry, *morceaux de musique.*

Aged nine and eight, the little Rae sisters made their first Communion in the summer of 1850, for which occasion, besides rosaries and fifteen yards of velvet ribbon, the account book records $15 for tulle veiling, easily the most expensive material appearing on its pages. White dresses for the occasion were perhaps produced at the McLoughlin home.

Lowering of transportation charges with increased shipping must account for the inexpensive school supplies and textbooks of 1850. Certainly mademoiselle's book bill, from syllabaire to science text, could not have given cause of complaint to the most parsimonious of fathers. Disappointingly, the titles are never given; instead, all the items handed to the eager student on a given date are set with economy on a single line, "Atlas géographie histoire," with no commas between; "grammaire cahiers plumes" are written together like a single title.

Fortunately, two texts have come down from Oregon City Academy days. *The Central School Reader: Being a Collection of Essays and Extracts from approved Writers,* was compiled by the Female Association for the Improvement of Juvenile Books, and published in Philadelphia by Thomas, Cowperthwait & Co., 1847, with an apology by the Female Association for producing another selection of readings for the more advanced classes "in this age when school books have been multiplied to such an extent, as to be spoken of as being 'too much of a good thing' . . ." Bound in tan leather and printed on tough paper, the book is still in good condition. Sister Mary Bernard took it to Marysville with her in 1856, where the inscription, *Srs. of Notre Dame, Oregon,* in her own strong hand, must have brought the tall, white academy before her as she built the towered, red-brick convent where the Feather and Yuba rivers meet.[10] Bryant and Wordsworth and lesser lights are represented in this old reader, with a preponderance of nature pieces in which the moral is usually obvious and sentimentally so. All of which is quite as one would expect from the Female Association for the Improvement of Juvenile Books.

The other text, *Inquiries Concerning the Intellectual Powers, and the Investigation of Truth,* by John Abercrombie, M.D., F.R.S., Fellow of the Royal College of Physicians in Edinburgh and First Physician to His Majesty in Scotland, was published by Harper Brothers in New York in 1843. Probing into the mental causes of physical ills, His Majesty's first pysician had produced this learned little book for the general reader some years before in Edinburgh. Then the American publisher, noting that it was being used in classes of "Intellectual Philosophy" in many "seats of science," furnished it with a complete set of examination questions for the convenience of teacher as well as student. And though the advertisement declares that these questions have been so constructed as "to avoid the evils of engendering the habit of mere mechanical recitation," the thoroughness with which they follow the text, sentence by sentence, would certainly guarantee a top grade to practiced memory without benefit of thought. For teacher and student, the effect must have been deadening; one can see them both checking off the known items, flattering security hedging their minds against investigation.

This is the method found in pupils' notebooks of succeeding decades, a study plan that made for assured success on exhibition days, as parents listened enraptured to their offspring answering every question with finality. But the method that produced this fine showing at the annual public examinations hampered the learning process and prevented even a Sister Mary Aloysia from knowing the greatest joy of teaching. With their answers smugly tucked away in notebook or memory, locked treasures awaiting the key of her question, her students would hardly engage her offhand in the garden with young Socratic challenge.

So this little "Investigation of Truth," closed thus ironically against further investigation in the "seats of learning," must have been used by Sister Mary Aloysia's few advanced "science" students. Between two pages in the chapter on reasoning, there is a faded violet, its petals spread carefully, no doubt by her artistic fingers, and in the corresponding question section is a tiny paper marker. As the bristol-board cover shows a great deal of wear, this uninviting, black text-book may have seen some years of use in San José, in which case the discourse on reason may be graced by a pueblo violet instead of one from Willamette banks.

Whatever Doctor Abercrombie thought about the part played by the mind in physical ills, Sister Loyola set high practical value on hygiene and medical care. Among her records of doctor's visits and various medicines and drugs, loom the ominous English words that sent quavers down academy spines—Castor Oil. And without attractive bulletin reminders to spur them to their duty, the mesdemoiselles, little and big, brushed their teeth; that is clear from the frequent account book entries of *brosse à dents*.

CHAPTER 14

Beacon to the South

The walls of Sister Loyola's academy had scarcely risen when the land of gold began to attract her. Not later than the spring of 1849, she announced to Mère Constantine that her plans for a foundation "in the mountains" had to be abandoned, and offered California as an alternative. Some of the Jesuits, she said, had already transferred their efforts to this land of promise. Soon she wrote again that she had been offered a house in San Francisco. But the notion of abandoning Oregon and her academy had probably not as yet occurred to her when she first speaks of this new enthusiasm.

At once Mère Constantine applies a more than usually cautious curb. California seems beyond the Sisters' strength, she writes. And for the same reason she is very happy that the mountain venture has been frustrated. Go slowly; the same thing may happen to the California project. Wild stories from the gold fields have trickled through to her; California doesn't seem a proper place for Sisters. The rush for wealth makes the place dangerous, and law hasn't been established as yet.

Then a little later the Mother General herself becomes somewhat intrigued, perhaps as a result of letters from Father Accolti to which she refers. In December, she playfully concludes that since there is now so much gold in the West, there will soon be no further need for the Oregon purse at Namur. Presently she will ask Sister Louise at Cincinnati for English-speaking Sisters in case Sister Loyola finds it necessary to start this third foundation. While waiting for this reinforcement, Sister Loyola must keep the California plan in mind, for

216

now the cautious Mère Constantine herself feels a longing
to help in this wonderland.

In March, 1850, in response to another plea from Sister
Loyola, the Mother General admits that she is more drawn
to the idea than ever. She will send four Sisters presently,
but at the moment she cannot give financial aid; in fact,
she hopes the journey expense "will not devolve on us,"
for if it does, she "will have to borrow money." Then for
some reason, she changes her mind and counsels waiting until
the gold rush subsides, notwithstanding the advantages California has to offer. At the year's end, when the four recruits
are on their way, she states her opposition explicitly; even
after their arrival, she writes, the Sisters would still be too
few for so great a venture. In the light of more recent information and advice, she opposes any new risk for the time.
Referring to the Archbishop's "great enterprises," she warns
Sister Loyola against precipitation, advice which was perhaps
the effect of Father Boldoc's recent visit to the Mother
House.[1]

Through these two years, Sister Loyola's interest in California was in proportion to inducements laid before her by
members of the Oregon clergy who had gone south, at first
temporarily. The exodus started when Father J. B. A. Brouillet, then Vicar-General of Bishop A. M. A. Blanchet, left
for San Francisco at the end of 1848 with the hope of solicit-
ing funds from charitably inclined miners. Perhaps, too, his
going was in response to a recent appeal to Archbishop
Blanchet for priests to care for the crowds flocking into a
land in which the fine Christianity of mission days had sadly
declined. In reply, Archbishop Blanchet made it clear that
while he deplored the dearth of priests everywhere, he was
still not in a position to furnish missionaries; there were
still too few in Oregon.[2] Nevertheless, he approved of Father
Brouillet's absence for a time, especially as funds were so
badly needed in his brother's diocese. It was otherwise in the
case of Father Anthony Langlois, who at this point declared
his intention of becoming a Jesuit.

With his Archbishop's full permission, Father Langlois
left Oregon to go to Canada by the roundabout way of San

Francisco. But the aspirant never reached the distant novitiate; instead, he stopped to assist Father Brouillet in establishing the first American parish in the new city by the bay. There, swept along by a new enthusiasm and the success of their enterprise, he could not understand Father Brouillet's dutiful determination to return to Oregon at the end of his allotted time. Unable to persuade him, Father Langlois now appealed to the Oregon Jesuits to come to his aid and offered to send them $200 for passage money.[3] He must have known Archbishop Blanchet's stated desire to keep the priests who were then in Oregon; certainly he knew how their departure would affect him. This effort, then, to attract priests away from Oregon Territory seems inconsiderate. One would think that, recalling his earlier altercations with the Archbishop, he would be unwilling to cause him further pain. However, it is true that Father Brouillet also appealed to the Father General of the Jesuits to establish the Society in California, knowing, as he said, the desire of some of the Oregon Jesuits to labor there.

Fathers Accolti and Nobili went to San Francisco in early December, correctly assuming the Father General's response to that appeal.[4] The permission to go to California was based on the hope that greater good would be done where there were greater numbers, a viewpoint which did not appeal to Archbishop Blanchet. First and last, he held to the claim that there were not priests enough in Oregon. And while it is true that the first wild rush for the California mines took almost "everyone who had a shovel," a counter movement soon set in as prospectors learned to prefer a steadier income from the production of goods needed by the miners.

Immigrants had slipped through Oregon to California during the height of the rush; as the excitement died, they began to remain in Oregon. Outside of Oregon City, the Donation Land Law spurred immigration, and the discovery of gold in Southern Oregon called back many prospectors from the mines of California. The presence of an active clergy among these immigrants and miners would have created good will and prevented the hostility, based on ig-

norance, encountered by later missionaries in the territory.
Besides, the departure of missionaries from Oregon left the
Indians along the rivers unshepherded; for though they re-
treated later to the deep forests, in the early fifties they still
maintained villages along the Willamette, one of them within
sight and, alas, within sound of the convent in Oregon City.

On the same page of memoir or letter one finds the statement that the missionaries had no longer enough to do in
Oregon, with expressions of regret that their departure left
so many without instruction and ministry. The contradiction is not so puzzling as it seems. Little churches emptied
suddenly by the gold rush account for the statement; the
times that followed hard upon it account for the regret. Yet
as there was no time when the ministry was not needed, the
decision to let the Jesuits leave for California must have been
a difficult one.

The sudden bright hope in California accentuated, too,
trials that the missionaries accepted in earlier days as part of
their lives. Now the sufferings of Father Nobili in British
Columbia, extreme as the sanctity with which he bore them,
extended by repute to the entire area. But his subsisting
for a year on the flesh of dogs and wolves, on moss and grasses,
justifying as it does the order in 1848 to abandon that wild
country, is an extreme picture not paralleled in other parts
of Oregon. In fact, prospects seem to have been bright
enough when in that same year Governor Lane was greeted
in Oregon City with twelve guns.[5] Just before the fire at
Sainte Marie, Sister Loyola reported a degree of prosperity
to Mère Constantine.[6] And in that same year she was able
to purchase a tract of 240 acres at Multnomah for $1500.[7]
Even the losses sustained in the fire did not leave the Sisters
destitute. For a time, laundry and baking were reduced to
primitive conditions, but the community soon began improvements again, including buildings. The Sisters in general were less affected by the promises of California than were
the clergy. Sister Marie Catherine's long letter from Oregon
City in early 1850 does not even mention the land of gold.
Though, as always, she stresses the trials, the hard work, the
sometimes ugly dispositions of the children at Sainte Marie,

it is still "our dear little house at Willamette." It is there that "her heart always recalls her." [8] But in time some of the Sisters, too, began to see their difficulties in the intenser light of reports from the South.

The murder of Presbyterian Marcus Whitman, his wife, and eight other Americans at Wailatpu on the Walla Walla River, in 1847, by a band of angry Cayuse Indians, and the subsequent floods of accusations against the Catholic clergy, cast a more depressing shadow than did the exodus to California mines, a shadow which would have been more readily dissipated had they remained.

The tragedy was due partly to Doctor Whitman's method of hurrying the native away from his primitive notions and forcing on him the white man's attitudes. Ignoring their feeling toward the unsuccessful medicine man, he attempted and failed to cure those stricken with one of the recurring epidemics. With their anger whipped up by a malicious half-breed, who made them see Whitman and his associate, the Reverend H. H. Spalding, as their mortal enemies, a band of natives entered the Whitman home and carried out their revenge. Father Brouillet came upon the scene in time to save Spalding's life by appealing to the murderers, an act which Spalding repaid by accusing the Catholic clergy, who could wield such influence over the savage, of instigating the murder.[9]

The air was at once charged with accusations against all Catholic missionaries; poor Sister Renilde had scarcely drawn her last breath when gossip attacked even her fair name. In Oregon City, however, natives as well as whites rose up in the dead Sister's defense. She was completely vindicated, and from then on bigotry spared the Sisters in the little capital. Sister Marie Catherine was more disturbed by the fate of the five Cayuses who paid for the crime with their lives in Oregon City in 1850 than by all the furor. They were mere children, she said; and so they were, giving the frightened, confused evidence of children at their trial. Still they faced death bravely, fortified by baptism and First Communion at the hands of Archbishop Blanchet and Father Veyret.

The unfortunate affair brought about the end of the Presbyterian mission; if anything, it left the Catholic clergy in a stronger position with the natives. But despite the efforts of Hon. Peter Burnett and the honest opinion and testimony of some Protestants, the bitterness of many against the Catholic clergy continued. For this very reason, the continued friendly presence of missionaries was desirable.

Materially the Sisters' affairs were declining the spring of 1851, yet they had known much worse times. The number of boarders had fallen, as might have been expected, with the return of parents from California. But the house was not in great debt; Sister Loyola's book showed a small balance, and she held lots in Portland where land was beginning to be valuable. Thus it is hard to tell whether she thought of the California foundation as the first of a series of steps leading to the abandoning of Oregon. Circumstances demanded patient waiting, and she always found waiting as difficult to bear as failure; her need of security called for one glowing iron in the fire. And there was the offer of a house in California.

In the leather-backed account book, made by WCB & Co., London, Sister Loyola's neat and delicate writing offers some guide to conditions as she saw them through the early fifties. She considered prices at the time very high, and they were high as compared with those at the HBC stores before American competition entered the country. Yet she managed several improvements, such as the sinking of a good well, and the installation of a pump at the cost of $101. This put an end to the daily trudge to the river each morning at dawn, when the Sisters stood in a line on the steep bank handing buckets up from one to another, a duty which Father Accolti called "Via Crucis." And that before breakfast!

Four blankets cost $12, which Sister Loyola thought exorbitant. A blacksmith bill for "utensils" was $29. A carrier named Mr. Brown was often paid for services; one month his bill was $46. Wood for a shrine of St. Anthony was $35. A supply of dried apples cost $46.50. Butter was fifty cents a pound in February, 1851. The account registers satisfactory sales, too. Now Sister Loyola disposes of a horse, probably

one raised on the farm, for $80, exactly ten times the value
of a horse in the idyllic pre-American days. Another time
it is "un taureau" that brings in $30. Sister Loyola drove
good bargains, and at the time of her first trip to San Francisco her accounts show a fair balance.

Looking at the academy's decreased enrollment, Sister
Loyola may have come to share Doctor McLoughlin's dark
forebodings about the effect of the Donation Land Law on
Oregon City. She may have foreseen that immigrants staking claims in the valleys under its secure and generous provisions, and miners returning with gold, could not give back
leadership to the one excluded area where even the doctor
considered himself as living on sufferance. Actually he was
never forced to leave his claim, nor did business in Oregon
City ever come to a complete standstill. As late as October,
1851, Sister Loyola paid her share in a street improvement.
Only McLoughlin's land was adversely affected; those who
had purchased land from him might sell it if they wished. But
listening to the doctor's fulminations against Samuel Thurston, all the missionaries, as well as Archbishop Blanchet,
may have seen in the action against McLoughlin's claim a
cloud of ill will darkening and threatening the entire territory.

There was certainly enough opposition to Doctor Mc-
Loughlin in the report sent by Thurston to the House of
Representatives in June, 1850, after his election as Territorial Delegate from Oregon. Oregon City, he said, the capital of the Territory, situated on the best water power in the
world, had been wrongfully wrested from the Americans by
the doctor. Thurston claimed that the Methodist missionaries had first taken over the site, that they had been forced
to leave it under fear of having the Indians let loose on
them. McLoughlin had forced many citizens to leave the
claim while he was yet head of the HBC fort at Vancouver
with Indians at his command, he added; besides, up to March
4, 1849, the doctor had sold lots to the amount of $200,000.
Further, the doctor was still a British subject, still connected
with HBC, and was still refusing to file his intentions to become an American citizen. Thurston made other accusations

equally false. On the floor of the House, he referred to Doctor McLoughlin as another Benedict Arnold and an enemy of Americans.[10]

The Oregon Donation Law, passed September 27, 1850, was all Thurston could desire. By its terms every white settler, including aliens, either then resident or to become resident before December 1, 1850, had a right to a claim except Doctor McLoughlin. His claim would be used by the Territory for a university, this to prevent it reverting to his family. Doctor McLoughlin spent the year before the law would go into effect in bitter protest. His reply to the accusations appeared in the *Oregon Spectator*, September 12, 1850. Others, too, made efforts in his favor, but the law was not altered. Even after the law went into effect, protests were made, but though Samuel Thurston was drowned shortly after its passage, there were others to keep alive the devious inventions started by Waller. On the one hand, the university was not even begun, and property holders in Oregon City were not molested; on the other, the growth of the little city was stopped. Worst of all, the bigotry aroused by the Whitman massacre was fanned to flame by Thurston's revival of the Waller affair, and this conflagration extended far beyond Oregon City.

Actually, through those later years in Oregon City, the Sisters were carrying on an apostolate which would have satisfied the dreams they had as they paced *l'Infatigable's* deck. By simple instruction, sometimes formal but mostly casual, by acts of charity, but chiefly by patient understanding, they were making a deep and grateful impression on the Indians. Perhaps simple and gentle Sister Francisca knew best how to deal with them. She never confused them with explanations. They never feared to interrupt her household chores when they needed her help.

One morning an old Indian appeared in the kitchen, holding in his arms his little sick grandchild. Sister recognized the colic and administered a simple remedy. Then knowing that grandpa, too, had to be quieted by a much more elaborate display, she selected a soothing ointment, took baby on her lap, and applied the salve with great concern and

ado. It was medicine-man technique and Sister thought it
the right approach to grandpa's mind, poised between native
cult and Christian faith, and with only the dimmest notion
that medicine poured from a bottle might have a scientific
relation to pain. And Sister had no fear of an ugly reaction
should the child fail to respond. She knew the Indians
trusted the Sisters, though she did not realize her own special
success with them, success arising from her willingness to
allow them sufficient time to attain the white man's standards. And she loved the humorous incidents that marked
the waiting.

Another convert was the good-natured native that Sister
Loyola hired to help Sister Francisca in the academy garden.
Before long he was attending Mass and Vespers at St. John's
as he had done for a brief span before in one of Father
DeSmet's mountain missions. But one Sunday afternoon he
arrived too late even for Benediction, and as the Sisters filed
out they saw him standing dejected at the door. Sister Francisca offered her sympathy for she knew how he loved to
join in the Latin hymns, his lusty voice almost drowning
out Sister Mary Aloysia's efforts at the organ. They had
missed his singing, she told him. At her words his face
brightened. It was no matter, he said, as he knew the hymns
perfectly and could sing them alone. In proof of this ability,
he entered the church, knelt reverently, and sang the Benediction through, standing in dignity at the end for his own
resounding Doxology.

Every Sunday afternoon, the Sisters sang Vespers in the
church at His Lordship's request, and at this ceremony they
could always count on the attendance of a number of natives
as well as of the McLoughlins and other pious persons. One
Sunday eighteen stalwart Indians, strangers from the village
across the river, marched in and stationed themselves with
tremendous dignity in the back benches, their stolid expressions midway between threat and awe. Sister Loyola
and Sister Mary Aloysia exchanged questioning glances.
Was this an attack? Father Accolti signalled to the Sisters
that all was well. The savages approved the singing by their
continued solemn mien, and at the end their leader prayed

aloud in Chinook. Then they filed out, bowing at the Sisters in great seriousness.

Like children, Indians, big and little, used to bring prized articles to Sister Francisca for safe keeping. As she was cooking, a head would bob in at the kitchen door and a trusting native would beg permission to hide a treasure in the garden. Some of these would show her the little crucifixes that their other friend, Father DeVoss, had given them, their proudest boast being that he had baptized them. Many a time, as Sister pointed out a hiding place for fishing rod or blanket, the owner trusted her with his spiritual secrets as well. Christ had died for the Indian, too, one of them told her and went away happy in her smiling agreement. Often they brought her gifts of fish and game; one morning she found a fine salmon lying on the community room floor.

A garden enterprise on which Sister Francisca and Sister Aldegonde embarked in the spring of 1850, though a failure agriculturally, reads also as a golden page in the native apostolate. The site of this kitchen garden was in Block 169, on Jackson Street, between 11th and 12th, a tract which Doctor McLoughlin had assigned to the church in 1846 as a cemetery.[11] Later on, when the Sisters' affairs seemed to be progressing, he dedicated this block "to educational purposes," which may have meant Sister Loyola's short-lived plan for a second school, a day school perhaps. The garden may have been Doctor McLoughlin's idea, for he wished to bring as much as possible of his claim under improvement. At any rate, he sent two Indians to clear the block and prepare the soil. But though the Sisters came only to supervise, they found, as usual, a good deal of hard work to do before they could plant their seeds. They supplied the tools, carrying them back and forth each day, as theft of implements was as certain as their high price.

Between summer rains, they could almost see their garden grow. But alas, they soon noticed small holes in the soil and near each a little hillock of upturned earth. Next they observed here and there a luxuriant potato plant shaking nervously. Then one day Sister Francisca saw a shy little head emerge from a hole and suddenly disappear. "Squirrels!" Thus she translated the Indians' term for Sister Odelie's benefit. And as neither of them knew about gophers, the "squirrels" were blamed as the plants wilted one by one. Sister Loyola sighed, too, for their St. Paul potato crop could not now be marketed in toto as she had hoped.

But Sister Francisca could reckon a greater gain than a store of fine potatoes. There were all the kind words the two Sisters had spoken to curious natives who stopped at the garden. She loved to tell of one good Indian sent there by Doctor McLoughlin to work. He set up his wigwam at the scene of action, and when a heavy rain made the Sisters seek shelter under a tree, he came quickly and invited them to share it. To prove his trustworthiness, he took from his pocket a little roll and spread it out before them. The *Catholic Ladder!* Archbishop Blanchet had given it to him, he explained in a mixture of French and Chinook. With this he had passed on the word of light to forest friends and sent them to the Archbishop. Here was a chosen soul, who prayed daily and would walk long distances to assist at Mass.

For the others, one had to build up confidence by not complaining about their wild din far into the night on the river bank, an uproar that made sleep impossible blocks away. Worst was when the pagans called in the aid of the medicine man. Then the Sisters knew some poor sick one was lying in a hollow in the ground with the grim watch around, his head splitting with the screams of the healer. And who could tell how many converts were there watching the frenzied gestures, with the old darkness lurking in their simple minds? One must just "take patience" and pray for all of them. The healer would be exhausted by midnight; as for the patient, if he could endure that din, he had strong hopes of recovery.

The best of the converts needed an unfailing fund of understanding. One of the little orphans at the academy went for an early morning run in the garden. Finding the grass quite wet, she took off the new shoes of which she was very proud, hid them under a bush, and ran off. They disappeared. Next morning, an Indian woman from the nearby encampment called to see Sister Francisca. Quite unashamed, the simple creature was wearing the lost shoes, and spying them, the irate loser demanded her property. The Indian woman was greatly dismayed at the girl's accusation of theft, and it was really not theft, Sister Francisca said; to the woman, the garden was the great outdoors; anything found there was common property. Others, even churchgoers, took clothes from the laundry line. Why not? When one wished to hide something, the Sisters' grounds were sacred; at other times, they were a part of everywhere. One must not expect logic, and the more successful missionaries insisted least on the syllogism, and never showed astonishment at the Indian's surprising way of fulfilling obligations. When a group went fishing on Sunday morning, and piously substituted a visit to the Sisters' chapel for the duty of assisting at Mass, they were pleasing enough to the Lord, said the edified Sisters. No reproof, just a kind word; sometime they would understand.

There was the poor wretch who had been beaten almost to death in an Indian brawl, and who dragged himself to the academy. He must see the Lady Superior. He was surely going to die; he must be baptized and go to Heaven. The Lady Superior must, of course, be the one to perform the ceremony. But she was away, and the girl who opened the door merely told him so and waited for Sister Loyola's return to report the visit. Sister Loyola set out at once with what remedies she had at hand. Finding the man dying in a hovel, she made him as comfortable as possible and sent for Father Veyret, who came directly and baptized him. When the poor Indian died, another gentle deed was topic for almost wordless conversation around the campfire.

But aside from these opportunities among the natives, the promise of the academy should have offered reason for content in Oregon City in that quickened era when miners were returning with gold. Yet from the day in January, 1849, when settler Hugh Cosgrove stirred the quiet convent with the story of his eighteen pounds of gold acquired in a few days, and the *Oregon Spectator* announced that gold dust was selling in Valparaiso for $18.00 per ounce, California was a magic word even to Sisters.[12] Protestant clergymen who had families to support became miners for a while. There was the Reverend Ezra Fisher, who wrote to his Baptist sponsors that he had left his Oregon project for the time, to raise money to give his children "something of the bare comforts of life." Already, in July, 1849, he had made $1000, a clear sign that God was pleased with his venture.[13] Everyone talked of gold, especially as payments began to be made in gold dust, which Sister Loyola entered in her accounts as distinct from cash.

Sceptics thought the dust, poured out recklessly on counters for a time, would never have any value. It was like dirt, reminisced one pioneer, who saw a four-quart pan of it collected in a single day in an HBC store in Oregon City.[14] But traders allowed $16.00 an ounce for it, and thus honored, it had to be accepted. The wonder was the ease, the quickness of acquiring it; it was not like waiting for an uncertain crop to mature. In the land where it was plentiful, churches and schools could be erected as quickly as gold was acquired. To one who liked accomplishment, the measured ounces spoke eloquent words.

With her mind on several ventures, always including a house in San Francisco, Sister Loyola did not see that the academy was itself a factor in social change in that golden year of 1850. Under its roof met Canadian, American, and English maidens given more or less to studious pursuits. Though they certainly did not meet one another's brothers and friends under that roof, they as certainly talked of them the more for that reason. The Cosgrove family furnished four brides in the 1850's. In 1851, Margaret married the Canadian T. Poujade, and Ann married F. E. Eldridge. Later their brother married Mary Cavanagh, an academy girl. 1851 marked the weddings of Christina Klinger to Clifton Callaghan and of her sister Matilda to Andrew Poujade. In the fall of 1850, Doctor McLoughlin's ward, Mary Spence, married Charles McKay. Two years later, his sister Christina married J. N. Harty. Perhaps the most fashionable of these weddings was that of Ada Pambrun, second daughter of P. G. Pambrun of the Honorable Company, in May, 1852, to Captain Edward H. Beard of Baltimore, the young officer who lost his life less than a year later when his ship, the *Vandalia*, was wrecked on the bar.[15]

As the year 1850 rounded out, the Sisters had little time to consider social changes. The deadliest epidemic, typhoid fever, swept up from the south, turning their schools into hospitals. Indian and half-breed seemed more susceptible and defenseless than American settler. At Sainte Marie only one child escaped, and the Sisters waited through a terrible week before a doctor arrived to diagnose the disease and direct treatment. The sick children, he said, must be isolated at once, but this was not easy since only one pupil had a home.

Across the road was the deserted St. Joseph's College which Father Boldoc had abandoned in complete discouragement after the closing exercises of 1849. Since then its staring windows had reminded the Sisters sadly of good Mr. Larocque, its benefactor, of Father DeSmet's pleasure at finding the school "very prosperous," and of the English commander of the frigate *Modeste*, an interested visitor to this little college. Now Sister Mary Cornelia used the empty building as a hospital and sent the first dozen cases there with Sister Mary Albine and Sister Aldegonde as nurses, hoping thus to check the spread of the disease. As more cases developed, Sister Marie Catherine joined the hospital staff. To her dismay she found strong Sister Aldegonde delirious with fever. The others came at once, but with all their care, they had to look on helplessly as eleven of their charges died. As the pastor anointed them, he remarked to Sister Marie Catherine on their excellent understanding of the sacraments. To her this seemed a great fulfillment. Had not the Sisters come to teach the children of the forest?

Sister Aldegonde's Belgian constitution carried her through her ordeal. The other Sisters escaped contagion despite the long hours of nursing that left them all exhausted. But when the trial was over, Sister Loyola found generous Sister Marie Catherine in so weakened a condition that she took her back with her to Oregon City for a few weeks' rest. There, as her strength returned, she pondered over Sister Loyola's wonderful plans and schemes. A hospital! Perhaps on the claim that she had acquired at St. Louis on Grand Prairie, or on her recently purchased lots in Portland. In either case, to staff it would involve closing the house at St. Paul. What would Mère Constantine say to that? What would she say to a hospital project at all? Certainly a hospital was needed, but it would require funds and here was Sister Loyola complaining about the drop in resident pupils, about her still unpaid bills. Besides, Notre Dame was strictly a teaching congregation.

Was Sister Loyola speculating too much? There was the recently acquired Block 138 for which she had promised to pay $2,400 in four years.[16] There was also Block 19, and the tract in Multnomah. What did it all mean? And now the promise of a house in San Francisco, or a tract of land there if she wished to build. Sister Loyola had asked Mère Constantine which she preferred.

Sister Marie Catherine went home to St. Paul somewhat puzzled and worried. She wished Sister Loyola were a little more like Sister Mary Cornelia. Yet she admired Sister Loyola. Perhaps California would afford her the scope she needed. She was a real missionary, she loved souls as Mère Julie had loved them, but she wanted quick and tangible proofs of success. This talk of closing Sainte Marie! Sister Marie Catherine disliked that most of all. What would His Lordship say to that? What would the poor orphans do without the Sisters? But Sister Marie Catherine checked her critical thoughts and was soon lost in her usual round of duties.

PART VI

ALTERED
DESTINY

CHAPTER 15

Adobe Beginnings

Ten more Sisters of Notre Dame left Antwerp for America in July, 1850, eight of them bound for Cincinnati and two for Oregon. With these two, Sister Louise was to send two of her Sisters with teaching experience in American schools, the plan being that they should meet the Belgians in New York and proceed by way of Panama under the care of Bishop Alemany who was on his way to assume episcopal duties in California as Bishop of Monterey. But plans miscarried somewhat as the ship, *Fanny,* was held at Antwerp for lack of wind until September.

Gifted and saintly but extremely gullible Sister Mary Alenie wrote a most delightful account of that sea voyage,

made possible (despite Mère Constantine's "slender purse")
by the generous 10,000 francs of Lady Petre, the future Sister
Mary of St. Francis. Thus furnished forth, the ten Sisters
were the only cabin passengers and, evidently all a bit over-
credulous, they believed every word of the mischievous captain's tall stories. To the end of her life, Sister Mary Alenie
told the preposterous tale of mutiny led by the first mate,
who, to confirm the captain's words, came and stood before
the Sisters displaying in silence a large lantern containing a
skull. But the captain, she said, loaded eighteen pistols and
guns, and sharpened as many swords, knives, and daggers.
Besides, he fired off the two cannon to establish his authority,
and thus the ten cabin passengers crossed the Atlantic safely.[1]

But as Bishop Alemany had not been able to await the
arrival of the Sisters at New York, all ten of them were taken
to Cincinnati, Sister Mary Alenie praying all the way to be
sent on to Oregon. She had no wish to remain in "the United
States," which she considered "too near Belgium in civilization." Like her first missionary Sisters, she wanted real mission life. Still, as there was an academy in Oregon, she studied
English and practiced piano daily until at last the word
came. For some reason, one of the Cincinnati volunteers was
unable to set out for Oregon, and thus the band of four comprised the recent arrivals, Sister Mary Aloysius, Sister Donatilde, and Sister Mary Alenie, with German-born Sister
Catherine, educated and professed in Cincinnati. In May
the four left New York for Panama on the steamer *Empire
City,* traveling with two Dominican Sisters, Sister Louise and
Sister Francis, en route to California. The friendship then
formed between Sister Louise and Sister Mary Alenie on that
eventful journey was lifelong. The "tramp of the Isthmus,"
wrote this Dominican pioneer to Sister Mary Alenie nearly
half a century later, made them "near and dear."

The Panama route, which had come into use to oblige
the headlong haste of gold seekers, presented five weeks of
epic dangers. Twenty-six-year-old Sister Mary Alenie, as head
of the Oregon-bound group, was afraid of nothing. She had
lived through a mutiny at sea; she had watched the would-be
assassins, with their bags and bundles, disappear in a crowd

on a street in New York. She would never worry again! But they must not cross the Isthmus in religious habits, they were told on the *Empire City*. Not prepared for this contingency, the four Notre Dame Sisters took counsel together. As the ship docked at Chagres, they emerged from their cabins wonderfully transformed in billowing nightgowns of purple calico, and large sunbonnets intended to protect their black veils from the sun while working in Oregon gardens. Thus they set out in company with the Dominican Sisters, a certain Mr. and Mrs. Heffernan, and Father Eugene O'Connell, the future Bishop of Grass Valley.

How Sister Mary Alenie would have enjoyed a good Western! Near tragedy lurked at every turn. Jewish Doctor Rabbe and another gentleman prevented the murderous intent of a band of Indians by presenting pistols. God sent these two good men, she said, but one feels she trusted the pistols, too. That night the Sisters' room, furnished with a calico curtain for door, was safe enough as Father O'Connell and Mr. Heffernan, armed with loaded pistols, so at least they told Sister Mary Alenie, stationed themselves at the entrance.

One minute the travelers enjoyed the scenes from the deck of a river steamer; next they were horrified as "murdered bodies" floated past. Leaving the boat, the party hired mules at the cost of $16 each, to convey them and their baggage over the dangerous roads to Panama. A boy was sent along as guide, but he turned out to be of little help because of the varying temperaments of the mules. Some of these animals seemed in a great hurry; others went at a snail's pace when they went at all; the boy could not be every place at once. Poor Sister Donatilde was thrown from her mount. Little Sister Mary Aloysius got caught up in the branches as her mule sauntered on placidly without her. That incident was amusing since Sister was not injured. A poor man in another party fared worse when he was robbed of his passage money to California and left fastened to a tree on the last lap of the way to Panama. He was almost dead when the missionary party released him, took him to the city, and made up his passage money between them.

At last the party reached Panama where they had a Spanish supper that scorched the Sisters' Belgian tongues. In the torrid tropic heat, with rats running about the "hotel," they listened through a sleepless night to the weird cacophony of chattering monkeys and scolding parrots. The six Sisters spent the next few days in a poverty-stricken convent where the beds were wretched hammocks. Their poor hostesses placed their only mattress on the floor for Sister Mary Alenie, whose sudden illness they diagnosed as Panama fever. Fortunately she responded to the remedy they gave her and was up and about before their ship was ready to sail.

The *Sarah Sands,* an English vessel making her last run up the coast before returning to England, and carrying forty-five cabin passengers besides a large number in the steerage, all seeking California wealth, was riding at the entrance to Panama Bay and had to be reached by a tugboat. But as there were no wharves, the tugboat could be boarded only by trusting oneself to the arms of a strong Indian hired for the purpose. Sister Louise objected to this mode of trans-poration, tried to make it out to the tugboat herself, and was rescued willy-nilly from near drowning by one of the Indians. Thoroughly drenched by Pacific waves, she ceased her objections.

Meanwhile, with Mère Constantine's strong December letter before her, Sister Loyola waited for further news of the third band of Sisters. If she were not to make a foundation in California, there would be the problem of transporting this new group from San Francisco, which was the port of ships up from Panama; but it seems quite clear that through these months Sister Loyola was still intrigued by the California project, despite Mère Constantine's objections. Certainly she was corresponding with Father Langlois, for he sent her passage money for herself and a Sister companion before April, and this with the understanding that she would look over the possibilities as well as meet the four new Sisters. His invitation was in the name of the recently arrived Bishop Alemany. If Sister Loyola should accept it, the four new missionary Sisters could be detained for a California foundation. And certainly Father Langlois, with his great zeal for

San Francisco, would not approve of their wasting their energies in a region in which he had lost interest.

Sister Loyola's decision to make a foundation in California should not be interpreted as opposition to her higher Superior's decision against it. There was no time at which Mère Constantine did not allow her freedom for short-notice action. The time lag in communication, though not at all as great as in the first years, was still considerable, and Mère Constantine knew she could not hope to see the actual picture at a given time. When she finally heard that the Sisters were settled in San José, her comment was, "If it is the will of God, it is also mine." [2] On the other hand, her letters through the early 1850's indicate a growing worry about Sister Loyola's manifold planning. There was, for one thing, the matter of incorporation of the two schools.[3]

The Territorial Government, in its new capital in Salem, was beginning to incorporate institutions. Builders of young western greatness, they bolstered it by legalizing, in high-sounding terms, infant institutions which came to maturity, if ever, many a decade later. But though the gold-framed document in ornate penmanship proved little about the educational status of the "college" in which it was enshrined, it furnished a security of ownership desirable in an era of conflicting claims, and titles thus confirmed would present advantages in the event of disposal. The idea appealed to Sister Loyola, and she further decided on single incorporation of the property at St. Paul with that of Oregon City. In proposing this measure to Mère Constantine, she stated that Sainte Marie might soon have to be abandoned because of losses in population.

Perhaps the Mother General saw in this proposal a move toward the sale of the property at St. Paul as independent of the mission. At any rate, she wrote in strong disapproval to Sister Loyola and to Sister Mary Cornelia as well. As she had recently learned, in a visit from Bishop Demers, that Americans were settling near Willamette as well as in other parts of Oregon, she warned against a hasty withdrawal from the mission. She was mistaken, of course, about the Americans at Willamette; those who did come in soon joined the new

stampede to Jacksonville. However, some weeks before Mère
Constantine's letter could have reached Oregon, Sister Loyola
herself consented to separate incorporation, perhaps with
legal advice, perhaps because Archbishop Blanchet insisted
upon it. He had never interpreted the contract he had signed
as giving Sister Loyola the right to dispose of the land held
by the Sisters at St. Paul. Thus at the end of January, 1851,
the House of Representatives and Council of the Territory
passed bills incorporating the Young Ladies' Academy of
Oregon City and St. Paul's Mission Female Seminary, the
changed title of the latter being perhaps significant.[4]

Sister Loyola's next suggestion was that they leave St. Paul
and build on the grant at St. Louis. To hold a grant, she
argued, one must improve it and live on it. This was true,
and in presenting her reason Sister Loyola was undoubtedly
sincere, but it is not difficult to detect in the suggestion a
subconscious desire to be rid of Archbishop Blanchet's control in secular matters. She must have been somewhat cha-
grined, then, by Mère Constantine's reply that both she and
her counselors disapproved of the plan since the land at St.
Paul, being also a grant, was in the same position. Moreover,
there was already a house on their holding at St. Paul, they
were making a fairly good living, and they were cared for
spiritually.[5] This was logical thinking. It must have seemed
strange that Sister Loyola, complaining of hard times, should
have thought of building again, particularly in a place where
the mission had been closed for over a year.

In opposing the union of the properties and in dealing
directly with Sister Mary Cornelia about Willamette, Mère
Constantine was also continuing the policy she had begun at
Sister Loyola's first mention of a provincial organization; her
plan from the first was to keep the two Superiors on an equal
level of authority. As the mission years passed, her early
estimate of Sister Mary Cornelia seemed justified by her stability and uncomplicated thinking. Her letters, as the Mother
General wrote later, were clear and consistent. On the other
hand, Sister Loyola, with all her zeal and ability, had presented to her a tortuous planning that she found hard to
follow. It is plain that at this time Mère Constantine would

not consent to a step that would increase Sister Loyola's authority or lessen Sister Mary Cornelia's.

Sister Mary Cornelia had scarcely replied to Mère Constantine's letter about the Willamette property when word came from Sister Loyola that four Sisters would arrive in San Francisco in April, that she meant to meet them there, and that she wished Sister Marie Catherine to accompany her. They would wear secular attire on the journey. Would Sister Mary Cornelia see to the necessary dressmaking? Sister Mary Cornelia began at once to assemble a traveling outfit, and the high excitement caused by the announced missionaries subsided into ripples of merriment at the sight of full skirt, fichu, shawl, bonnet, and carpet bag modeled by Sister Marie Catherine at community recreation.

At the academy, Sister Marie Catherine found Sister Loyola in a whirl of preparation. Quickly she inspected her traveling companion's ensemble to make sure it would not present too great a difference from her own. Then she hurried her off to the chapel to pray that the journey would result in the greater glory of God, but not before Sister recognized the symptoms. Sister Loyola's face, Sister Marie Catherine recalled, "shone with an amiable, joyous vigor." Always a Land of Promise!

For the moment, at least, Sister Marie Catherine was swept along. For there was that little dream she had recently had, the only visionary indulgence of her adult life, of a lovely chain of mountains and a valley beyond. And as she gazed at the delightful picture, she heard a voice telling her she must go beyond into the valley. Yet as she knelt to pray, her mind shifted suddenly from the romantic to the practical. She added a prayer that she should "not commit any imprudences on the trip, the result of which I did not know."

Father Accolti spoke encouragingly if vaguely next morning after Mass, but from his references to Father Langlois and the city of golden opportunity, Sister Marie Catherine shrewdly guessed that he knew of a second reason for the journey. Prone as she was to conjecture, she still disapproved of examining one's Superior's reasons; she would assume for the present that there was no second reason; and she hurried into her traveling costume with Sister Mary Aloysia's assistance.

El Camino, a kind of "ferry-boat that looked more like a shell on the river," huffed and coughed and filled the air with black smoke as the two travelers scrambled down the bank through weeds and bushes. Would they ever reach Portland in that? Well, they must have patience! Only a few hours! Alas! The contraption chugged along for some seven or eight miles and then grounded on a sandbank. They had to wait for assistance, spending the day and most of the night on the river. So this was a steamboat! And for another reason, this introduction to the machine age was unfortunate; the engine occupied so much space that passengers found themselves inescapably close to its uncomfortable heat, as well as being in the midst of the crew. But Mr. Cook, the father of two day pupils at the academy, gallantly came to the aid of *El Camino's* two women passengers by curtaining off a corner of the deck for them.

Toward morning a tugboat helped *El Camino* off the sand, and presently she deposited her passengers at Portland, where the Sisters boarded the *Goliath,* bound for San Francisco with a couple of stops en route. The sight of the Columbia, which they had not seen since their arrival, made Sister Loyola so reminiscent of the terrors of the bar that she began to recount them play by play; in fact, "she seemed to enjoy going over those days of agony," and this for the benefit of a companion whom the rolling expanse led into depths of silence.

Sister Marie Catherine's meditative voyage moods had often been broken by near tragic incidents which she loved to recall, beginning with the morning when she lost her footing on the deck of *l'Infatigable* and, wrapped up in her cloak, rolled helplessly toward a break in the railing, prevented from a plunge into the Atlantic only by the quick action of a crewman. But now on the *Goliath,* the tragedy was all too real. First the captain's mate fell overboard. The current bore him down at once; not all the shouting, whistling, and discharging of cannon could bring help in time to save him. A great sadness fell over the ship, for the mate was "a very good man," everyone's friend. One of the firemen, more deeply stricken than he could bear, jumped into the ocean that night to end his sorrow. Telling it, Sister Marie Catherine could never find words for her horror at such an abysmal lack of trust in God. Her next tragic recording, however, had a happy ending.

Leaving Humboldt Bay next day, they saw floating timbers and soon sighted a ship caught on the rocks. The captain of the *Goliath* rescued the almost starved crew, gave them first aid and a good dinner, and turned back to port to put them ashore. And here, as usual, follows a comic bit. As the ship was to ride at anchor for some hours, Mr. Cook invited the Sisters to go ashore and have a taste of Pacific sea food. Clams! But wasn't it a barbarous custom to eat them from the shell? It seemed a savage practice, but as Mr. Cook and others were enjoying them it was probably American instead. Sister Marie Catherine really loved novelty, but she knew her companion did not. It was so enjoyable, she said, to observe Sister Loyola's polite composure as she downed the meal. Sister Marie Catherine was sure they would accept no more invitations to dine.

The Golden Gate welcomed the *Goliath* with sunshine, and presently the Sisters were "feasting their eyes on the grand amphitheatre which presented istself," from their anchorage at the foot of California Street. The captain courteously offered to escort the Sisters to the new St. Francis Church, adding that though he was not acquainted with San Francisco, he knew that Catholic churches were always surmounted by crosses. They accepted this kindness gratefully, especially since, like Mère Constantine, they had heard something of the little city's reputation; thus guarded against lawlessness, they approached a likely looking church and were led by the captain to what seemed to be the parish residence. The young man who answered the captain's knock snapped a contemptuous "No" to his inquiry, and slammed the door.

They tried another church, small and mean, with a residence still smaller and meaner.[6] This time the porter was a gentleman. He was sorry Bishop Alemany was not present, but he would call a priest. The Sisters bade a grateful farewell to the captain and turned to receive the cordial greeting of Father Langlois.

How delightful, Father Langlois said, to think that he had succeeded in bringing the Sisters of Notre Dame to California! Quite ignoring the fact that they had come only to meet their Sisters, thought Sister Marie Catherine, but presently she wondered whether perhaps Father Langlois knew more than she herself.

Explaining that the Bishop would not arrive for a couple of weeks, Father Langlois offered the Sisters hospitality for the night and promised to procure them more comfortable lodging with a good family. But first of all they must meet Father John Maginnis, who was then forming the nucleus of St. Patrick's Parish by celebrating Mass in a little room at Fourth and Jesse streets. Father Langlois went straightway to summon Father Maginnis, and Sister Loyola took the opportunity to prepare Sister Marie Catherine's mind for the proposed San Francisco foundation, about which the two priests would doubtless speak in her presence. Sister Marie Catherine showed less surprise than she expected. Instead, she remarked to her Superior that comparing their attire with that of ladies they had encountered on the streets, she found theirs at least a decade behind the times and a bit outlandish even at that.

Father Maginnis greeted the Sisters with dignity but withdrew at once. How strange! Was their appearance really that bad? But Father Langlois made up for this chilly reception by inviting the Sisters to dinner with him and by talking in his rapid and jovial manner of the parish and the little church, which he said was named for St. Francis Xavier; in fact, Father Langlois considered the great Jesuit, not the Saint of Assisi, the patron of San Francisco, for he had not yet given up his desire to join the sons of St. Ignatius Loyola. The two Sisters spent the afternoon in that church, making up, Sister Marie Catherine said, for their hours on the steamer "where there was no sign of religion or faith." But in that quiet place, certain distracting questions teased Sister Marie Catherine's mind.

Recalling Father Accolti's words of farewell, she felt sure

that he, too, must have known of the intended foundation
and approved of it. Now what of the four new Sisters? Would
they ever see Oregon? But four would not suffice for a
foundation. Would the house at St. Paul be closed to staff
the new house? What about the children? Her little savages?
And poor Archbishop Blanchet. He was away when they
left, but the Sisters would give him Sister Loyola's message.
Would he be told about the house in San Francisco? Sister
Marie Catherine suddenly gathered up her scattered thoughts;
it was not her duty to know the answers. Beginning with
Mère Constantine, she repeated slowly the names of all the
principals in this little drama of her mind. With eyes on
the white wooden tabernacle, she prayed that wordless, tremendous sort of prayer of which only the Sister Marie Cath-
erines are capable, not a prayer as such, but an intense willing
that all of these should know the peace of Christ in doing
His will. As her thoughts blurred after the clear, bright
focus of that moment, she saw a saintly, old man asleep in
an armchair with a paint brush in his hand.

Sister Loyola tapped her on the arm. They must go directly to their room in the residence, she said, and see what
could be done to improve their costumes. For one thing
the bow hanging limply from Sister Marie Catherine's bonnet
looked quite silly.

They could do very little to improve matters; in fact, Sister
Marie Catherine expected that the lady of the "good family"
would refuse to accept them as guests. That she did welcome
them kindly was "doubtless due to the imposing gravity and
noble countenance of Sister Loyola." At any rate, they would
not have thought of wearing religious habits on the streets
of this wild, new city, that Father Accolti sometimes called
a madhouse.

On his arrival, Bishop Alemany received the Sisters most
cordially, telling them of Father Langlois' high praises of
their work in Oregon. Then he invited Sister Loyola into
another room for what seemed to her companion an endless
interview. No, of course, it was not her affair. She tried to
recapture her detachment of a few days back in the little
church, but there was the closed door behind which decisions

were being made, decisions that might mean closing the only home her orphans knew; and she was not even asked her opinion, the one person who would put in a word for the poor savages. Had Sister Loyola, fearing her loyalty to the Oregon mission, asked for this private interview? There she was, criticizing again! As she asked forgiveness for this lapse, Sister Loyola emerged from the office "looking very pensive." Worse still, she had no intention of discussing matters.

On the way back to their little apartment, Sister Marie Catherine began to take heart; perhaps after all they would return to Oregon and take the four new Sisters with them. She saw pairs of black eyes smiling from the windows as she walked up the path. Mops of black hair tied back with bits of clean ribbon. Hair clean and free from troubles. Children clean and wholesome, body and soul.

When Sister Loyola regained her composure, she said briefly that His Lordship did not wish them to found a house in San Francisco, but that he had suggested San José, the capital, and had invited them to go down and find a location while waiting for the Sisters. Sister Marie Catherine thought better of her impulse to ask why, and later her patience was rewarded by accidental discovery. Father Maginnis had invited the Sisters of Charity; little San Francisco could not yet afford the two establishments at the same time. So that explained Father Maginnis' lack of interest! And this new, golden city! It was poor, too!

Father Langlois adjusted his mind to the new plan with surprising alacrity. An excellent idea! San José, only three miles from Santa Clara, where Father Nobili was founding a college at Bishop Alemany's request!

A college! Sister Loyola saw its counterpart for women in the capital three miles away. A large building, much larger than her academy on the Willamette. In the capital, not in a city that had ceased to be one, not even in this port town, too small to allow for two convents. She began to talk now in her old, gay manner, and listening, Sister Marie Catherine thought more and more of her dream of hills and a valley beyond. Perhaps!

Settler Martin Murphy made the Sisters as comfortable as

possible in his big family carriage and tried to make up for miles of bumping and jogging by talk of the Santa Clara Valley with its wealth in its soil, and of the wisdom of fortunate prospectors who bought its acres with their gold instead of risking it in uncertain enterprises in San Francisco. He talked of Father Nobili and his plans, but mostly he talked of the great need of Sisters, of his own three daughters, of his wife's great happiness at the thought of their being properly educated. But as Sister Loyola's enthusiasm mounted, her companion grew more silent. Afternoon wore on into a tiresome journey, for whether or not their route kept closely to El Camino Real, it was rough and hard all the way. But at last they reached the Murphy rancho at Mountain View, where Mrs. Murphy greeted the Sisters with joy and a servant set a good dinner before them.

Somewhat later the servant announced another guest, Bishop Alemany, who was on his way to Santa Clara, where he intended to celebrate a Pontifical High Mass next morning. Palm Sunday, Sister Marie Catherine reminded herself, but she learned presently the official reason for His Lordship's visit. He was placing the parishes of San José and Santa Clara in the hands of the Jesuits, the transition being marked when in the solemn Mass a Mexican Franciscan and a Jesuit acted as deacon and subdeacon. This, Sister Loyola said, was a sign of the blessing of God; if they settled in San José, they would have their accustomed spiritual guidance.

When the Sisters went to the parish church in San José for services on Holy Thursday, they were happy that the transfer was taking place there, too. The Mexican pastor, somewhat "original" liturgically, seemed unperturbed by the irreverent manners of his congregation. Even at the altar railing, they talked and pushed and elbowed one another. The Sisters understood somewhat the pastor's toleration when they began to experience manners in this capital-pueblo with its Spanish-Mexican miners, soured and disillusioned by American sharpers. Religion in the pueblo was at a low ebb; men never attended Mass; women and children were present without knowing its meaning.

Santa Clara was quite different. Here the Sisters saw honest settlers like the Murphys attend Mass reverently, reliving the goodness of early days under the saintly padres. What an aura of sanctity about this church, on the wall of which hung the crucifix that spoke to the holy man Catala!

Mrs. Murphy's sister, Mrs. Thomas Kell, took the Sisters to her rancho just outside of San José. Here they met Mr. Charles White, in whose home they enjoyed hospitality, and their Oregon City friend, the Honorable Peter Burnett, as well as Senator Caius T. Ryland and others, among them the Spanish Don José Suñol, who had cast his lot with the new American government. Together, these leading citizens presented Sister Loyola with a petition to start an academy for young ladies, a step which Mr. White declared would put an end to the evils of San José. This time Sister Marie Catherine was present, and as Sister Loyola faced the decision, she also faced her companion's grave reluctance. For once Sister Loyola lost her grip on assurance. She postponed the decision.

Sister Marie Catherine had been inquiring about the local cost of building materials. Now she could give her Superior the benefit of her somewhat frightening findings. Lumber was either brought around the Horn or hand-sawed; building costs in general were prohibitive. But, regaining her usual confidence, Sister Loyola laughed and said that progress was beginning and would be rapid. Sister Marie Catherine saw that argument was futile. There was no point in speaking of Willamette and the orphans; Sister Loyola knew as well as she did that they could not maintain three houses. And at the thought of her orphans, Sister Marie Catherine's latest and most harrowing intuition scattered her other worries. Did Sister Loyola mean to leave her in San José with the four new Sisters?

Sister Loyola decided to discuss matters with Father Nobili. She could see that her companion was reading her mind too accurately, that she was struggling to accept her plans docilely, but really not succeeding. Besides, she had reason to respect Sister Marie Catherine's judgment. What if she were right this time? She would place the problem, point by point, before Father Nobili. If he favored the foundation, surely Sister Marie Catherine would be satisfied.

Father Nobili had just heard news of Oregon from Father Anthony Goetz, who had shared hardships with him in British Columbia. On his way from Idaho to California, Father Goetz had stopped at St. Francis Xavier at Willamette and gathered material for a very gloomy report to Father Nobili, a report including difficulties facing the Sisters should they remain in Oregon. So Father Nobili advised Sister Loyola to make the foundation in San José. When she mentioned her Superior General's injunction, he said that he himself was in the same position, but since time was pressing, numbers were increasing daily, and both invitation and property had been offered, he had acted and trusted his Father General to ratify his act. The Fathers were leaving Oregon; they would replace the departing Franciscans. They would seize the opportunities which California presented. If his General should order otherwise, they would at once obey. The Sisters, he thought, should do likewise. Sister Loyola left the interview with a decided mind; she would accept the foundation in San José. One cannot help wishing she had written to Archbishop Blanchet at this point, and thus spared him the distress of hearing of her action from another quarter.

There was nothing for Sister Marie Catherine to do but to go along with the "valiant Sister Loyola." In her memoir, she tells of their announcing "our decision" to the leading citizens, who were now offering assistance. The phrase may have been playful, or a little ironical, but certainly that decision produced a crisis in her mind. On the one hand, she felt obliged to accept her Superior's point of view; besides, she admired and respected Sister Loyola enough to find doing so quite easy. On the other hand, she was the same Sister Marie Catherine who had thanked God on *l'Infatigable's* deck that she was drawing closer to her "dear savages." She never solved the problem. When Sister Loyola said that it would have been useless to remain in Oregon, Sister Marie

Catherine accepted that statement and quoted it in her memoir. Yet had she been in Sister Loyola's place, she would certainly have kept a community there.

Struggling in this predicament, Sister Marie Catherine accompanied Sister Loyola next day when Mr. Martin Murphy conducted a tour about the pueblo in search of a site. Again she was very silent as the other two chatted about the various possible locations. Finally Sister Loyola asked sweetly in French for her opinion. Sister's reply, also in French, was not so sweet. As though she had forgotten "our decision," she asked abruptly how they could go headlong into arrangements without their Mother General's consent. Then she realized that Mr. Murphy understood French and was laughing at both her temper and Sister Loyola's embarrassment. Now a double load weighed her conscience; besides abandoning her orphans, she had scandalized a good Christian, who was polite enough to laugh at her outburst. To repair this scandal, she added quickly that the tract they were then passing would seem especially well fitted for a boarding school because of the avenue of willows in the rear. And thus the lovely plot on Santa Clara Street was her selection. There, largely because of the business acumen that fitted so oddly with her nature, poor adobe beginnings developed into one of California's finest early schools.

When Sister Marie Catherine says that she and Sister Loyola came to San José penniless, she is, as often, speaking figuratively. They could not, however, have made the first payment on the ten lots on Santa Clara Street without first disposing of their Oregon possessions, had not California's first governor started a subscription in their behalf. Bishop Alemany headed the list with $300, the Murphy family added $600, a few donated $100, and there was a fair list of lesser gifts. One donor gave a lot that was later very valuable as business property, but the high tax made it impossible to hold. The entire subscription was not, however, at all what one might expect in the land of gold. Prices were unbelievably high, but the small house on the property was almost beyond repair; a new building would have to be started at once.

Sister Loyola set about things with her usual speed. Undaunted at the disappointing subscription, she told Sister Marie Catherine they would soon have a few boarders and all would be well. She asked Mr. Murphy to purchase the lots in the name of the Sisters of Notre Dame; she notified Bishop Alemany, including in the letter a note telling the four new Sisters to remain in San Francisco until she should come for them. She found temporary lodging for herself and Sister Marie Catherine in an unused hospital belonging to the Belgian Doctor van Canoghan. Thus located within walking distance of Santa Clara, they attended Father Nobili's Mass each morning at the Mission and accepted gratefully his invitation to breakfast of bread and coffee in a little adjoining room. They spent the days trying to make their one little house habitable, watching in fascination as the workman erected their "boarders' dormitory" of adobe bricks. They made purchases in the local shops, and when Sister Marie Catherine winced at the exorbitant prices Sister Loyola roundly denounced "the demon of cowardice."

But once she had set her hand to the work, Sister Marie Catherine gave it all her ability, which in practical matters was always superior to Sister Loyola's. And somehow she managed a new attitude; the Mexicans of the pueblo, she reflected, were in even greater need than the Willamette Indians. She even faced the new language problem with equanimity. Here she would need English, which she still found difficult, and Spanish, which she "ignored." When Sister Loyola told her, as she had expected her to all along, that she would be one of the "foundation stones," she accepted it as the will of God, assuring Him, however, that she was in no wise responsible for the change.

Subscriptions were paid so slowly that Sister Loyola was almost at her wits' end when Doctor van Canoghan presented her with her first boarders, three-year-old Johnnie Towsend, his nurse Bridget McCue, and a maid. Johnnie's father, Doctor Townsend, had met with a fatal accident, and, as his godfather, Doctor van Canoghan charged himself with the child's care. So for a short time and because she needed funds so badly, Sister Loyola accepted the three, using the advance payment for their board to purchase beds, tables, and chairs.

When the original building was roughly ready for habitation, this strange assortment of five persons left the hospital with their carpetbags and walked to Santa Clara Street. There was no welcoming committee. No zealous group of parish ladies had stocked the larder; the cupboard, like the rest of the tiny house, was bare. From the Peralta estate adjoining the property, came devout Doña Josepha, bearing a statute of St. Anthony, as her gift. They had only to turn to this saint in all their needs, she said, and all would be well. It did not occur to the señora, it seems, to play the role of the helpful saint herself beyond the modest extent of her promise on the subscription list. The Sisters, however, were grateful for her beloved San Antonio and attributed to him an immediate blessing in the shape of a message from Father Langlois. The Sisters had just arrived on the *Sarah Sands*.

Bishop Alemany chuckled as he told Sister Loyola of Sister Mary Alenie's insisting on going directly to Oregon. They really must not stay in San Francisco, she told His Lordship, thanking him kindly for his invitation. No, not even two of the four might stay; they were under very strict orders from their Mother General. But they were happy enough, he said, to have an end of sea voyaging when they saw Sister Loyola's note.

Looking at the three Belgians, Sister Loyola recalled Mère Constantine's description, "not learned persons but very virtuous souls." So Sister Mary Alenie was the one with boarding school experience who "understood singing." Sister Donatilde, with less English than the others must be the "good housekeeper." This very frail and very youthful Sister Mary Aloysius, what a determined look. And three of them could hold their own in English conversation. Sister Loyola thought of her own first encounter with an American!

In astonished French phrases these Sisters registered their disappointment in the drab little city of San Francisco. What of all the gold they had heard about? And the Bishop's house! Only a hovel in which he had to receive his guests in his bedroom, he seated on his bed, and they on chairs brought in from his dining room, which was really a tiny storeroom expansion of his kitchen. They had been lodged quite comfortably at the homes of the French Consul, Mr. Dillon, and of Judge Barry. But a Bishop living in such a squalid place! This they could not understand. What would they think of the wretched little house in San José? Sister Loyola made use of the long ride down to explain their altered destiny and to prepare them for conditions which she assured them would quickly improve. It really mattered little, they said, now that they knew Sister Marie Catherine was there. For weeks they had listened to Sister Mary Alenie's praises of her former teacher.

Despite all their drawbacks, things moved very rapidly on Santa Clara Street through spring and summer. While Sister Loyola went out on good-will tours, signing up day pupils in the pueblo and boarders on the ranchos, the others hurried the narrow, new adobe building to completion. The row of classrooms and parlors, all opening on the long corridor, had to be finished before August. That done, they started their first frame building, a tiny convent of hand-sawed redwood. Their good carpenter neighbor, Mr. Godrich, gave all his free time to its construction, and late summer evenings were loud with hammer and saw as he worked. The new missionaries quickly became good artisans, too, as they fitted benches and tables to the dimensions of the adobe classrooms, varying this activity with shopping excursions with Sister Marie Catherine to piece out sets of plates and forks in the local stores, which never had enough of one pattern.

In her methodical way, Sister Loyola opened her accounts. She repaid Father Langlois his $170, knowing how badly he needed it, and entered as loans from the house in Cincinnati the passage money of the four Sisters from New York to San Francisco, as well as the sum of $205 for a piano. On this total debt, $2,000, a staggering one at the moment for her, she figured the interest, after her return to Oregon, and sent the statement to Sister Marie Catherine, who pinned it into the account book.

But Sister Loyola was unafraid. She entered an announcement in *Alta California* before classes opened and waited in assurance.[7] In the casual manner of the day, boarders straggled in, twenty-six of them, before she left, in quite high spirits, late in September. All would go well in the new boarding school under Sister Marie Catherine's care. In case they kept the academy in Oregon City, Sister could be left in charge in San José. She must make that suggestion to Mère Constantine. It was true that Sister's patience ran a little short at times, and it was also true that both Spanish maidens and newly rich American girls possessed resources of expression unknown to Maggie Clatsop. These would be better for a firm hand. In a crisis, Sister Mary Alenie's fund of love could be counted on to neutralize both Sister Marie Catherine's frankness and Sister Mary Aloysius' insistence on perfection. It was well to have Sister Mary Alenie in charge of the boarding pupils, and what a fine Mistress of Novices she would be later on! As for the small subscription list, well, it was just the times. Miners suddenly wealthy could think of pleasanter ways of letting gold slip through their fingers than helping Sisters to build schools.

CHAPTER 16

Farewell Willamette

A few days before Sister Loyola's return to Oregon City, Archbishop Blanchet wrote a most conciliating letter to Mère Constantine. Hurt though he was at not being consulted, or even told about the foundation in San José, his fear of losing all the Sisters impelled him to state his satisfaction with their work, especially with that of Sister Loyola.[1] And there was a fairly cordial meeting between His Lordship and Sister Loyola on her return, at which she explained both her long absence and her reasons for accepting Bishop Alemany's invitation.

Whatever Sister Loyola planned for the future, Mère Constantine's strong letter waiting for her in Oregon City was enough to hold her hand for the time; besides, it was best now to wait for her Superior's reaction to the new foundation, her announcement of which seems to have been tardy enough, since Mère Constantine did not respond to it until October.

It was discouraging, though, to enroll only twelve boarders, and no new ones, despite the elaborate ad in the *Oregon Statesman*. Though the academy's two largest debts were paid in August after the sale of the Portland lots, the outlook was not too bright since little harvest income was to be expected from St. Paul. This failure may have been due to Sister Marie Catherine's absence as manager; whatever the reason, Sister Loyola gave Mère Constantine a poor report of the farm and house at St. Paul a short time after her return. As she waited through the autumn months for a reply, she found some reason for discouragement in the

251

pages of her account book. The few boarders for whom anything like the full amount was paid were the Costellos, wards of Hugh Burns, and one or two others. This period was also darkened by much talk of complete dispossession of Doctor McLoughlin. Archbishop Blanchet was, in fact, so greatly worried over the church property itself, that he entered it in a memoir which he besought Governor Lane to present in his name in Washington.[2] It speaks for his kind relations with the Sisters, too, that he made their disputed claim at Multnomah an article of that memoir, thus strengthening Sister Loyola's own plea to Governor Lane in October.

Sister Loyola's letter on conditions at St. Paul crossed Mère Constantine's almost stormy letter of October eighth. Accepting the San José foundation as the will of God, the Mother General accuses Sister Loyola of purchasing too much and too hastily, of acting with too few Sisters. Sister Loyola's letters present puzzling contradictions, she asserts, and to convince her of this fact she includes a few instances. She repeats her advice not to leave Willamette, where the Sisters already have property which has cost them "so much trouble." The Mother General is plainly worried at what she considers real indiscretion and rashness.[3]

But she wrote again and in a milder vein in November; for one thing, she had just received Archbishop Blanchet's letter of September twenty-first, and she wished to prove to Sister Loyola that though His Lordship might seem a bit unreasonable at times, he was still in the long run her admiring friend. She had also weighed carefully Sister Loyola's reasons for wishing to close the Willamette house, reasons perhaps confirmed by Sister Mary Cornelia. If that house must be closed, very well; in that event, the Sisters may be divided between the other two houses. Then she adds most emphatically that Sister Mary Cornelia is to be sent to San José as Superior even though the Willamette house is not closed. This decision, arrived at with her counselors, is an order, and an order intended to keep Sister Mary Cornelia in office as Superior, which was clearly not Sister Loyola's plan in the event of the closing of her convent. Mère Constantine hastens to add her confidence in Sister Marie Catherine, whose fine qualities she recognizes, but insists that the new post in San José is better suited to Sister Mary Cornelia than is Willamette. She adds that Sister Mary Cornelia will learn Spanish much more readily than Sister Marie Catherine and, summing up, that she is better suited to San José.[4]

This is a significant letter, emphasizing as it does the decision to establish Sister Mary Cornelia at the head of the most promising mission house. It seems incredible that its unconditioned meaning should have escaped Sister Loyola. The letter throws light also on the Mother General's attitude toward the Sisters' possible abandonment of Oregon City, a matter which Sister Loyola must have mentioned as a possibility. It may perhaps have to be abandoned, she concedes, because of lack of good will among the inhabitants; she does not mention poverty as a reason.

In the light of present-day attitudes among Catholic religious, the phrase about lack of good will has a strange ring. To leave an area where ill will exists is to create a vacuum in which it will most certainly increase and flourish. To remain in it in the spirit of good human relations, to spread the good odor of Christ, is the smiling response of religious to ill will today. As a rule, it succeeds. But even Mère Constantine shared the strain of caution that marked the most apostolic of her time, a distrust of which the high stone walls of the period, the locked iron gates with little wickets, were outward symbols.

When Sister Loyola received Mère Constantine's letter, she at once took steps toward the closing of the Willamette house. What part Sister Mary Cornelia played in the arrangements, and what her attitude was at the time, it is impossible to say. She was informed by Sister Loyola, and undoubtedly by Mère Constantine, of her mission to San José. She and her community prepared to transfer all the orphans and the few boarders to Oregon City, and the departure took place very soon after Archbishop Blanchet was notified of it. Later he remarked the suddenness in a letter to Mère Constantine, complaining at the same time that she did not consult him before sanctioning this "departure to California" in 1852.[5] Certainly Sister Mary Cornelia deplored the pain that this and the final leaving caused the poor Archbishop. In her early California days, she could not be at peace about it until she heard he had secured the Sisters of the Holy Names for his mission.

In her simple manner, Sister Laurence tells the sad little story of the departure on a blustery day in March. They wept, all of them, Sisters and children together, when, after Mass, the Canadian Father Cenas removed the Blessed Sacrament from the tabernacle. Father Cenas wept, too, and at this the children sobbed aloud. It was their home; the academy would be different. Good, kind Sister Mary Cornelia was going very far away. After breakfast, the families that still lived nearby came to take the Sisters' baggage down to the boat, but the children and Sisters had to walk in the rain, which fell in torrents before the sorry procession reached the river.

Like other river "steamers" this little craft was chiefly engine, and now the captain made good use of that fact. He stood his drenched passengers around it, assuring them they would soon be dry, the Sisters "taking patience," and praying their charges would come through it all without colds. Presently someone spied their big black dog swimming bravely after the boat down the river. Thinking it better not to take the huge fellow to the "city," the Sisters had asked their neighbors to keep him, but he would not be kept. In the face of such loyalty, the captain stopped the boat, took the dog on board, and thus earned the gratitude that lit up all the sad, black eyes, as their happy favorite shook great splashes of water about, as though the scene were not quite wet enough.[6]

It must have been with His Lordship's permission that Sister Loyola leased the forty acres at St. Paul to the farmer Antoine Rivet. That she did so seems to indicate that she meant to keep the academy open at least for a time, for the orphans and such boarders as remained. As a means of income for the orphans, it was a wise arrangement; the harvest of 1852 shows that Rivet became a very efficient farmer when he himself became a partner in the gain.

In April, Sister Loyola and Sister Mary Cornelia set out for San José, taking with them Sister Norbertine and Sister Aldegonde. Whether the trip was eventful or not, there was no Sister Marie Catherine to tell the tale; instead, she gaily awaited their arrival; her expansive reception was certainly the crowning event of their travel. At St. Paul, she had come to admire Sister Mary Cornelia's quiet government and now, in her jubilant bluntness, she stated her joy in superlatives.

In Sister Marie Catherine's simple telling, Sister Loyola's installation of Sister Mary Cornelia was made with a temporal clause; she was to direct the project "while waiting what Divine Providence would enable us to do later." If Sister Loyola did insert this condition, she did so sincerely; it did not occur to her that in the event of closing the academy, she would cease to be the head of the mission band. In fact, it seems not to have occurred to anyone concerned, least of all to Sister Mary Cornelia.

For the next few weeks, Sister Loyola was deep in plans with Sister Mary Cornelia and Sister Marie Catherine, enjoying betimes the hilarious stories of the latter. Their first Christmas dinner, when the five Sisters sat down to a feast of bear meat and cabbage. And the statue of St. Anthony that neighborly Doña Peralta had given them as a talisman! The good Saint, unknown to his client, was now suspended high in a branch right above her property. To round out a tract for convent and boarding school, it was desirable to annex that remnant of a great rancho, a transaction of which the good lady would not hear. Never worry, Sister Marie Catherine insisted. Saint Anthony must remain in the tree until he changed the Doña's mind, which at last he did.

And there was the unpredictable workman, the Indian whom she named Don Juan, and who often made merry with his friends, the roving Indians of the valley. With no better understanding than the others of property restrictions, to say nothing of convent enclosures, Don Juan invited his cronies one night to share a cup at his little shack on the grounds. Terrified at both sight and sound of the roisterers, the four inexperienced Sisters took to the attic of the convent, there to barricade themselves against attack. Not so Sister Marie Catherine. Seizing a stick, she rushed out shouting "Police!" and commanded the Indians to leave the place. They left, even Juan. When the Sisters saw him again, he was working soberly at his usual tasks.

Sister Marie Catherine had nothing good to say for adobe buildings or rather for the beamed roofing and badly fitted tiling with which they were finished. At St. Paul it had been at least possible to locate the leaks and plug them with moss. Here the leaks were everywhere, and instead of clean rain water, a muddy liquid oozed through, making weird patterns on the children's bedspreads. Their little frame buildings were more satisfactory. The "convent," known through the years as the 1851 House, its hand-sawed boards expertly fitted together with wooden pegs in lieu of nails, was at least rainproof, and convenient, too, with its big, all-purpose room and the stairs at the back leading up to its dormitory attic.

With very good boarding-school prospects, Sister Loyola began to talk of a fine brick edifice. It was futile to remind her that they were paying interest to Mr. Davidson on their land and to Martin Murphy on a loan of $2,300. She could see that in San José the Sisters would have to be independent whether they liked it or not. The subscription list was disappointing; there were no new signers and many of the original ones seemed to have forgotten their promises. But the number of pupils had almost tripled during the year. Yes, they must build. Trust the Lord and build.

In June Sister Loyola returned to Oregon City, where she found both Sister Mary Aloysia and Sister Mary Bernard quite ill with malaria. Nine of the twelve academy boarders were withdrawing, either of necessity or because the school had become predominantly native. Only the two Cavanagh sisters, wards of the Archbishop, and one or two others were staying on, and only one new pupil had entered. This was the lowest moment in the academy's brief history, but impatient though she was, Sister Loyola did not act at once. For one thing, there would not be room in San José for all the Sisters until the completion of another frame building. She also wished to convince Mère Constantine that the move was necessary, for this step was far more serious than making the San José foundation. Archbishop Blanchet had not yet returned from the First Plenary Council in Baltimore. She did not wish to leave in his absence, besides, she wished to have an understanding with him about the Willamette property. She began straightway, however, to make what preparations she could. She advised Charlotte Seymour, who was near the end of the academy courses and was now a good musician, to transfer at once to San José. But she did not, as might be expected, send even one of her three best teachers on ahead.

Sister Loyola's effort was now directed toward disposal of all holdings for the benefit of the third foundation. As a claim against the land in St. Louis prevented its sale, she consulted Mère Constantine in July about taking legal steps to clear the claim, as well as about other holdings.

Mère Constantine counseled her against lawsuits in a land of conflicting claims. Moreover, she wished that land bought recently from Doctor McLoughlin be returned to him before departure. This was, of course, in reference to the property purchased in 1850, but on which Sister Loyola had not as yet begun to make payments. If they were to leave Oregon, Mère Constantine wished them to sever property connections. At this point, the Mother General thought she would not regret seeing them leave Oregon, "if the Good God in the least manifested His Holy Will." We must prefer a greater good, she said, when it presents itself to us in a more permanent manner. However, she still spoke of the move as a remote contingency; she wanted greater reason for it; and she reminded Sister Loyola that there are crosses everywhere. Either Sister Loyola had not made clear the urgency she felt at this time, or Mère Constantine was minimizing it and allowing for time to improve conditions.[7]

At about the same time the Mother General wrote a stern

letter to Sister Mary Cornelia, who had again complained
to her about her inadequacy. This time she sums it all up
as want of simplicity. But in her little scolding, she is
strengthening Sister Mary Cornelia's confidence in herself
and preparing her for continued leadership. It is also clear
from this letter, as well as from her letter of October twenty-
seventh to Sister Loyola, that she has quite set aside the
thought of abandoning the Oregon mission. She is preoccupied now with improvement in communications. Her
high hope is a transcontinental railroad; then Namur will
be in close touch with the distant missions, and she will be
able to send assistance more easily.

Sister Loyola must have cleared her title to the St. Louis
property and sold it some time between June ninth and
August twenty-third. Her balance shows over $400 on
the earlier date, and it is interesting to note that, even at
that low point, her account is not in the red; on the second
date she reports a gain of over $1,200. She lays in supplies
of meat and firewood for some months and purchases 5,000
feet of finishing boards, wainscoting for corridors perhaps,
and pickets for fencing, improvements that would make
the house more salable. In September and October she
pays to a certain Mr. Beauchemin what seems to be the last
of her debts, about $1,200, but during the fall and winter
she realizes a gain of over $1,800 from the farm at Willa-
mette, the greatest single item being the sale of most of
the herd in March for $960. In all, the lease arrangement
has been profitable, and the farmer seems satisfied.

There was much business connected with all this marketing of produce, and securing of storage for wheat, oats,
hops, and potatoes. One of Sister Loyola's expenses was a
canoe for the farmer for his trips down to Oregon City.
The Sisters, too, made trips to bring down articles from
the now vacant Sainte Marie, and experienced a bit of surprise there one day when, reaching through an open window
for an article left on a table, they felt instead the soft, winter
coat of a fox.

This handling and selling of produce was not occupation
proper to Sisters, but it was part of Sister Loyola's plan to

rescue as much as possible of her investment in money and labor through nearly a decade, for use in the new and promising house in California. In her accounts, there are even two entries, not large, of proceeds from "la boutique," where the Sisters were making leather articles, even saddles, using a tooling outfit sent from Namur at their request; its original purpose, of course, was to teach a "branch" of usefulnes to the young native. As academic classes dwindled, the Sisters gave more time to this work, to finish up their supplies as well as to turn an extra penny.[8] As they sat at their work through those last months, when all but the most elementary class books stood closed on the shelves, they thought often of the July program from San José, with its First and Second Crowns, its premiums in natural history and philosophy, its vocal and piano, its painting and drawing. Best of all, its list of names. There was a school!

But here now instead were Kalispels, and Clatsops, and Chinooks, some but recently "rescued from the wild animals of the forest," some who had grown into adolescence at Sainte Marie and who, despite their streak of opposition, thought of the Sisters as the center of their existence. But though the Sisters had come primarily for these Indians, their own lack of psychological preparation still found them often frustrated and worried when black eyes flashed elemental thunderings. The most respected, Sister Mary Aloysia, suffered from native impudence and inertia, both of which she found harder to bear after her brief span of academy teaching. They told one another, perhaps, as they worked on their leather pieces, that from the day the orphans arrived the academy was doomed, regardless of the fortunes of Oregon City. The presence of so many "savages" would of itself have emptied the boarding school; the Raes for instance, had become "externes" after the arrival of the orphans.

Between recurring attacks of fever and loss of his missionaries, Archbishop Blanchet was becoming more saddened and worrisome. Irritability turned small misunderstandings into greater ones. The very mention of California troubled him, and considering Father Accolti's enthusiasm for San

Francisco it was perhaps inevitable that the strain between them should reach the breaking point. Mère Constantine must have had many complaints of disagreement from Sister Loyola, for now in endeavoring to avoid friction as much as possible, she offered advice which ran counter to her own usual policy. In case departure from Oregon became necessary, she counseled, the Sisters should maintain secrecy until their plans were complete.[9] She may have considered this course best partly because she felt that Sister Loyola had missed too many opportunities of conciliation, and partly because she knew of the Archbishop's prostrating illness. It was not her own way of acting with the hierarchy, nor was it in accord with her earlier advice. She held that an institute with central government must be ruled by that government; still she had always counseled a confiding and dependent attitude and she herself was accustomed to seek the advice of the Bishop of Namur. Yet while her February letter indicates that she realized how brittle the situation was, it presents her as still wishing to see the Sisters remain in Oregon.

Long before Mère Constantine penned that letter, however, Sister Loyola had begun preparations for the final move without advising the Archbishop. In fact, Mère Constantine's reference to secrecy may easily have been in response to Sister Loyola's claim that it was necessary.

These furtive preparations certainly influenced the Providence Sisters from Montreal, who stopped by mistake in Oregon City at the end of November en route to Vancouver. Led by the Canadian Father G. Huberdault and their Superior, Sister Larocque, these Sisters were responding to Bishop A. M. A. Blanchet's call for missionaries, when they found themselves instead in his brother's austere little residence in Oregon City. Despite his illness, the Archbishop welcomed them warmly, and sent word of their coming to the Sisters of Notre Dame, who thoughtfully brought blankets that evening with their greetings. Next morning, they returned, told the visitors "discreetly" that their presence would exhaust the Archbishop's small food supply, and invited them to the academy.

The archiepiscopal larder was not really so badly off; the visitors noted that their unexpected coming "seemed not to embarrass" their host. His Lordship's housekeeper, their annalist wrote, was an elderly woman relative; his young nephew was his attendant.[10] His lot at the time was comfortable as compared with that of his early mission days. The annalist must have misunderstood some little ruse of the Sisters of Notre Dame to bring the visitors to the academy where it would be easier to offer them hospitality.

The account of the Providence Sisters relates the "fine religious friendship" that sprang up between the two groups, the charity of the Sisters of Notre Dame, the happy Christmas and New Year's, when Sister Loyola shared with her guests a huge Christmas box from Namur and gave them the duplicate copies from her library as well as material for vestments. But the picture is also a sad one. The "one diversion" of the guest community was "to watch their hostesses prepare for a speedy departure" to California, as they themselves waited for communication with Bishop A. M. A. Blanchet, all the while becoming more fearful about accepting a foundation in his diocese. Being nurses, they cared for the ailing Archbishop and his also ailing elderly relative; otherwise they were unemployed and fearful of remaining so. They were shocked to hear how the Sisters had worked at St. Paul. They thought that all the natives were withdrawing to the deep forest, taking their children with them, that presently there would be no native children to care for.

That fear was ungrounded; there would always be native orphans; before leaving, the Sisters of Notre Dame had to find homes and adoption for their younger native charges and service in good families for their older girls. No matter how far the Indians withdrew, the few Canadian priests would reach them as always, would always need Sisters to whom they might entrust these abandoned waifs. Father Brouillet assured Father Huberdault that there would be children to teach, and though he did not minimize the poverty of the northern diocese, he certainly thought the foundation possible, as within four years another group of Provi-

dence Sisters found it was. But Father Huberdault had talked
with Father Langlois in San Francisco, and apparently with
others whose view of Oregon was pessimistic. And now he
and the Providence Sisters took counsel together, decided
not to remain, and notified their Superiors in Montreal of
their decision.

When Bishop A. M. A. Blanchet returned from his long
journey, his brother offered to escort the Canadian missionaries to meet him at Ft. Vancouver.* To his surprise, only
Father Huberdault, Sister Larocque, and one other Sister
appeared to make the journey, and they offered no explanation. At Ft. Vancouver, Bishop A. M. A. Blanchet was still
more surprised and asked at once where the other Sisters
were. That night Father Huberdault explained. They had
merely come to tell His Lordship that the mission was impossible. The stupefied Bishop of Nisqually wondered, says
the annalist, "whether he was not the victim of a horrid
nightmare." He had given their Superiors in Montreal the
true picture of his diocese, before his long journey, he said,
and while it was true that Oregon had suffered greatly since
then, still there was much good to be done, and there were
sufficient resources for a living.

At this the Sisters were "deeply moved." They began
to think they were perhaps viewing the matter "through
their grievances." But they held to their resolution, and
unfortunately the three departed "without remitting their
obediences to Mgr. Blanchet," and without being provided
with letters from him authorizing them to withdraw from
the diocese of Nisqually. On that fateful January twenty-
first they returned to Oregon City, where Sister Loyola was
preparing for an advance move to San José on February
first. Her guests and Father Huberdault decided to leave
on the same ship. Thus "after eight days of sadness passed
since the refusal of the Vancouver mision," they set out
with her, Sister Alphonse Marie, and Sister Mary Albine.
Later, again and again, they deplored their act. Yet who

* In 1850 the Diocese of Walla Walla was suppressed. A. M. A. Blanchet
then became Bishop of Nisqually with headquarters at Ft. Vancouver. The
Providence annalist mistakenly refers to the "Vancouver Mission."

could blame them? The departure of those who had spent almost a decade in Oregon was a persuasive argument.

In the crowded quarters of the Sisters of Charity in San Francisco, the Providence Sisters shared poverty, gracious but real; with two mattresses for their whole number, they used "width for length" and tried to sleep, their carpetbags for pillows. As school was opening, even this hospitality could not last. Worse, because they could not produce letters of obedience from Bishop Blanchet, Bishop Alemany refused to accept the Sisters' services in his diocese and forbade Father Huberdault the exercise of his priestly functions. This matter was ironed out through Father Langlois' good offices, but there was still no place for the harassed Sisters of Providence. Even the French Consul, who had been so kind two months before, now "made excuses." These poor Providence Sisters began to accuse themselves of leaving the northern diocese for reasons that "'seemed questionable at best." They thought of the grief of Bishop Bourget and their community in Montreal when they would "hear of such a defection!" They wanted to return now to Ft. Vancouver and "to implore Bishop Blanchet" to accept their services. But instead they set out for home by way of Chile in an unseaworthy old vessel.

Their terrible voyage pales the story of *l'Infatigable*, the worst trial being the presence of a vicious officer. Father Huberdault risked his life to protect the Sisters from the advances of this terrible individual. Safe at last in Chile, the group accepted an assignment there instead of returning to Montreal. Finally, after a period of stress which perhaps Oregon could not have paralleled, some of the Sisters returned to Montreal, the others remaining in Chile as a separate community.

In San José Sister Loyola took over with her usual enthusiasm, happy to note an increased registration. The enrollment of Governor Burnett's daughter especially pleased her; with a few such names, the school would acquire tone and make possible the building scheme she had in mind. For Sister Loyola had no patience with the temporary makeshifts that Sister Marie Catherine's ingenuity was producing, as when she created a chapel by extending a roof between two buildings and purchasing a counter from a dismantled store for an altar. However, the students did not complain of such living quarters; for many of them they were not too unlike their own homes.

The picture in Sister Loyola's mind was a large and imposing brick building, her masterpiece. For once Sister Mary Cornelia spoke up. Scarcity, she said, made the cost of material and labor exorbitant. Why not wait a while? It was the wrong time for any but the very wealthy to build so expensively, and endowment or subsidy of any kind was not to be expected. Besides, the times were unsettled; in this new country, a shift in population might leave their school deserted, and they might easily lose their whole enterprise in mortgage. The school itself was the important thing. If Mère Constantine would send a few English-speaking teachers, with language and training suited to America, the school would soon acquire a very fine reputation even in a group of temporary buildings. Sister Loyola laughingly brushed the arguments aside. Where, she asked, was Sister Mary Cornelia's faith? And with plans set in motion, she returned once more alone to Oregon in March.

Her first step was to insert in the *Oregon Statesman* of March twelfth, her announcement of an auction sale, a six-inch inventory which reads like the closing out of a small but quite elegant Victorian school with farm attached. The announcement includes all the movable articles at the academy: dining room sets, all sorts of household furniture, linen tablecloths, toweling, carpets (one "Turkey" carpet), dinner and tea services, and pewter plate. The two pianos, harp, and guitar are listed, as well as articles "suitable for ladies' boudoirs," art supplies, and even lamp oil. The list includes "eight cows with their calves, five at St. Paul Mission [not included in the earlier sale of the herd], and three at the academy; "all of American blood, but three which have 1/4 Spanish." The academy block and buildings are for sale or rent. The garden is "under the most perfect cultivation, well stocked with fruitbearing trees of various kinds, garden vegetables, etc., etc."

And before this ad appeared in print, Sister Loyola visited Archbishop Blanchet to advise him of the community's impending departure. He had perhaps expected it but not the shock that accompanied the announcement. The Mother General, Sister Loyola told His Lordship, wished the acres at St. Paul to be returned to the mission despite his having signed them over to the Sisters. That was only just and right, he said; the property should not be sold for the benefit of a foundation in California. Sister Loyola was willing to relinquish her claim to the land, but she wished to be reimbursed for buildings and improvements, and she furnished him with an estimate, which with the unsold stock, pigs, horses, etc., amounted to $2,500. The lease, which she held, would run for another year, but on condition of payment of the sum, she would hand it over at once. His Lordship was astounded, as certainly Mère Constantine would have been had she known of the demand. Of what use, he asked, would a vacated school and buildings be to him? He could only watch them and the implements deteriorate. And he did not want the animals. If she wished to hold the lease, she might have the profit of the land until its expiration.

That offer was generous, but seeking the justice of dollars and cents, Sister Loyola did not think so. She failed to see the lack of logic in demanding so much from a mission which was, according to her estimate, too poor to sustain her community. She did not consider that if the lease were renewed, the problem of marketing would fall on the Archbishop; nor did she realize the irony of his having to send money out of his poor diocese to a community that had left it for a more thriving location.

Thinking he had yielded enough, Archbishop Blanchet notified farmer Rivet to leave the farm at the expiration of the lease. Sister Loyola straightway placed the matter in the hands of a lawyer, perhaps Amory Holbrook, who managed other business for her. It was all most regrettable. Here were two very good persons unable to come to terms, both holding out for what each considered absolutely just, the one brooding over injury, the other objectively figuring investment and returns. Nothing more is heard of the matter until a few months before the expiration of the lease; then the Archbishop laid the matter before Mère Constantine.

Sister Loyola's next move was her auction on March seventeenth, when she disposed of pianos and harp and "Turkey" carpet and all the rest of the movable property, and entered in her book $1,630, a very good sum for that day. House and land were sold three years later to William Buck, long after Sister Loyola had ceased to be interested in them.[11] Perhaps new tradesmen from Portland attended that sale; perhaps new settlers purchased harp and pianos for their daughters; perhaps a prospector, lately returned from Southern Oregon mines, bought up the "Turkey" carpet. But the fact that there were buyers on that March day of 1853, as well as for trees and a good sized herd a few months before, points to new beginnings of life. Those were hard years and beginnings were slow, but others lived through them, wondering perhaps at the departure of those who had lived heroic early days. If there had been no California, no contrast, no Father Langlois writing eager letters about the immense good to be done in little San Francisco, Sister Loyola might have led her Sisters to Portland, and with its development found scope for her unusual zeal and ability.

If Sister Loyola had kept even a small community in Oregon and allowed the stronger foundation in San José to assist it through the "dark decade," she would have won the undying gratitude of the Archbishop whose fretfulness was partly due to fear that she would take his Sisters away. And there would always have been the work for young souls which their Foundress desired for them. Neither the Archbishop nor the people, says Sister Marie Catherine, ever would have believed that the Sisters would really leave them.[12] Where such trust existed, there was opportunity for good. This opportunity is essential to the daughters of Mère Julie, who taught happily in a wheatfield; flourishing academies are not. Yet in her memoir Sister Marie Catherine writes loyally that no one but Sister Loyola "could have terminated so painful and delicate an affair." Sister Loyola could and did. She concluded her affairs and set out on April twelfth with all the remaining Sisters.

As no entries were made in Sister Loyola's accounts after the auction sale, one must suppose that payments, perhaps on the pianos, were made after that date, since the sum of $3,200, which she transferred to the San José house in April, is larger than that of the last Oregon City statement. This was a fairly sizable sum to bring to the new undertaking, and the Willamette property contract in her handbag was a guarantee that the Archbishop would finally pay her claim. To businesslike Sister Loyola, all this seemed right and just.

Epilogue

Sister Mary Cornelia yielded her authority to Sister Loyola again, too self-effacing even to notice the look of regret on her Sisters' faces. They accepted the change as an arrangement of higher authority and they admired Sister Mary Cornelia's humility. On the other hand, they were dismayed by such an easy dismissal of her suggestions. They admired Sister Loyola's fine qualities; they looked on her as their appointed Superior, but as she talked of her plans with no regard for the opinions of Sister Mary Cornelia and Sister Marie Catherine, the peace and security that marked Sister Mary Cornelia's superiorship began to give way to uneasiness.

It did not improve the general feeling when Sister Loyola drew up a plan on so grand a scale that the builder refused to consider it in view of the Sisters' small capital. Thereupon she modified it somewhat and satisfied the builders by borrowing amounts that alarmed Sister Marie Catherine. At the end of the year, the loans amounted to over $24,000, and the plan had to be sustained by further loans as the total cost of the building mounted to $54,000. Debt was not a chronic state, as now, and the little receipt book which records payments of interest year after year to Martin Murphy and the Peraltas, caused many a worried hour. That

268

solvency was attained at last was due, as in many another academy story, to the simple and frugal lives of the community.[1]

As the walls of that building rose, Archbishop Blanchet sat thinking long, sad thoughts. When the harvest was under way, and the expiration of the lease was approaching, he wrote at last to Mère Constantine, sending her Sister Loyola's itemized bill with his reasons for considering it too demanding. He wished to "get back the land," for pending payment of her bill Sister Loyola still held the contract he had signed in Namur. He wanted, he explained, to be able to use the buildings "raised at great expense to the mission," as he hoped for another community at St. Paul. He wished especially the return of Mère Constantine's good will, which on account "of her long silence," he feared he had lost. He protested his admiration for the Sisters of Notre Dame, as well as his kindness to them in their years in Oregon. He had never willingly caused them pain. On his side, he wished to be just, to pay whatever was owing the Sisters, and to this end he desired "to come to an agreement." Sickness and troubles, he said, had combined to prevent his making this request before.[2]

Mère Constantine's reply is unfortunately not extant, but she acted quickly, and the more so as certain complaints had reached her from San José. In late November or early December, Sister Loyola was notified of her transfer to the Cincinnati Province. She was to depart at once with Sister Mary Donatilde. And now the true Sister Loyola emerges in the grand humility of which only the very fine are capable. Quite gaily she set aside the authority to which she had grown so accustomed. Sister Mary Cornelia, and the community, too, found that parting very hard, for despite the edgy tension of the past weeks, every one of them loved Sister Loyola. For her too often brusque manner, her judgment too often blinded by her aggressive spirit, her insistence that her opinion must be right, all these went hand in hand with thoroughgoing unselfishness. In her four foundations, said one of the older Sisters who remembered Ixelles, she had reached so far beyond need and means as to touch frustration. Idle carriage and horses at St. Paul, Turkish carpet at auction in Oregon City, a debt of $45,000 in San José, more staggering than a present million dollar debt! Yet the Sisters knew that in all this there had never been the slightest personal motivation.

In her new location, under the direction of Sister Superior Louise, Sister Loyola's unusual ability found its perfect milieu. The older province was now entering an era in which expansion gave justifiable scope to her genius. Here her activity supplemented the gifts of government which she willingly acknowledged in another. By all accounts, the last decades of her life were very happy; perhaps they were never happier than when in her last days she sat of an evening in the garden at the Sixth Street Convent, telling stories of Oregon and feeling for the time on the unglassed face of her big silver watch, as she had so often done in the dark cabin on *l'Infatigable*.

At the Panama crossing, the vessel that bore Sister Loyola and Sister Mary Donatilde down the Chagres to the Atlantic, passed the one that carried the fourth colony of Sisters of Notre Dame to the West, this time five Sisters, two of them well-educated British subjects, but all welcome additions at San José. For two years, Sister Mary Cornelia had been pointing the need of teachers speaking fluent English without an accent; thus the arrival of Sister Aloyse of the Cross and Sister Mary of St. George seemed special good fortune. But the five new Sisters could, in fact, very well have been ten, for the large brick building, with its endless pine floors to be waxed, created "charges," the successors to the "branches" of Oregon days, which called for many hands. The elegant edifice had to be kept shining and spotless, and the maidens of this boarding school, most unwisely of course, were not expected to contribute to the shining.

To the amazement of the newcomers, Sister Mary Cornelia introduced herself as being only in temporary charge of the house. She insisted that surely Mère Constantine had appointed a Superior among the five. All the Sisters, of course, considered Sister Mary Cornelia already appointed. Then one day Sister Laurence received a letter from Mère Constantine stating that Sister Mary Cornelia's appointment in 1852 had been final, that her tenure should never have been interrupted. With real joy Sister Laurence shared her letter with Sister Mary Aloysia, who needed no further proof but gathered the community to pledge their loyalty to Sister Mary Cornelia. It was a great day for the first Sisters of Notre Dame on the Pacific Coast. Still Sister Mary Cornelia protested her unfitness and continued to protest it until Mère Constantine, in one last good scolding, forbade her to speak of it again. Agreeing with her, in caustic terms that she would hesitate to use with another, she observed that lack of fitness is all the greater reason for dependence on God. Sister Mary Cornelia must now put an end forever to the "reasonings which I have heard for the last ten years," and submit to her Superior's decisions. After which outburst, she added in gentler tone the good news she had been receiving from San José, that there was now more peace and union in the house.[3]

Shortly after Sister Loyola's departure, there begins a series of payments extending through a period of somewhat over two years, and credited mostly to Archbishop Blanchet. All told, they amount to a little less than half of the sum for which Sister Loyola had asked. In the absence of letters it is hard to say whether the agreement for which the Archbishop asked was ever made. Under the circumstances, the Mother General would have absolved him completely, as also would Sister Mary Cornelia. It is more likely that the Archbishop, sincerely wishing, as he had said, to deal justly with the Sisters, himself renewed the farmer's lease and sent the proceeds, to his own figure of his debts, to San José. This seems likely since the greater sums are entered in the harvest of 1855. The entry of $1,600 in December, 1856, must have been the down payment at the purchase of Block 12 by William Buck.

Through these years, Archbishop Blanchet never quite relinquished hope of the Sisters' return. Early in 1859 Mère Constantine wrote that he had again asked for a community, but that she had had to refuse "at least for the present." In 1860 she comforted Sister Mary Cornelia with the news that the Willamette Valley was "no longer abandoned." The

Archbishop had secured the Sisters of the Holy Names. And that news brought comfort to Sister Marie Catherine, who never could forget her little savages, and to Sister Mary Aloysia, who said of her departure from Oregon, "ce coup . . . n'a pas laissé de résonner bien fort au coeur . . ." For though she had yielded a bit to discouragement in Oregon, it was her first mission and she longed to return to it. She regarded the Archbishop, "ce bon évêque," as an object of pity, deserted by all but three priests, and praying for others to take their places. How could that be otherwise, she asks; she herself is wrung with compassion at the sad plight of the young with their schools closed.

Gentle Sister Mary Aloysia, apparently ignorant of Sister Loyola's demand for reimbursement, regretted that the Archbishop had not written to them since their departure, concluding from his silence that perhaps their leaving so saddened his heart that he could not write. If Sister Mary Aloysia knew the reason for his silence, her unwillingness to criticize Sister Loyola prevented her stating it. At any rate, that letter, like the memoirs, presents the paradoxical statements of souls abandoned and missionaries with not enough to do. In the midst of things, she is puzzled by it all, but she blames no one. To Sister Mary Aloysia, all the actors in this little drama were admirable.[4]

And so they were. In each, some pardonable human trait proclaiming less than angelic origin serves only to intensify tremendously unselfish dedication. There was no mean spirit among them. Father Langlois with his volatile enthusiasms, now for Oregon, now for California; now ardently longing to become a Jesuit; again rushing off to the Dominican Novitiate and finally leaving that order, too, is sincere and unselfish. And at mention of the good Archbishop's occasional severe attitudes, one should recall that severity quite unthinkable now was common enough in those days among those charged with souls. And a tinge of irritability would be a quite understandable result of long and lonely hardships of his early years in Oregon. Achilles sulking loses no stature. The Fathers and Sisters whose *Ave Maris Stella* floated over Southern Seas, the Canadian missionaries in unhewed log huts, with earth for floor and fir branches for roof, were all of heroic mold and saintly, too.

On the one hand we wish the missionaries, or at least some of them, had stayed. For the foundations in California could have been made without the total abandonment of the Willamette Valley. And even materially their going ironically marked the beginning of a turn for the better. When Sister Loyola was closing her academy, new sawmills were busy along the Columbia supplying San Francisco's lumber demands. Passing through the valley only five years later, Father DeSmet was astonished by "the towns and villages, the rich and beautiful farms, vast apple orchards." [5] We would like to think of Sister Loyola leaving San José to Sister Mary Cornelia and starting a school in Portland, to which Oregon City would have given place had there never been a Donation Law, and of Sister Marie Catherine caring for her "dear savages" at St. Paul until the very house she had helped to build became, as it did a few years later, a boarding school for daughters of the Willamette and of Southern Oregon. But one misstep cannot dim the epic heroism of those missionaries in the Willamette Valley. They were no less heroic in California, where every early foundation of Notre Dame was made with unbelievable labor.

Notes

ABBREVIATIONS USED IN NOTES:

CR, *DeSmet: Life, Letters, and Travels of Father Pierre Jean DeSmet, S.J., 1801–1873.* H. M. Chittenden and A. T. Richardson.

F. N. Blanchet: *Francis Norbert Blanchet and the Founding of the Oregon Missions.* Sister M. L. Lyons.

La Mission de l'Oregon: Notice sur la Territoire et sur la Mission de l'Oregon.

Quebec Missions: Notice and Voyages of the Famed Quebec Mission to the Pacific Northwest. C. Landerholm.

CHAPTER 1

[1] The story of *l'Infatigable*'s long wait in the Schelde before her historic voyage is found in the Memoirs of Sister Marie Catherine and others, as well as in the first eight letters addressed by Mère Constantine to "the Missionary Sisters sent to Oregon."

[2] The first owners of *l'Infatigable* were David and Deboe of Antwerp, who sold her in 1850 to another Antwerp firm, Van den Bergh and Cie. After the voyage of 1844, Captain Moller was succeeded by Captain Richmers and later by Captain Cordier. The last mention of *l'Infatigable* is in 1855. There is no foundation for the legend that she was lost at sea. (The author is indebted to Mr. Jan-Albert Goris, Commissioner of Information, Belgian Government Information Center, New York, for securing data on *l'Infatigable* from the National Maritime Museum of Antwerp.)

[3] CR, *DeSmet*, II, 447.

[4] Brother George must have been a fugitive from the reign of Terror. If he had been a Brother Minor, as Sister Marie Catherine's memoir indicates, his continued residence in the Cabareaux home would be difficult to explain; he would have found his way to a house of his order. But as the Minims had expanded almost entirely in France, their order was almost wiped out of existence by the Revolution. Besides, Brother George's scholarly pursuits were more akin to those of the Minims; a Franciscan lay brother would hardly have built up such a library.

[5] The first missionary band of Sisters of Notre Dame de Namur arrived in New York on the ship *Eliza Thornton*, October 19, 1840, at Bishop Purcell's invitation. With Sister Louis de Gonzague as Superior, they made their first foundation in Cincinnati, opening classes in January, 1841.

6 Among other gifts made to Sister Loyola at her departure from Ixelles, was a handsome silver watch presented by the parents of a recently deceased pupil of the school. It was inscribed "In memory of Denise," and with Sister Loyola's name and the date. Sister took this large and heavy timepiece with her to Oregon and later to Cincinnati. As it had no crystal, she used to feel the time with her hand when the light was dim. A half-century after the gift of the silver watch to Sister Loyola, Sister Superior Julia of Cincinnati was looking about for a case for altar relics. The beautiful Gothic chapel at Our Lady's Summit, East Walnut Hills, Cincinnati, was nearing completion, and the relic case was the one thing wanting. Suddenly she had an inspiration; the old watch was just the thing. She had the worn-out works removed and the case lined with white silk. Thus the watch became the reliquary in the altar stone at Our Lady's Summit, and a relic in its own right of two valiant pioneer Sisters. *Among the Reapers in the Fields of Notre Dame,* September, 1894, 92–93.

7 Sister Mary Cornelia's appointment gave her a special status. Ordinarily a Superior can consult her higher Superior in important matters. At such a distance and with such poor communications, Sister Loyola would not enjoy this privilege and would thus need a special assistant. Besides, it seems to have been Mère Contantine's wish from the start that Sister Mary Cornelia should become a Superior if and when a second foundation should be made.

8 *The Life of Mère St. Joseph,* 222–35. But more particular details of this schism were withheld from publication until a century had passed; then a complete account, based on the depositions of those who had been deceived into following the misguided reformers, was issued in mimeograph form.

9 Maria Lucas, grandniece of the "Irish Don," Mateo Murphy of San Rafael, is still living, age 96, and relating lively stories of her girlhood at the College of Notre Dame in San José, California, in the 1870's. Don Mateo's rancho included the greater part of Marin County, California, and remained in the family's possession long after California's statehood.

10 Father John Nobili died in Santa Clara in 1856. His remains were interred in the students' chapel which he was constructing at the time of his death. Later they were removed to the Mission Church, where a marble slab recalls his memory.

11 W. L. Davis, "Peter John DeSmet, the Years of Preparation, 1801–1837," in *Pacific Northwest Quarterly,* XXXII, April, 1941, 167. Young DeSmet's restlessness was a source of worry to his relatives.

12 CR, *DeSmet,* I, 12–13 and 105–106. Father DeSmet is described as surpassing all his associates in physical strength and energy, and at the same time possessing an unusually attractive appearance. Though he was somewhat short for one of his heavy build, his presence was commanding and dignified. But he was far from enjoying constant good health. He used to jest about the number of persons who remarked his seeming robustness when he was in reality quite ill.

[13] W. N. Bischoff, S. J., *The Jesuits in Old Oregon,* 14. But Father Bischoff adds that despite his poor health, "the Abbé DeSmet begged, preached, and labored for his former brothers in Christ" during the ensuing two years. CR, *DeSmet,* I, 14, includes the grateful acknowledgment by St. Louis University of valuable contributions made by DeSmet, among them "Physical and chymical instruments."

[14] Mr. Paul Bakewell, Sr. (*American Catholic Who's Who,* 1938 and 1939), wrote his recollections of Father DeSmet in a letter to his grandson, Father Anderson Bakewell, S. J., of the Maryland Jesuit Province, in 1945. This letter appeared in *The Jesuit, Maryland Province,* April, 1956, p. 23.

CHAPTER 2

[1] Sister Helen Louise, S.N.D., *Sister Louise,* 83–84.

[2] Five letters written by Sister Louis de Gonzague, February 15, 1841, to May 9, 1843, deal with visits of Father DeSmet, and the desire felt by herself and her Sisters to found a mission in the West. Archives of Sisters of Notre Dame, Namur.

[3] L. B. Palladino, *Indian and White in the Northwest,* 55. Father Palladino here mentions also Father DeSmet's near appointment to episcopal dignity, and his suggestion that the honor go to Vicar-General Blanchet.

[4] Sister Letitia Mary Lyons, *Francis Norbert Blanchet,* 145–46.

[5] Letters of Mère Constantine, No. 2, December 10, 1843.

[6] Mère Constantine, No. 3, December 12, 1843.

[7] CR, *DeSmet,* II, 451. Here Father DeSmet speaks of the blasphemer as a passenger, but as there were no passengers aboard other than the missionaries, and as the mate is mentioned in this regard in the memoirs, he must have been the guilty one.

[8] Mère Constantine, No. 4, December 17, 1843.

[9] Mère Constantine, No. 5, December 22, 1843.

[10] Mère Constantine, No. 9, December 24, 1843.

CHAPTER 3

[1] C. Landerholm, *Quebec Missions,* 19. Here Chinook is described as easy to learn, and Father Demers is credited with mastering it in three months. But the Sisters found it very difficult, probably because of its lack of construction and because almost no one except a native could pronounce it. And 150, in which F. N. Blanchet goes into detail about the sounds of Chinook: some sounds as *r* are missing; the sound *h* is "so in the throat" that it cannot be imitated; it is quite futile to try to represent Chinook pronunciation in print. A note on the same page states that Chinook was once thought to have been invented by the employees of HBC as a means of communication with the several Indian tribes. But the jargon was in use before the arrival of the whites; it was based on the Chinook tongue which was the most widespread dialect in the Northwest.

2 Letter of Sister Louis de Gonzague to Mère Constantine, December 31, 1842. Father DeSmet told Sister L. de G. that it would require four years to learn the language of the Coeur d'Alène Indians. He thought only the younger Fathers with good memories should attempt to learn Indian dialects.

3 Sister Letitia Mary Lyons, *Francis Norbert Blanchet*, 22–23. Of his success in learning Chinook, Father Demers wrote to the Vicar-General, "God has given me the grace to learn the Chinook language in a short time. It is in this jargon that I instruct the women and children of the white settlers and savages who come to (me) from far and near." Letter dated January 23, 1839.

4 T. J. Farnham, *Farnham's Travels,* in Reuben C. Thwaites. *Early Western Travels,* XXIX, 90. Farnham's report on HBC farms at Nisqually and Cowlitz. The Indians told Farnham that they succeeded well with but little work.

5 Letters of Mère Constantine, No. 8, December 31, 1843.

6 CR, *DeSmet,* 410.

CHAPTER 4

1 CR, *DeSmet,* 419. For Father DeSmet's account of the voyage from Antwerp to Valparaiso, CR, *DeSmet,* 408–20. For Sister Mary Aloysia's account, *La Mission de l'Oregon,* 66–78, and translation in C. B. Bagley, *Early Catholic Missions,* 63–69. Sister Marie Catherine gives a vivid account in her memoir.

2 *La Mission de l'Oregon,* 81. Sister Loyola wrote that Fathers De-Smet and Vercruysse and she herself suffered much from seasickness, but that the others were less afflicted after the first few days. She also states that none of them knew what a really rough sea was until they reached Cape Horn. In C. B. Bagley, *Early Catholic Missions,* 71.

3 *La Mission de l'Oregon,* 69. CR, *DeSmet,* 412–13.

4 *La Mission de l'Oregon,* 74.

5 Sister Loyola's letter of April 27, 1844, from Valparaiso, states that the storm carried away two of the sails as also a quantity of the sailors' clothing. *La Mission de l'Oregon,* 82. C. B. Bagley's translation of this letter adds that the wind was seventy or eighty miles an hour (p. 81), but the original does not give the velocity.

6 *La Mission de l'Oregon,* 77, and on p. 82, Sister Loyola's statement that the Sisters all went to bed at eleven despite the storm, that those who remained awake continued their prayers, but that fear had so little effect on some of them, they went to sleep in the midst of it all.

7 CR, *DeSmet,* 420.

CHAPTER 5

1 CR, *DeSmet,* 420–34. Father DeSmet's account of the somewhat lengthy stops at Valparaiso and Lima is a fascinating study of Chile

and Peru as well as of these cities. It indicates his breadth of interest and his ability to make excellent use of his time. For Sister Mary Aloysia's story of this phase of the voyage, *La Mission de l'Oregon*, 78–80, and 86–91. In C. B. Bagley, *Early Catholic Missions in Old Oregon*, II, 69–70 and 74–76. Sister Marie Catherine's memoir is especially detailed for Lima.

2 Sister Loyola's letter of April 27, 1844, to Mère Constantine, *La Mission de l'Oregon*, 81–84, reviews the voyage to Valparaiso briefly. In C. B. Bagley, *Early Catholic Missions in Old Oregon*, II, 71–72.

3 This missionary expedition was led by Bishop Rouchoux, a member of the Congregation of the Sacred Hearts (Picpus), who as Vicar-Apostolic held general jurisdiction over the two prefectures of the Vicariate Apostolic of Eastern Oceania, which the Sacred Congregation of the Propaganda had established in 1833 under the care of his Congregation. Bishop Rouchoux left Honolulu early in 1841 to secure missionaries in France. In December, 1842, he sailed with his large group of volunteers in the brig *Marie-Joseph*. The ship was never heard from again. Sister Letitia Mary Lyons, *Francis Norbert Blanchet*, 133 and 152; Ralph S. Kuykendall, *The Hawaiian Kingdom*, 1778–1854, 342.

Archbishop Blanchet believed the *Marie-Joseph* was wrecked rounding the Horn. When he and his missionaries, including seven Sisters of Notre Dame, rounded the Horn in *l'Etoile du Matin* in 1847, he asked them to join him in prayer for the repose of the souls of Bishop Rouchoux and those who lost their lives with him. Sister Mary Laurence, who wrote the account of the voyage of *l'Etoile du Matin*, relates that one of the crew, a certain M. Aubrey, told the Sisters he had seen two large church bells taken aboard the already heavily loaded *Marie-Joseph*, and had feared the ship would not reach its destination.

4 For these requests and inducements, *La Mission de l'Oregon*, 82–83.

CHAPTER 6

1 CR, *DeSmet*, II, 434–41. Father DeSmet's account of the voyage from Lima to the Columbia. For Sister Mary Aloysia's account, *La Mission de l'Oregon*, 92–106, and translation in C. B. Bagley, *Early Catholic Missions in Old Oregon*, II, 77–84. And Sister Marie Catherine's memoirs.

2 CR, *DeSmet*, II, 436.

3 J. Gibbs, *Pacific Graveyard*, 5. "The first official survey of the river awaited the arrival of Lieutenant Charles Wilkes of the U. S. Navy in 1841." (One of Wilkes' ships was wrecked there at a point subsequently known as Peacock Spit.) "Among the findings of the Wilkes Expedition was the continual movement of the sands around the mouth of the river, which constantly changed the channel depths. This dis-

covery revealed why it is so difficult to make accurate navigation charts of the bar."

For earlier charting of the Columbia: Broughton's chart of the river entrance appears in *OHQ*, v. 18, opposite p. 231, and is followed by T. C. Elliott's article on charting of the river.

"Sketch K," located between pages 206 and 207 is found in "Report of Prof. Alexander D. Bache, Superintendent of the Coast Survey . . . , 1850," *H. Ex. Doc. No. 12*, 31st Cong., 2d Sess. This "preliminary survey of the mouth of the Columbia River," is based on findings of the Hydrographic Party under the command of Lieutenant W. P. McArthur, U. S. Navy and Assistant U. S. Coast Survey, 1849. On p. 51 of the Report, Bache quotes McArthur as follows: "I have examined all the charts that have been made of the Columbia River from the time of its discovery to the present, and find that there have been continued changes going on, but at all times has there been a good deep channel at the mouth of the river. To these changes in the channel is to be attributed the great dread which navigators have had of the Columbia, and I have recommended a lighthouse on Cape Disappointment, and five buoys to be placed in such a manner as best to point out the channel. I would also recommend that these be placed under the superintendence of the pilot, who will always know when any change in the channel takes place, and can move the the buoys to such positions as he might think best."

It would seem that at any time before the construction of jetties at the mouth of the Columbia, the presence of a skilled pilot was more important than the possession of a chart.

Though "Sketch K" was made five years later than the Wilkes Chart, it may not for that reason approximate less closely the position of banks and channels in 1844. But as it represents only the mouth of the river, while the Wilkes Chart represents the river to Portland, it gives a more detailed picture. For this reason and because the soundings are marked on it, "Sketch K" probably offers a better idea of Captain Moller's predicament.

A note appended to a letter by Father J. B. Z. Boldoc, C. Landerholm, *Quebec Missions*, 143, (1845), states that crossing the bar was possible only in fair weather and with the sounding line, and that even at that there were frequent wrecks; that vessels often waited for a month and a half before being able to cross, whether entering or leaving.

[4] CR, *DeSmet*, 437. Father DeSmet mentions a suggestion made to him a day or two later. "They [probably the ship's officers] even came to me and proposed taking us to the Sandwich Islands." This proposition was made just outside the bar, July 29. Neither Father DeSmet nor Sister Mary Aloysia mention the "plot" related by Sister Marie Catherine, but it is easy to see that the worried sailor who warned the Fathers may have overheard this talk of going to the Sandwich Islands.

[5] There is no foundation for the legend that the Sisters added a

promise of their own to Father DeSmet's vow formula to erect a chapel in honor of the Immaculate Heart of Mary in gratitude for a safe landing. If they had made such a promise, Sister Mary Aloysia would certainly have entered it in her detailed account of the vow, *La Mission de l'Oregon*, 98–99. *American Foundations of the Sisters of Notre Dame de Namur*, 135, states that this promise was a condition of the vow on the part of the Sisters, and that the beautiful chapel of the College of Notre Dame in San José was its fulfillment. The vow included the clause that each priest should celebrate Holy Mass and each Sister receive Holy Communion on certain feasts in honor of the Immaculate Heart of Mary.

[6] C. B. Bagley, *Early Catholic Missions in Old Oregon*, II, 81. Mr. Bagley here inserts into Sister Mary Aloysia's account worry felt by the Sisters about whether their "storm-beaten vessel with its tattered sails and broken masts" would get through the seething waters of the bar. But Sister Mary Aloysia said nothing at all about the ship at this point. *La Mission de l'Oregon*, 101. Mr. Bagley found this quotation in *Harvest Fields*, 66. Both Father DeSmet and Sister Mary Aloysia say *l'Infatigable* entered the river with sails spread. Aside from the main topsail ripped off by the gale, p. 99, she suffered no serious injuries between Lima and the Columbia, and the sail was probably replaced before she reached the river.

[7] Sister Mary Aloysia's account mentions Captain Moller as losing self-control at this point. *La Mission de l'Oregon*, 104. Father DeSmet states that it was the mate who cried, "We are between life and death," addressing the captain, and that he added, "but we must go on at any price." CR, *DeSmet*, 439.

CHAPTER 7

[1] CR, *DeSmet*, 486, note. Letter of Father DeSmet to Senator Benton, Nov. 3, 1849, in which he reports his conversation, June, 1846, with a British officer on the *Modeste*. But Father DeSmet himself held that Oregon was being unjustly taken from its rightful owner, the Indian. (Letter to Bishop Hughes, Aug. 17, 1845, same page.)

[2] O. O. Winther. *The Great Northwest*, 71. The "Coasting Trade" scheme was evolved by Simpson and carried out by McLoughlin. . . . Arrangements for marketing at Canton were made through the East India Company.

[3] O. O. Winther, 71. The Fort Vancouver "Skin Book" illustrates this decline in its record of Snake River expeditions from 1826 to 1852. The first party venturing into this region returned with 2,744 skins. Twenty years later, returns from the same area were 1,454. Returns from other points show the same falling off. And 120, McLoughlin's statement that the trade "must diminish" with settlement.

[4] O. O. Winther, 73–74. But Simpson's chief reason for encouraging

agriculture on a large scale was that "every pursuit tending to lighten the expense of the Trade is a branch thereof." At the outset, it was perhaps McLoughlin's sole motive, too. In the case of Oregon, they were both greatly impressed by reports of giant trees and other signs of very fertile soil.

5 Dr. B. B. Barker, *Letters of John McLoughlin,* 1829–32, Introduction, iii. "On reading these letters one is impressed with the infinite details of the business which Dr. McLoughlin had to supervise."

CR, *DeSmet,* IV, 1556. Father DeSmet noted the firmness, tact, and knowledge of people that made McLoughlin so successful an administrator.

Frederick V. Holman, *Dr. John McLoughlin,* 26, remarks that when McLoughlin came to the Northwest, it was not safe for the company's parties to travel except in large numbers, but that in a few years there was almost no danger. Yet he had no trained soldiers to govern that great area.

6 The HBC charter, as well as the statute passed by British parliament in 1821, gave the company, as was necessary, a great deal of power. Sister Letitia Mary Lyons, *F. N. Blanchet,* Introduction, xv, and note: G. W. Fuller, *A History of the Pacific Northwest,* 110. T. J. Farnham, *Travels,* in Thwaites. *Early Western Travels,* 29 and 61.

7 J. Schafer, *Oregon Settlement,* 39–42. Even after Astor's inflence subsided, there were always some interested enough to keep Oregon before the eyes of Congress. Lord Ashburton thought that Americans were concerned with getting a good harbor on the Pacific. He thought that Indian tribes that had been pushed west would for years be an obstacle to Americans settling in Oregon. However, Sir George Simpson noted in 1841 that though the British subjects were still more numerous in the Willamette Valley, the Americans were showing "a strong feeling of nationality," and were entering into a struggle with HBC for the water power at Willamette Falls.

8 W. I. Marshall, *Acquisition of Oregon,* 353. McLoughlin gave Lee the use of horses, oxen, and milk cows, and furnished him with all supplies. If the cattle died while in his possession, he would not be charged with them. Horses had to be returned in kind, or the sum of eight dollars, the current value of a horse. McLoughlin granted this start to all settlers who asked for it. And p. 26 notes generous treatment of all Americans at all HBC posts, if they were not fur traders.

9 Gary had been assigned to replace Lee, whom the Mission Board had transferred to Honolulu.

10 W. I. Marshall, *Acquisition of Oregon,* 384–85.

11 E. M. Lynskey, *The Government of the Catholic Church,* 65.

12 T. J. Farnham, *Travels,* in Thwaites, *Early Western Travels,* 29. Farnham thought the white population (1839) of Oregon fairly orderly and industrious, though many of them had lived dissolutely (before the companies merged in 1821 and HBC forbade the sale of liquor). He praised especially the settlers in the Willamette Valley for their

stand against the vice of drunkenness; he commended HBC for buying up the whole cargo of a vessel that carried liquor to prevent its going to the natives, and for interdicting it as an article of trade though its sale would have been profitable to the company.

[13] Sister Letitia Mary Lyons, *F. N. Blanchet*. Note on pages 23–25 gives the chief points of Bishop Signay's instructions to his two first missionaries to the Northwest. Point 1 deals with the "first object" of the mission, regaining the natives from "barbarism and its disorders." But after four years' experience Vicar-General Blanchet wrote to Bishop Signay, Oct. 28, 1842, that it was clear the conversion and reform of the whites should come first, and that of the savages would follow naturally.

[14] Blanchet's account of the journey was published in his *Historical Sketches* in 1878, in which he added a description of Fort Vancouver to his journal letters. C. B. Bagley, *Early Catholic Missions in Old Oregon*, I, 28–46. Sister Letitia Mary Lyons, *F. N. Blanchet*, 1–17, relates the appointment of the two missionaries and the events of their journey, and includes excerpts from letters of both.

[15] C. B. Bagley, *Early Catholic Missions in Old Oregon*, II, 39, and 119–22. The illustration opposite page 119 is a photograph of an original *Ladder* which Mr. Bagley found in a collection at Fort Nisqually, but which had disappeared from the Fort at his time of writing, 1932. He recalled that it was about six feet by eighteen inches, and that the design seemed to have been made with a small paint brush and India ink. Actually the pictured *Ladder* is narrower in proportion to its length.

Vicar-General Blanchet used his first *Ladder* at the Cowlitz Mission in the summer of 1842. Pleased with the results, he either made, or had made, copies for other missionaries, furnishing a key or manual with these. The *Ladder* illustrated in Bagley's volume was made in 1842 or possibly 1843. Centuries and decades are represented by bars and dots, and the paper being broken at the top, it is impossible to say which year is indicated. Thus the *Ladder* treasured at the old fort might have been the first one.

[16] Sister Letitia Mary Lyons, 64. "We have done nothing for a year but hold our old position. Our efforts to extend the reign of Jesus Christ among the savages have failed. . . . We await the arrival of Reverend Father DeSmet who has not yet returned." Blanchet to Signay, Nov. 6, 1843, QAA.

CHAPTER 8

[1] The narrative here follows CR, *DeSmet*, 440–49. *La Mission de l'Oregon*, 104–20, for Sister Mary Aloysia's account. C. B. Bagley, *Early Catholic Missions in Old Oregon*, II, 83–89. Memoirs of Sister Marie Catherine. Life of Sr. Mary Cornelia.

2 How *l'Infatigable's* cook obtained enough water to make even sufficient coffee for the passengers would present a problem if he did not draw it from the river, since no one is reported as bringing water aboard. The first assistance of any kind came later in the day. On the other hand, would river water so near the mouth be salt-free? Research Associate Priscilla Knuth of Oregon Historical Society took this question to U. S. Engineers, and was assured that in July water in the main channel would be fresh, perhaps with a negligible fraction of salt water, and that it need not be muddy, since the mud would have slacked off in June.

3 *La Mission de l'Oregon*, 105. Nous avons nommé le canal où nous sommes entrés et que nous avons traversé les premiers, *le canal Saint-Ignace.* CR, *DeSmet,* I, 441. Father DeSmet says they named this channel, which had just been crossed "for the first time," in honor of Saint Ignatius. C. B. Bagley, *Early Catholic Missions in Old Oregon,* "Historical Sketches," I, 116. F. N. Blanchet says this channel was "never attempted before."

4 *La Mission de l'Oregon*, 105.

5 *La Mission de l'Oregon*, 106. Sister Mary Aloysia says the chief of the Clapsapes (sic) sent the food. Father DeSmet says the American who led the first band of Indians to the ship was the donor. CR, *DeSmet,* 442.

6 CR, *DeSmet,* 441. Father DeSmet says they had observed all these signals, but adds that they were suspicious of them. Sister Mary Aloysia says they did not understand the signals. *La Mission de l'Oregon,* 105. C. B. Bagley, II, 83, says none on board saw the flag nor heard the guns, and that they saw the beacon but feared it. He seems to be guided here by *Harvest Fields,* 69.

7 *La Mission de l'Oregon*, 111. ". . . avec toute sa famille." And on p. 113, Sister Mary Aloysia mentions small children in the McLoughlin family, probably those of Eloisa McLoughlin and William Glen Rae, who lived in San Francisco but may have been visiting at Fort Vancouver.

8 Sister Mary Aloysia refers to this epidemic as "la maladie." *La Mission de l'Oregon,* 112. Father DeSmet called it dysentery. CR, *DeSmet,* I, 451. C. B. Bagley, translating Sister Mary Aloysia, calls it smallpox. *Early Catholic Missions in Old Oregon,* II, 87. Here again, he is quoting *Harvest Fields,* 71. The symptoms indicated dysentery.

9 This bell was blessed December 22, 1839, PR, 3, OHS. It weighed eighty pounds and was brought to Oregon, probably by ship, with a fifty-pound bell for Father Demers' church at Cowlitz. The Vicar-General and Father Demers started from Fort Vancouver, December 10, with their respective bells in two canoes, stopped for supper together at the mouth of the Willamette, and parted, each with the happy prospect of hearing the Angelus three times a day at his mission. Rowing up the Willamette, the Vicar-General worried about the risk his co-worker was taking on the more dangerous Columbia, in a light canoe

laden with a heavy bell, but Father Demers reached Cowlitz safely and in four days had his bell raised on a forty-foot frame and blessed. C. B. Bagley, I, 31. When the present brick church was built at St. Paul in 1845, the Archbishop's bell was placed in the tower from which it sounds the Angelus and summons parishioners today.

CHAPTER 9

[1] For the narrative of the Sisters' first months at St. Paul: Memoirs of Sisters Marie Catherine and Mary Albine, and *La Mission de l'Oregon*, 120–32. C. B. Bagley, *Early Catholic Missions in Old Oregon*, II, 91–97.

Sister Mary Aloysia's long letter beginning on page 92, *La Mission de l'Oregon*, and Sister Loyola's supplement, page 120, were accidentally run together under the latter signature. C. B. Bagley corrected this error.

[2] Not malaria as in *Harvest Fields*, 76, and in C. B. Bagley, 90. Sister Loyola termed the sickness *maladie régnante*, which as in other instances, indicates the epidemic that took so many lives in Oregon that summer. The sudden and violent attack also points to the epidemic and not to malaria.

[3] See page 123 and note for Blanchet's original *Ladder*. The second development of the Blanchet *Ladder* was the pocket size as here described. Some of these were made by the Sisters of Notre Dame shortly after their arrival in Oregon. Leaving Oregon for California in 1853, they brought with them two of these small *Ladders*, one of which is in the Notre Dame Archives at Saratoga. The other was donated some years ago to the Bancroft Library, and is reproduced in C. Landerholm, *Quebec Missions*, opposite page 44. On these small *Ladders*, the symbols are explained by hand-printed captions in French. They are more detailed than the Blanchet original given by Bagley, II, opposite 119, and they show many individual differences. The printing at the top of these *Ladders* was done with block-letter type, as is clear from unevenness. It is possible that Sister Marie Catherine may have done this work with the large and varied type set that she inherited from her friend, Brother George.

In 1860, Archbishop Blanchet had an engraving of his *Ladder* made for printing, this time with more elaborate pictures and explanations.

The *Ladders* are convenient historic documents, since they date themselves. After the fourth decade of the nineteenth century, three dots, indicating three completed years, date the document 1844.

[4] Father Mengarini had accompanied DeSmet to the mountains in 1841. Biographical account of Father Mengarini in W. N. Bischoff, *The Jesuits of Old Oregon*, 228.

[5] Blanchet Letter No. 8, September 19, 1854, in Portland Archdiocesan Archives. Mère Constantine was opposed at first to the Sisters'

autonomous holding of property in the mission. Letter No. 16, October 4, 1846.

6 Sister Letitia Mary Lyons, *F. N. Blanchet,* 150–51. Excerpts from Blanchet's letter to Bishop Turgeon, April 8, 1844 in QAA, and note regarding Langlois' criticism of Blanchet as related by Demers in his letter to Father Charles Cazeau, November 19, 1843. Demers was annoyed at both the conduct of Langlois and the patience of Blanchet.

7 C. B. Bagley, *Early Catholic Missions in Old Oregon,* I, 121.

8 C. B. Bagley, II, 56. Blanchet gives detailed wage rates and notes on high prices of manufactured goods, furniture, etc. The cost of transportation multiplied the cost of imported articles. He gives the wage of farm hands as 1,200 to 1,500 francs a year; teachers as 1,200 to 1,800 francs.

9 CR, *DeSmet,* I, 450, and W. N. Bischoff, *The Jesuits in Old Oregon,* 46–47.

10 Father Anthony Ravalli would have been an asset in any mission field; he had supplemented his theological studies with medicine and mechanics. He brought with him to Oregon a set of buhrstones twelve inches in diameter, which an Antwerp merchant had presented to him at his departure, to insure the mission a supply of flour for altar bread, but to his surprise, he found flour mills there. However, he took the set with him on his mission to the Flatheads. L. Palladino, *Indian and White in the Northwest,* 60.

11 The stove was given to Champoeg Museum by J. G. Alpin of Woodburn, Oregon. His mother, Marie Wagner Alpin, used to assist Vicar-General Blanchet in teaching the Indians, probably at Fort Vancouver, as well she might have done, according to her son's boast that "she spoke and sang in four languages, French, Latin, English, and the Indian jargon." But then, she was the daughter of a certain Peter Wagner, Indian interpreter. Alpin's father was George Chipman Alpin, a trapper in the employ of HBC until his marriage, when he took up a claim between Champoeg and St. Paul, December 26, 1850. Hearing that the Sisters were about to dispose of their four original stoves and replace them by new French stoves, the elder Alpin bought one of them to heat his new cabin, because it threw more heat than a fireplace would. When he moved to Woodburn, apparently during a flood as he moved out by boat, he left the old stove. The flood destroyed the cabin. Long afterwards, his son came back, put the pieces of the stove together, and turned it in to the Champoeg Museum as a relic. The story of the stove, related by Grace Bell Jones Austin, of Woodburn, Oregon, in an old news clipping, hangs in a little frame near the stove in Champoeg Museum.

12 Early in the year Blanchet stated his views in a letter to Signay. While he emphasized the need of a bishop in the Northwest, he suggested that a Canadian priest be consecrated and sent out. The new bishop could learn all he needed to about the country in a few months, and this measure would not necessitate a long absence for consecration

on the part of a missionary already there. He also suggested the choice of a bishop from the United States for the Columbia area, since all progress due to immigration would likely develop south of the river. The letter makes clear Blanchet's own distaste for the position. Sister Letitia Mary Lyons, *F. N. Blanchet*, 149. Blanchet to Signay, March 24, 1844, QAA.

[13] In a letter dated Namur, October 4, 1846, Sister M. Aloysie, writing for Mère Constantine, advised Sister Loyola that the matter of the land at St. Paul had been settled in accordance with her wishes. Letters of Mère Constantine, No. 16.

[14] L. Palladino, *Indian and White in the Northwest*, 65, says Accolti had "no predilection for work among the Indians . . ." Subsequent events verify this statement.

[15] C. B. Bagley, *Early Catholic Missions in Old Oregon*, II, 54.

[16] C. B. Bagley, I, 121.

CHAPTER 10

[1] The account of the first years of the school at St. Paul is related in letters to the Mother House by Sister Mary Aloysia, March 3, 1845, and Sister Loyola, October 14, 1845 and July 23, 1846. *La Mission de l'Oregon*, 131–70, and C. B. Bagley, *Early Catholic Missions in Old Oregon*, II, 97–114. Also in Sister Marie Catherine's memoir.

[2] *La Mission de l'Oregon*, 133, . . . dix piastres (cinquante francs). C. B. Bagley, II, 98, . . . ten dollars.

[3] . . . les trois Rois qui furent ornés de schalls (sic) et de diadèmes de carton . . . *La Mission de l'Oregon*, 140.

[4] . . . elle passe pour un phénix dans ce genre. *La Mission de l'Oregon*, 136.

[5] Le sifflement des serpents, le rugissement des tigres, le hurlement des loups. . . . *La Mission de l'Oregon*, 139.

[6] In his article, "The First Fruits of the Land," *OHQ*, vol. 7, March, 1906, J. R. Cardwell gives on p. 28 a list of indigenous fruits including apple, plum, and grape and various berries. Also he states that the first cultivated fruits were introduced by HBC in the 1820's. As Sister Norbertine planted some young trees each year, she may have obtained saplings of various kinds from the nursery started in Milwaukie near Oregon City in 1847 by the Luellings, who brought hundreds of live trees across the plains that year.

[7] C. Landerholm, *Quebec Missions*, 233–37. Letters of Father Demers to M.C., during the absence of Bishop Blanchet, and letters of Father Boldoc, 237–43, written during the same period, indicate how engrossed each was with the building program which they both hoped to have completed before the Bishop's return. Father Demers especially was overburdened; besides being in charge of the vicariate for the time, he was building up the parish in Oregon City, with the as-

sistance of Father DeVoss. He lamented that care of outlying missions prevented either of them remaining in residence in the parish.

In addition to their other burdens, both Father Demers and Father Boldoc here report worries and struggles caused by the illicit sale of liquor by Americans to Canadians and half-breeds, an abuse which the Provisional Government could do little to prevent beyond legislation. These letters are interesting, too, in that they present Father Demers as more optimistic than Father Boldoc. American immigrants are, for instance, a squalid lot to Father Boldoc, but very promising to Father Demers. Both fear the evil effects of continued international dispute over Oregon, but while Father Boldoc sees no immediate end of it, Father Demers thinks a peaceful solution may be in the making even while he writes.

8 CR, *DeSmet*, I, 475–76.

9 L. B. Palladino, *Indian and White in the Northwest*, 56; and W. N. Bischoff, *The Jesuits in Old Oregon*, 47–48, and for the work of Father DeVoss among the Kettle Falls Indians, p. 153.

10 Letters of Mère Constantine, No. 27, November 26, 1848. But Mère Constantine later altered her advice in this matter of outdoor toil. At the time of writing, she could not have realized what an onerous form it took at Sainte Marie de Willamette.

11 PR, January 6, and 21, 1839. (OHS, Parish Records.)

12 PR, December 25, 1839. (OHS, Parish Records.) B. B. Barker, *Letters of Doctor John McLoughlin*, Appendix A, 297–327, furnishes interesting data concerning the McKays and Montours.

13 *La Mission de l'Oregon*, 163. Father Demers' letter to Mère Constantine dated October 21, 1845. Translated in C. B. Bagley, *Early Catholic Missions in Old Oregon*, II, 111.

14 Sister Loyola's letter is dated October 14, 1845. She sent it probably in November, at any rate before Christmas, of which she would otherwise have included an account. The fortnightly paper, then, must have been the *Flumgudgeon Gazette*, published by Charles Edward Pickett. In an article on this paper, OHQ, vol. 40, 203, ff., the author, L. C. Powell, states that it was a manuscript newspaper. OHS has one issue, perhaps the only remaining one, vol. 1, no. 8, August 20, 1845. The paper ran to about a dozen copies each issue. During the sessions of the legislative committee at Oregon City in the summer of 1845, the paper appeared twice weekly.

Hugh Burns became the first official mail carrier, Oregon City, 1846. It is difficult to know what mail service Sister Loyola had in mind; she may have heard plans for this Oregon City regular delivery.

15 Letter of James Douglas to Sir George Simpson, Vancouver, March 5, 1845, in *Publications of the Hudson's Bay Record Society*, 3rd Series, 1844–46, London, 1944. Appendix A, p. 177–88. In the same letter Douglas expressed satisfaction with all the Belgian missionaries. While he regretted the loss of "good customers" among the departed Methodists, he hoped that "the Jesuits would richly supply the blank." The

newcomers, he noted, "are building on a large scale" on the Willamette, and "deal out their cash with a liberal hand."

CHAPTER 11

[1] Archbishop Blanchet gives the account of this journey, his consecration, and return to Oregon in his "Historical Sketches," in C. B. Bagley, *Early Catholic Missions in Old Oregon*, I, 125–29. See also II, 56–59. The story of the voyage by Sister Laurence is in Annals of the Sisters of Notre Dame, I.

[2] Letters of Mère Constantine, No. 16, October 4, 1846.

[3] Archives of the Sisters of Notre Dame in Namur. This "notice" of the life and death of Sister Renilde quotes from a letter, not extant, written in Oregon City shortly after she died.

[4] C. Landerholm, *Quebec Missions*, 212–33.

[5] This attitude toward the regular clergy is indicated in Bishop Blanchet's addition to his *Memorial*, which he presented to Cardinal Brunelli May 6, 1846. He seems to have been influenced by what he heard in Rome of difficulties between other prelates and regulars in their dioceses, as well as by word he had received from Father Demers regarding a boundary dispute, which must have been at St. Francis, with the Jesuits. Actually Bishop Blanchet had only very generous feelings toward the Jesuits up to that time. He even tried to persuade Father DeVoss to act as vicar-general during his absence. When Father DeVoss declined, he appointed Father Demers. The addition to the *Memorial* is given by Sister Letitia Mary Lyons, *F. N. Blanchet*, 163–64, note.

[6] Sister Letitia Mary Lyons, 165–67, for the opinions of both the Archbishop of Baltimore and the Father General of the Jesuits.

[7] Letters of Mère Constantine, No. 17, November 14, 1846.

[8] The purpose of the Oceanic Maritime Society was "to facilitate the passage of priests who were anxious to devote themselves to the work of the missions in parts of the world with which communication was difficult." Sister Letitia Mary Lyons, *F. N. Blanchet*, 168, note.

[9] Dr. B. B. Barker, *The Financial Papers of Dr. John McLoughlin*, 30. Captain Menes returned to the Columbia in 1849 or 1850 with a cargo owned by V. Marzion & Company of Havre de Grace, who planned to establish a French colony in Oregon. This time *l'Etoile du Matin* was caught on the bar of the Columbia and was so badly damaged that she had to be towed to Portland. There her cargo was unloaded and her hull burned. Captain Menes transferred the cargo to Oregon City, where he opened the "French Store" for the vessel's owners. In 1850 Dr. McLoughlin became a partner in this store.

Captain Menes settled in French Prairie where he died in 1867. His name occurs as witness, godfather, etc., a number of times in the old church records.

H. H. Bancroft, *History of Oregon*, I, 326–27, note 18, says that when no pilot appeared, the ship attempted to cross the bar, went aground and was pounded for nine hours. A pilot in the service of HBC, named Latta, towed her into Baker's Bay (shown on the Bache chart) by constructing a box rudder. Bancroft quotes *Oregon City Enterprise,* March 21, 1868.

[10] *Oregon Spectator,* June 25, 1846, No. 43. A letter to the editor, signed "An Observor," praised both event and sermon as impressive and noted that St. John's Church accommodated about 500 persons.

CHAPTER 12

[1] Letters of Sister Laurence, Willamette, August 29, 1847, Archives of Sisters of Notre Dame in Namur. The narrative of this chapter is based on this letter, as well as on the memoirs of Sister Marie Catherine and Sister Mary Cornelia, and the Annals of Sisters of Notre Dame of California.

[2] Letters of Mère Constantine, No. 25, August 23, 1848.

[3] Mère Constantine, No. 23, August 10, 1848.

[4] Mère Constantine, No. 18, December 18, 1846. Mère Constantine later withdrew this refusal. No. 28, May 28, 1849. This letter, written by Mère Constantine's secretary, Sister Aloysie, shows clearly the Mother General's realization that she was too distant to make adequate decisions. In general, her letters indicate her desire to adjust her directives to changing conditions in the mission. In her early letters, she warns against withdrawal from dependence on the mission, even though she knows Sister Loyola finds this dependence distasteful. No. 16, October 4, 1846. Later, when she thought the school in Oregon City was self-supporting, she approved of the community making improvements at its own expense as an act of charity toward the poor mission. No. 29, August 2, 1849. This last letter also indicates that she did not understand as yet how completely independent of the mission the school in Oregon City had been from its beginning.

[5] Old Land Office Records, Oregon City, page 410, Book 1. "Dr. John McLoughlin conveyed Blk. 12 Oregon City, June 6, 1846 to Sister Marie Caroline of the Order of the Sisters of Our Lady." Sister Mary Cornelia acted as Sister Loyola's secretary (Caroline Neujean).

CHAPTER 13

[1] Sources for students and their families: two account books begun by Sister Loyola in Oregon City in September, 1848, one for tuition and one for expenses; Parish Records, OHS in Portland; translated Parish Records in Appendix, M. L. Nichols, *The Mantle of Elias.* The narrative follows Annals of the Sisters of Notre Dame in Oregon and California.

[2] Daughters of William Glen Rae and Eloisa McLoughlin. Margaret

was born on the steamer *Beaver* coming from Fort Stikine in 1841. Maria Louisa was born in San Francisco in 1842. Their brother, John Rae, was born at Fort Vancouver in 1839. He was reared in the home of his grandfather, John McLoughlin, in the Orkney Islands, Scotland. He died in Portland in 1868. His Scotch kilts may be seen in McLoughlin House in Oregon City. On the death of William Glen Rae in 1845, his wife returned to Oregon City with her three children and lived there with her parents after the retirement of Doctor McLoughlin from HBC. One of the treasures at McLoughlin House in Oregon City is a rosewood melodeon given by Doctor McLoughlin to little Maria Louisa when she was an eight-year-old pupil of the Sisters of Notre Dame.

[3] C. H. Carey, *History of Oregon,* 505, and note on 506 quotes letter of Dr. W. C. McKay, February 11, 1892, in MSS, OHS.

[4] C. H. Carey, 507.

[5] C. B. Bagley, *Early Catholic Missions in Old Oregon,* II, 144, "Historical Sketches."

[6] Letter of Sister Marie Catherine to the Sisters in Namur, Oregon City, March 10, 1849. "Chronicles of the Sisters of the Holy Names of Jesus and Mary, Oregon City," in Provincial Archives, Convent of the Holy Names, Marylhurst, Oregon.

[7] See p. 186, and note 9.

[8] McLoughlin House was moved from its original site on Lot 6, Block 29, facing the falls, to its present location in McLoughlin Park, between Seventh and Eighth Streets. It was established as a National Historic Site in 1941 through the united efforts of McLoughlin Memorial Association, the Municipality of Oregon City, and the National Park Service of the United States Department of the Interior.

[9] *Oregon Statesman,* September 16, 1851, p. 3, col. 2.

[10] Long known as College of Notre Dame, Marysville, this historic landmark of the Sacramento Valley was razed in 1951 to give place to modern convent and schools.

CHAPTER 14

[1] Letters of Mère Constantine, Numbers 30, 31, 34, 35, and 36, dated respectively September 1, 1849, December 5, 1849, March 13, 1850, September 26, 1850, and December 12, 1850, offer a fairly clear picture of Sister Loyola's growing interest in California as she presented it to the Mother General.

[2] J. B. McGloin, S.J., *Eloquent Indian,* 5–6. The request was made by the Franciscan José Gonzales Rubio in 1847, through the British Vice-Consul, James Alexander Forbes. Archbishop Blanchet's reply is dated May 7, 1848.

[3] J. B. McGloin, 9, "Ecclesiastical and Religious Journal of San Fran-

cisco." A large part of this journal by Father Anthony Langlois is reproduced in *Eloquent Indian*. Father McGloin gives a bibliographical note on this journal, p. 336.

4 J. B. McGloin, 22.

5 Unsigned letter in the Archives of the Sisters of Notre Dame in Namur. The letter is dated Oregon City, February 26, 1849.

6 Letters of Mère Constantine, No. 29, August 2, 1849.

7 Autograph letter of Sister Loyola to General Lane, Oregon City, October 18, 1851, in OHS Lane Papers, in which she refers to this purchase from Hugh Burns in 1848.

8 Letter of Sister Marie Catherine to Mère Constantine, Oregon City, March 10, 1850. As always, Sister Marie Catherine's references to unproductive soil, unrewarding harvests, etc., must be seen in the light of one who wrote decades later.

9 C. B. Bagley, *Early Catholic Missions in Old Oregon*, I, 153–226. Here Father J. B. A. Brouillet's "Authentic Account of the Murder of Dr. Whitman . . ." is given in full, as well as an appendix, 227–38, of pertinent extracts from Rev. Gustavus Hines' *History of Oregon*, and the deposition of Sir James Douglas, Chief Factor of HBC, in 1847. Despite Father Brouillet's publication, 1853, the "Whitman saved Oregon" myth persisted until the publication in 1911 of William I. Marshall's "The Acquisition of Oregon." Brouillet's pamphlet was embodied in an official report made by J. Ross Browne to investigate hostilities between Indians and white settlers. United States Congress published this report as *Ex. Doc. No. 38*, Cong. 1 sess., 1859. Sister Mary Justine McMullen, S.N.D., *Career of Peter Hardeman Burnett, California's First Governor*, note, p. 124. (Dissertation, Catholic University, Washington, D. C., July, 1950.)

10 F. Holman, *Dr. John McLoughlin the Father of Oregon*, 124–30, followed by McLoughlin's answer in the *Oregon Spectator*.

11 Index to Territorial Papers, OHS, lists this block as given to Archbishop Blanchet. The location is according to the old plat.

12 *Oregon Spectator*, January 25, 1849. Hugh Cosgrove's account of his days in the California gold fields is recorded in an unsigned letter written in Oregon City, February 26, 1849. Archives of the Sisters of Notre Dame in Namur, Belgium.

13 C. H. Carey, *History of Oregon*, 507.

14 "Reminiscences of F. X. Matthieu," in *Oregon Historical Quarterly*, vol. I, 73–104. In 1900, at eighty-two years of age, Mr. Matthieu recalled his pioneer days in Oregon with remarkable clarity.

15 *Oregon Statesman*, March 5, 1853.

16 The signatures of John McLoughlin and Aloyse Vermuylen (Sister Alphonse Marie) appear in the Articles of Agreement drawn up June 8, 1850, for the purchase by the Sisters of Notre Dame of Block 138 in Oregon City. Robert Caufield signed as witness. This old document and another recording the purchase of Block 19 by the Sisters are in the Archives of the Sisters of Notre Dame of the California Province.

CHAPTER 15

[1] Journal of Sister Mary Alenie. The Life of Sister Marie Catherine is followed here for events in San Francisco and San José.

[2] Letters of Mère Constantine, No. 39, October 8, 1851.

[3] Mère Constantine, No. 37, January 20, 1851.

[4] These two items of Territorial legislation passed the House of Representatives January 29, 1851, and the Council February 1, 1851. The Speaker of the House was Ralph Wilcox; the President of the Council, William Buck, perhaps the same who purchased Block 12 from the Sisters of Notre Dame in 1856. The numbers of the two acts are 45 (the academy) and 46 (St. Paul's). On the same day were passed Bill 41, "An act to regulate incorporated literary and religious societies," and 48, "An act to incorporate the First Congregational Society of Portland."

The *Oregon Spectator,* February 20, 1851, p. 3, col. 1, gave notice of the incorporation of both academy and school at St. Paul.

[5] Letters of Mère Constantine, No. 38, June 2, 1851. An *Oregon Spectator* ad, offering a large lot of apple trees for sale, seems to indicate Sister Loyola's plan to leave St. Paul. *Oregon Spectator,* October 24, 1850, p. 3, col. 4, OHS.

[6] Bishop Joseph Sadoc Alemany was Bishop of Monterey before his appointment as Archbishop of San Francisco in 1853. Apparently Father Langlois had expected a visit from him and had notified Sister Loyola of the fact, assuring her of an interview. The small house in which Father Langlois welcomed the two Sisters was certainly an improvement on his attic quarters of 1849. It was also somewhat roomier than the shack in which the Bishop greeted Sister Mary Alenie and her companions a few months later, and which they described as a hovel.

[7] *Alta California,* July 25, 1851, p. 2, col. 6, The Bancroft Library, University of California.

CHAPTER 16

[1] Letters of Mère Constantine, No. 40, November 20, 1851, to Sister Loyola, quotes from Archbishop Blanchet's letter of September 21, 1851.

[2] "Memoire of the Archbishop of Oregon City," addressed to the Honorable General Joseph Lane, Delegate of Oregon Territory. Section 1 deals with the church property, which it states was donated *verbally* in 1845 or 1846. Section 2 is the request in favor of the Sisters of Notre Dame. Lane Papers, OHS. For Sister Loyola's request to General Lane for full right of possession of this property, see note 7, Chapter 14.

[3] Letters of Mère Constantine, No. 39, October 8, 1851.

4 Mère Constantine, No. 40, November 20, 1851.

5 Archdiocesan Archives, Portland, Oregon. Original letter of Archbishop Blanchet, No. 7, to Mère Constantine, dated Oregon City, September 18, 1854.

6 The narrative here follows the accounts of Sister Mary Laurence and Sister Marie Catherine.

7 Letters of Mère Constantine, No. 42, August 21, 1851.

8 The Sisters were not fending off starvation by this work; in fact, according to Sister Marie Catherine's account, living was more precarious at times in early San José than at this time in Oregon City.

9 Letters of Mère Constantine, No. 45, February 5, 1853.

10 *The Institute of Providence,* vol. III. Chapters 6, 7, and 8, pages 63–107, relate the arrival of this group of Providence Sisters in Oregon City, their two-months' stay with the Sisters of Notre Dame, their departure with them for San Francisco, and their fifty days of waiting there before their departure for Chile.

11 Old Land Office Records, Oregon City, Book D of Deeds, page 86. "The Sisters of Our Lady conveyed to Wm. W. Buck, November 4, 1856 Blk. 12, Oregon City, between 13th and 14th Streets on the River." William W. Buck served as Territorial Treasurer during the latter months of 1851.

12 Sister Marie Catherine's statement in her memoir, that the people would not be able to understand the Sisters' departure from Oregon, recalls her remark in her letter to the Sisters in Namur, March 10, 1849, that during her visit to Oregon City she was impressed by the great esteem for the Sisters on the part of both Protestants and Catholics. Archives of Sisters of Notre Dame in Namur.

EPILOGUE

1 Sister Marie Catherine's memoir gives a detailed and humorous account of the early days of the Sisters of Notre Dame in San José. The memoir of Sister Mary Cornelia has been followed here. Financial statements are from the first account books of the Sisters of Notre Dame in San José.

2 Archdiocesan Archives, Portland, Oregon. Original letter of Archbishop Blanchet, No. 8, to Mère Constantine, dated Oregon City, September 19, 1854, and to this letter is appended Sister Loyola's itemized bill. Letters No. 7 and No. 8 were written to Mère Constantine on two successive days.

3 Letters to Mère Constantine, No. 48, May 2, 1855.

4 Archives of the Sisters of Notre Dame in Namur, Belgium. Letter of Sister Mary Aloysia to Mère Constantine dated August 29, 1853, Pueblo San José. This letter was brought to Namur by Father Accolti in December, 1853.

5 CR, *DeSmet,* II, 740.

Bibliography

Archival Sources:

Archdiocesan Archives, Catholic Archdiocese of Portland, Oregon.
Clackamas County Records, Clackamas Court House, Oregon City,
Oregon.
Oregon Historical Society: Parish Records, Territorial Records,
Lane Papers.
Oregon State Archives, Oregon State Library, Salem, Oregon.
Provincial Archives, Convent of Holy Names, Marylhurst, Oregon.
"Chronicles of the Sisters of the Holy Names of Jesus and Mary,
Oregon City."
Provincial Archives, Sisters of Notre Dame de Namur: Namur,
Belgium and Saratoga, California.

Printed and Edited Sources:

Letters of Dr. John McLoughlin, 1829–1832. Edited by Dr. Burt
Brown Barker, Portland, Oregon, Oregon Historical Society, 1948.
Life, Letters, and Travels of Father Pierre Jean DeSmet, S.J.,
1801–1873. Edited from original and unpublished journals and
letter books and from his printed works by H. M. Chittenden
and A. T. Richardson. New York, Harper, 1905.
"The Correspondence and Journals of Captain Nathaniel Wyeth,"
in F. G. Young, Ed., *Sources of the History of Oregon.* Portland,
University Press, Eugene, Oregon, 1899, Vol. IV.
"T. J. Farnham's Travels" (Willamette Valley), in *Early Western
Travels.* Cleveland, R. G. Thwaites, 1906, vol. 29, and DeSmet's Let-
ters, in vol. 27.
"Historical Sketches," F. N. Blanchet in Catholic Sentinel, February
7 to September 12, 1878.
Authentic Account of the Murder of Dr. Whitman. J. B. A. Brouillet,
Portland, 1869.
Early Catholic Missions in Old Oregon. Clarence B. Bagley, Seattle,
Lowman and Hanford, 1932. Vol. I contains Blanchet's "Sketches"
and Brouillet's "Authentic Account." Vol. II contains letters by Sis-
ters of Notre Dame and others published in Brussels, 1847.
*Notice sur la Territoire et sur la Mission de l'Oregon, suivie de quel-
ques lettres des Soeurs de Notre Dame établies à Saint Paul de Wil-
lamette.* Bruxelles, 1847.

Publications of the Hudson's Bay Record Society. 3d Series, 1844–46. Edited by E. A. Rich, Cambridge, London, 1944.

"The Sisters of Providence in Chile, 1853–1863." Vol. III of *The Institute of Providence* (History of the Daughters of Charity Servants of the Poor), Montreal, 1930.

Notices and Voyages of the Famed Quebec Mission to the Pacific Northwest, 1838–47. Carl Landerholm, Portland, Oregon, Oregon Historical Society, 1956. Translation of the first of the five volumes of "Missions de Québec." In this volume, seven reports are assembled under the title, "Mission de la Colombie."

The Financial Papers of Dr. John McLoughlin. Edited by Dr. Burt Brown Barker, Portland, Oregon, Oregon Historical, 1949.

Newspapers and Periodicals:

Alta California (Bancroft Library, University of California)
Among the Reapers (Notre Dame Press, Cincinnati)
The Catholic Sentinel (Portland)
The Jesuit (Maryland Province)
Oregon City Enterprise (Bancroft Library)
Oregon Historical Quarterly
Oregon Spectator (OHS)
Oregon Statesman (OHS)
Pacific Northwest Quarterly

Secondary Sources:

Bancroft, H. H. History of Oregon, 1888.

Bischoff, W. N., S.J. *The Jesuits in Old Oregon.* Spokane, Gonzaga University, 1945.

Brosman, C. J. *Jason Lee, Prophet of the New Oregon.* New York, 1932.

Carey, C. H. *History of Oregon.* Pioneer Historical Publishing Company, 1922.

Fuller, G. W. *A History of the Great Northwest.* New York, Knopf, 1931.

Gibbs, J. A. *Pacific Graveyard.* Oregon Historical Society, 1950.

Holman, Frederick. *Doctor John McLoughlin the Father of Oregon.* Cleveland, Ohio, A. H. Clarke, 1907.

Kuykendall, R. S. *The Hawaiian Kingdom.* Honolulu, 1938.

Lyons, Sister Letitia Mary. *Francis Norbert Blanchet and the Founding of the Oregon Missions* (Dissertation). Catholic University of America, 1940.

Lynskey, E. M. *The Government of the Catholic Church.* New York, Kenedy, 1952.

Marshall, W. I. *Acquisition of Oregon and the Long Suppressed Evidence about Marcus Whitman.* Seattle, Lowman and Hanford, 1911.

McGloin, J. B., S.J. *Eloquent Indian.* Stanford, Stanford University Press, 1949.

McMullen, Sister Mary Justine, S.N.D. de N. "The Career of Peter Hardeman Burnette, California's First Governor" (Unpublished thesis). Catholic University of America, 1950.

Montgomery, R. G. *The White-headed Eagle.* New York, Macmillan, 1935.

Nichols, M. L. *The Mantle of Elias.* Portland, Oregon, 1941. This volume contains a valuable translation of most of the old French records in Oregon mission churches.

O'Hara, Bishop E. V. *Pioneer History of Oregon.* Paterson, New Jersey, St. Anthony's Press, 1939.

Palladino, L. B., S.J. *Indian and White in the Northwest.* Lancaster. Penn., Wickersham Publishing Co., 1893. Revised edition, 1922.

Schafer, Joseph. *A History of the Pacific Northwest.* New York, 1918.

Shea, J. G. *History of the Catholic Missions among the Indian Tribes in the United States.* New York, 1855.

Sisters of Notre Dame de Namur. *American Foundations.* Philadelphia, The Dolphin Press, 1928; *In Harvest Fields by Sunset Shores.* (Sister Anthony, S.H.). San Francisco, Gilmartin Company, 1926; Life of *Mère St. Joseph.* London, Longmans, Green, and Company, 1923; *Sister Louise,* Sister Helen Louise. Benziger Brothers, 1931.

Victor, Frances F. *The River of the West.* Toledo, Bliss and Company, 1870.

Winther, O. O. *The Great Northwest.* New York, Knopf, 1952.

INDEX